The Trinitarian Order in England

Excavations at Thelsford Priory

Margaret Gray

Edited by

Lorna Watts and Philip Rahtz

BAR British Series 226

1993

Published in 2019 by
BAR Publishing, Oxford

BAR British Series 226

The Trinitarian Order in England

ISBN 9780860547419 paperback
ISBN 9781407318516 e-book

DOI https://doi.org/10.30861/9780860547419

A catalogue record for this book is available from the British Library

This book is available at www.barpublishing.com

BAR Publishing is the trading name of British Archaeological Reports (Oxford) Ltd.
British Archaeological Reports was first incorporated in 1974 to publish the BAR
Series, International and British. In 1992 Hadrian Books Ltd became part of the BAR
group. This volume was originally published by Tempvs Reparatvm in conjunction
with British Archaeological Reports (Oxford) Ltd / Hadrian Books Ltd, the Series
principal publisher, in 1993. This present volume is published by BAR Publishing,
2019.

BAR
PUBLISHING

BAR titles are available from:

BAR Publishing
122 Banbury Rd, Oxford, OX2 7BP, UK
EMAIL   info@barpublishing.com
PHONE   +44 (0)1865 310431
FAX   +44 (0)1865 316916
www.barpublishing.com

The Trinitarian Order in England
Excavations at Thelsford Priory
by Margaret Gray

With contributions from Lawrence Butler, Mary Berry, Blanche Ellis, Ian Goodall, the late Ralph Harcourt, Tim Pestell, Philip Rahtz, the late Stuart Rigold, the late William Seaby, David Walsh and Susan Wright.

This report includes a gazetteer of all the Trinitarian sites in England.

CONTENTS LIST

MICROFICHE

To view microfiche go to https://doi.org/10.30861/9780860547419_microfiche

LIST OF FIGURES

MF : only in microfiche

LIST OF PLATES

LIST OF TABLES

Chapter 1
SUMMARY

This report describes two excavations at the Trinitarian priory of Thelsford, Warwickshire. The first was undertaken to find the extent of the priory in order that the site might be scheduled; this located the church and claustral buildings, and indicated the size of the enclosure. The second excavation was on the line of a new road and recovered details of the water management, perimeter ditches and ancillary buildings of the priory. From synthesis of both excavations, the outline of the layout of the priory complex can be suggested, together with its water systems, gardens, and land, in relation to local topography and hydrology; there is evidence for the materials used in construction and use. Finds include worked flints (some in prehistoric pit), coal, utilised stone, structural ceramics (roof tiles and brick); floor tiles, decorated and plain; mortar, burnt daub and iron slag; objects of glass (including window glass), iron, copper alloy, lead, and silver; coins and jettons; pottery; clay tobacco pipes; wood, charcoal and fibre; human and animal bones; and bone objects. Of especial interest are a lead shroud, associated with a silver belt buckle and plate, chape and eyelet stud; the skeleton was possibly that of Edmund Lucy, who died c. 1498, or that of his wife Joan, who died in 1514.

There is also a gazetteer of Trinitarian sites in England, which includes the results of recent documentary research and fieldwork.

Editors' Note

This report has been arranged for publication according to the conditions laid down by the Historic Buildings and Monuments Commission. We are grateful for their generous grants for post-excavation and publication. This has involved putting most of the archaeological detail into microfiche, and including in print only a summary with synthesis. The historical section and the gazetteer of other Trinitarian sites in England have been printed in full, as being of more general interest. The contents list and bibliography refer to the whole report, and the former indicates what will be found only in microfiche.

Chapter 2
INTRODUCTION

The priory and the majority of its estate was concentrated in the upper Avon valley (figs 1 and 2). The site (SP 271583) is in the parish of Charlecote and lies close to the A429 road between Barford and Wellesbourne. It was reported in 1965 to the Avon-Severn Research Project that ploughing was destroying the earthworks of the priory, which decided to undertake an excavation to determine the limits of the monastic features in order that the site might be scheduled, to prevent further destruction. With the help of a grant from the (then) Ministry of Public Buildings and Works (later the Department of the Environment, now the Historic Buildings and Monuments Commission), an excavation took place for nine weeks during June and July 1966. The labour force for the first four weeks was provided by ten boys from the Norton Remand Home at Kineton, under the supervision of their master, Mr. A. Walker. The work was completed by students from Birmingham University (School of History) and by local volunteers. In 1969 the site was scheduled within the area shown by the dotted lines on the site plan (fig 3).

In the 1970s a gas pipeline traversed the site. A watching brief was kept on the course of the whole line by the Department of Field Archaeology, Herbert Museum, Coventry, but 'no significant finds or structures' were reported where it crossed the priory.

In 1971 the Warwickshire County Council proposed that the A429 road should be realigned to avoid the narrow Thelsford Bridge; and that the new road should cross to the west of the buildings found in the 1966 excavations. Once again the funds were provided by the (then) Department of the Environment, and an excavation took place for three months during April to June 1972. The labour force was supplied by students and local volunteers.

In September 1972 the area to the south of this excavation was examined by Mr. P. Saunders, as traces of parallel ditches showed on air photographs. It was not possible to find any evidence of these on the ground, nor were any archaeological features observed by him when this area was under road construction.

I would like to thank Mr. F. Whetter, the owner of the site, for his kindness in allowing excavation to take place on his land and the interest he showed in the results. I am grateful to Professor Philip Rahtz for his help during the 1966 excavation and also, together with Lorna Watts, in the preparation of this report; and to Dr. S.M. Wright for her advice on the historical section and tiles. I would also like to thank the following who worked with me on the site: in 1966, Gerry Lewis (site assistant), Eileen Ross (finds assistant), A. Walker, Adrian Oswald, Horace and Julie Sanders, Heather James (then Wanstall), Ian Saunders, David Brown and Jane Dent. In 1972, Nicholas Clayton (site assistant), Heather James (then Barney) and Kristine Orr (finds assistants), Peter Saunders, John Burman, Regina Haldon, Stephen Hughes, Brian Hodkinson, Peter Kerr-Jarrett, Julie Sanders, John and Sue Sadler, Karsalie Fraser, and the staff from the National Vegetable Research Station at Wellesbourne. I am indebted to Melvyn Card and Lucy Matthews for publication drawings of the pottery and small finds; and to Lawrence Barfield, Mary Berry, Blanche Ellis, Ian Goodall, the late Ralph Harcourt, Philip Rahtz, the late Stuart Rigold, the late William Seaby and David Walsh for their specialist reports. I am also grateful to the Colt Fund (administered by the Society for Medieval Archaeology) for a grant for my research into the English Trinitarian sites.

The finds and slides have been deposited in the County Museum, Warwick, together with any site records, negatives, photographs and drawings not included in this publication (the archive) (Warwick access no. 124/1981). A copy of the latter has also been deposited in the National Monuments Record.

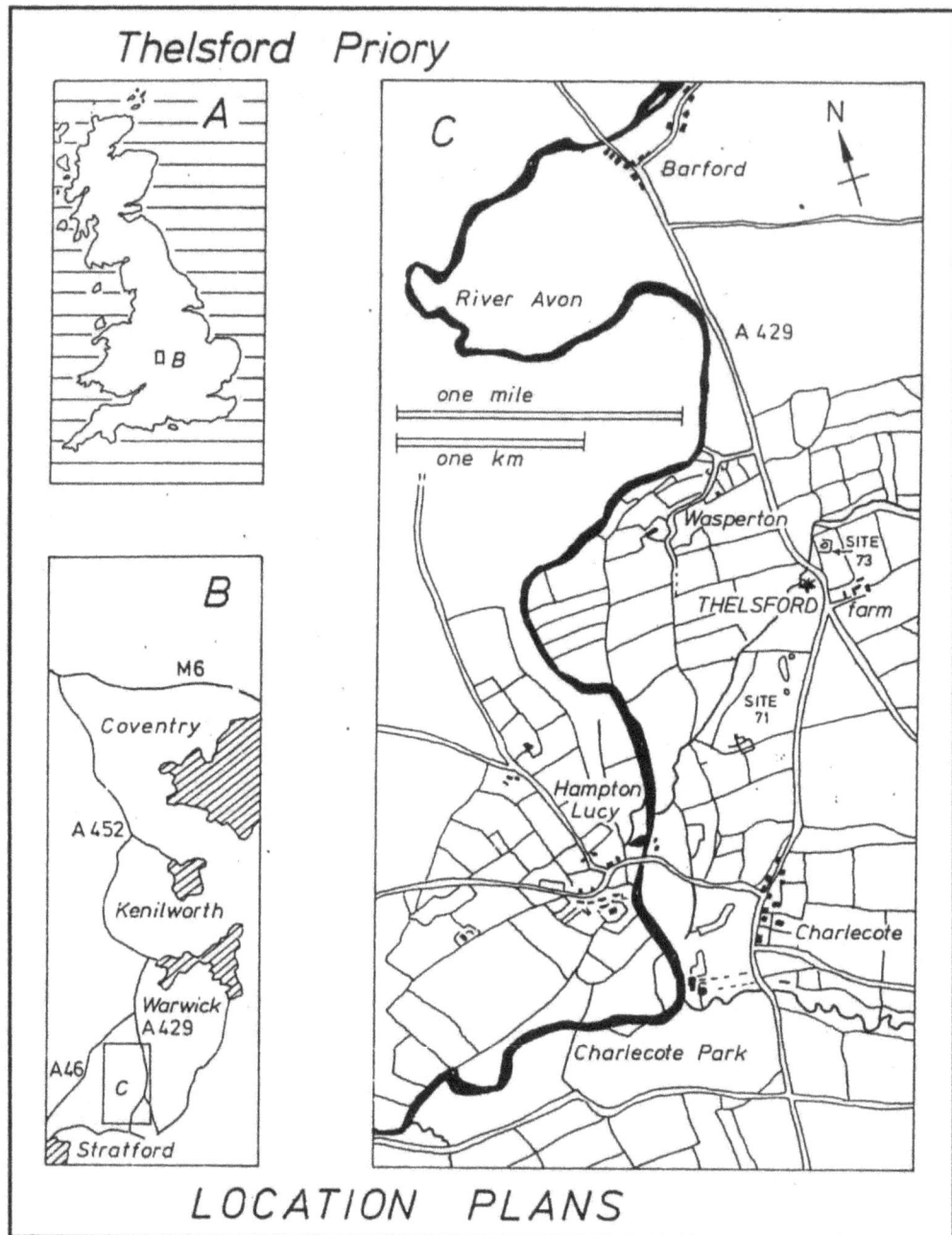

Fig 1

THELSFORD PRIORY ESTATES

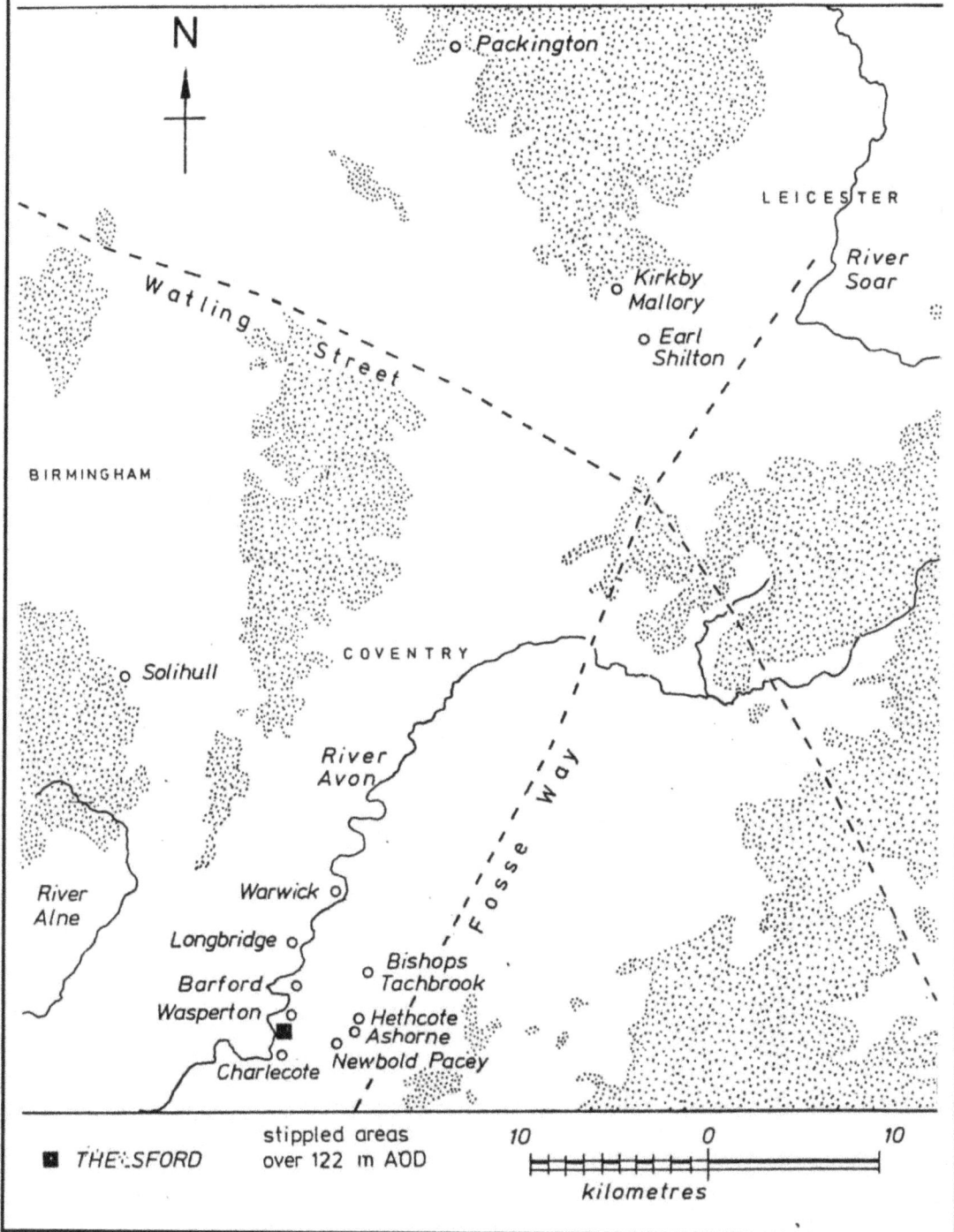

N

Packington

LEICESTER

River
Soar

Watling Street

Kirkby
Mallory

Earl
Shilton

BIRMINGHAM

COVENTRY

Solihull

River
Avon

Fosse Way

River
Alne

Warwick

Longbridge

Bishops
Tachbrook

Barford
Wasperton

Hethcote
Ashorne
Newbold Pacey

Charlecote

■ THELSFORD

stippled areas
over 122 m AOD

10   0   10

kilometres

Fig 2

Chapter 3
GEOLOGY, SOILS AND TOPOGRAPHY

The priory was situated on a gravel terrace on the south side of the Thelsford Brook (fig. 3). There is a difference in level of six metres between the water level of the brook (42.19 m above OD in 1966) and the bench mark on the Thelsford Cottages (48.19 m above OD). Most of the buildings were on the flattest part of the site near the road, with the ground rising to the south behind them. The brook is fast flowing with sharp meanders, and shows traces of canalisation.

The underlying natural strata are of red gritty gravel with patches of stiff red clay in the lower areas. In some places the gravel is mixed with coarse yellow or red sand. These materials are components of a glacial terrace gravel, containing Bunter pebbles, sandstone and limestone, which is typical of the terrace gravels of the Avon valley (Beaver 1968, 54-5). A large periglacial ice-wedge cast (442) traversed the site (below, 6.4b and fig. 6). On these basal glacial layers of sand, clay and gravel lay a buff-yellow sandy soil, with flecks of dark brown, but with no gravel or building debris (layer Q). This was mainly defined in the lower-lying areas of the site, and was cut away extensively in areas of the medieval occupation. This sandy soil is interpreted as a pre-medieval buried soil, probably augmented by alluvial deposits.

The building stones used in the priory were either of green sandstone or yellow-grey limestone from an unknown, but probably fairly local, quarry.

The priory is shown in the 1925 6" O.S. map (Warwickshire sheet XXXIX.13) as being close to the fishponds on the west side (fig.3), indicated by an 'antiquity' mark. Excavation showed however that the buildings lay further east within the former bend of the road, which probably deviated from its line here for this reason.

The area enclosed by the perimeter ditches of the priory was about 1.6 ha, with the fishponds extending beyond this to the west along the valley bottom. These fishponds were in 1966 the only visible remains of the priory; but until the 1939-45 war there had been extensive earthworks, which have since been ploughed down. Considerable earth moving has also taken place to fill up hollow places caused by water courses and possible small ponds.

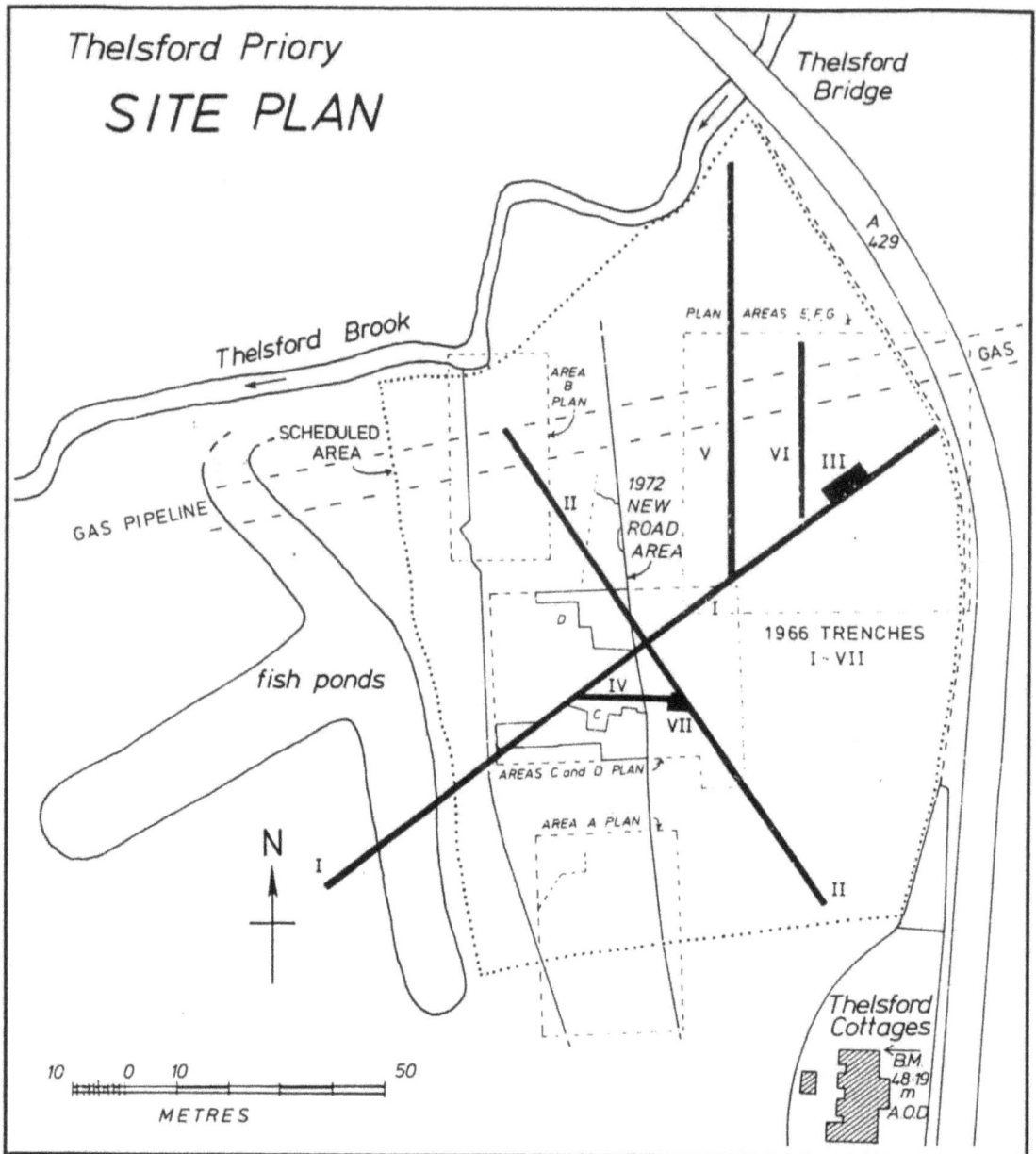

Thelsford Priory
SITE PLAN

Thelsford Bridge

Thelsford Brook

A 429

GAS

PLAN AREAS E, F, G

AREA B PLAN

SCHEDULED AREA

GAS PIPELINE

1972 NEW ROAD AREA

II

V

VI

III

fish ponds

D

I

1966 TRENCHES I - VII

N

C

IV

VII

AREAS C and D PLAN

AREA A PLAN

I

II

Thelsford Cottages

BM 48·19 m A.O.D.

10   0   10   50
METRES

Fig. 3

Chapter 4
HISTORY

The history of the Canons of the Holy Sepulchre and of the Trinitarians has for the purposes of this report been taken from secondary sources and no attempt has been made to add to this information from primary sources. This outline has been included to provide a background to the structural sequences established by excavation.

4.1 History of the Canons of the Holy Sepulchre of Jerusalem

In its first phase, Thelsford Priory belonged to this order. The secondary sources for the history in England of this short-lived order are few, the main one being Dickinson (1950, 83-4). The history of their first foundation in Warwick is found in Dugdale (1730, 454-5); and the history of each of the six foundations is in the relevant volumes of the *Victoria County History*, with a general summary in Knowles and Hadcock (1971, 137-82), listed with the Augustinian Canons of which they were a component. There is a distribution map of the houses in Robinson (1980, 58), who also includes a short summary of their history. There is also some information in Walsh (1967), and an unpublished history by P.L. Daniel (Daniel 1991).

A small but important minority of Augustinian Canons Regular belonged to independent congregations, with their own constitutions and different machinery of government. The heyday of the majority of these orders was in the 12th century, the Order of Arrouaise starting in c. 1090, that of St. Victor of Paris in 1108, and the Canons of the Holy Sepulchre in 1114. The latter were instituted in the Church of the Holy Sepulchre at Jerusalem in 1114, traditionally by Godefroi de Bouillon, and may have had connections with an earlier institution of the Canons of Mount Sion. Dickinson (1950, 83) places their institution at the Holy Sepulchre to 1114 but Daniel 1991 says that their earliest constitution was given to them by Patriarch Jibelin in 1108. They owed their existence to the crusading movement, with the specific purpose of guarding the Holy Sepulchre and supplying the chapter of the Latin Patriarchate. The order attracted lay members, and the founders of houses were often noblemen who had been on crusade. The habit of this order was the same as that of the Canons Regular except that they had a red double cross on their cloaks and, as pictured in Dugdale (1730, 455), they were bearded.

The Canons of the Holy Sepulchre were the first of these three branches of the Augustinian Canons Regular to found a house in England and this was their house at Warwick. Knowles and Hadcock (1971, 178) dispute the date of 1109 given by Dugdale (1730, 454) for its foundation, the order not being instituted in Jerusalem until 1114. If Daniel's date of 1108 is correct, the earlier date is a possibility. The Warwick priory was begun by Henry de Newburgh, Earl of Warwick, who died in 1119, and probably was connected with the First Crusade (1096-99); it was finished by his son Roger, who became earl in 1123. The house, which lay close to, or on top of, St. Helen's parish church, was dedicated by Simon of Worcester in 1125. Chatwin (1926, 53) says that the building was supposed to be similar to the church of the Holy Sepulchre in Jerusalem. The buildings lasted until the Dissolution but the rebuilt Priory House was sold and moved *en bloc* to Virginia, U.S.A. in 1925. Northgate

House is on the site of the Priory Gatehouse and the County Record Office is over the site of the church and part of the foundations can be seen. This was excavated in 1970 (Webster and Cherry, 1973, 175-6) and part of the nave, the south aisle and the chancel were uncovered. Substantial walls to the west of the church were thought to be part of a west range, with a square chapter house. Beneath this was a circular structure which the excavator, W.J. Ford, interpreted as a limekiln. The site has not yet been fully published. This house is referred to as a hospital and Knowles and Hadcock (1971, 178) add that the canons especially cared for pilgrims to the Holy Land. Although the prior and Chapter remained as Canons of the Holy Sepulchre until 1280, they later became indistinguishable from the rest of the Augustinian Canons Regular. It was in 1200-12 that, as 'Canons of St. Radegunde of Theulisford' they received a grant from Henry de Bereford for a hospital at Thelsford (c.f. 4.3 below).

The other houses of this short-lived order are shown in Robinson (1980, fig. 15,58) to be concentrated in the East Midlands. They are listed and described in Daniel 1991 with a comprehensive Bibliography for each site. There was a house at Thetford, still with remains, which was excavated in 1969 (Wilson and Hurst 1971, 169). The first church was aisleless with a graveyard to the south; the second phase showed an enlarged church with transepts of late 12th century date and with cloisters to the north of the church. Daniel 1991 gives a foundation date of 1109-19 but Robinson (1980, 59) says that its foundation was connected with the Second Crusade and dates this to 1139. The order, like that of the Trinitarians, was connected with hospitals. Apart from the hospital at Thelsford founded 1200-12 and its dependent hospital at Stafford (c.f. 4.3. below) there was a leprosaria at Hedon (East Riding) founded 1205, a hospital at Stamford, founded 1170-89 for pilgrims to Jerusalem and one at Nottingham, founded 1170, which continued as a hospital for some time after the canons had left it, although Stamford ceased in 1227.

Robinson (1980, 59) states that all three of these independent orders of Augustinian Canons lost contact with their continental origins in the later medieval period, but from their arrival in England they were hampered by distance and the smallness of their numbers. The collapse of the Angevin Empire under King John (1199-1216) was probably more of a cause for their demise than the failures in the Holy Land.

It is a misconception that all of their lands and revenues were transferred to the Trinitarians (Midmer 1979, 302). Although there were certain aims which the two orders shared, such as the provision of hospitals, and the fact that they both followed the Augustinian Rule, the reasons for their institution were different. The only priory to be transferred was that of Thelsford and its dependent hospital at Stafford, both of which were in decay when they were taken over (c.f. 4.3) Daniel 1991 lists the Trinitarian house at Hounslow as having been in the possession of the Canons of the Holy Sepulchre. Although there was possibly a hospital on this site, V.C.H. Middlesex (1962, 191) gives no indication of the order, if any, to which it belonged.

4.2 History of the Trinitarian Order

The secondary sources for the Trinitarian's history are mainly continental. Deslandres (1903) and Antonin (1925) have written histories of the French houses, and von Kralik (1919) the German. Deslandres uses as source material chronicles of some of the ministers of the order from the 15th century onwards, as well as registers from some of the priories; he has a useful chapter on the bibliography of his subject (1, vii-xxvii). Antonin uses five 13th century sources, three from the 15th, two from the 16th and one from the 17th centuries (c.f. his bibliography, 1925, 13-19).

There is no published history of the English Trinitarians, nor of those in Scotland and Ireland. Dugdale (1730, 498-9) includes some general history of the order. Part of the English material has been worked on by Chettle (1947) and Bate (1924), when they were writing the histories of Easton Royal and Hounslow respectively. A comprehensive historical summary is included in Pestell 1991. A summary of the post-Reformation history is found in the *Encyclopaedia Britannica* (1982 11, 928), in Walsh (1967, XIV, 293), and in Hebermann *et al* (1907, 46).

The concept of the Trinitarian movement, 'The Order of the Most Holy Trinity for the Redemption of Captives', originated in Northern France with the saint John de Matha and the hermit Felix de Valois in 1198. This was just after the Third Crusade and at a time when the effects of the Muslim advances into North Africa and Spain of the previous centuries were still being felt in Western Christendom. The Muslim threat continued as piracy against Mediterranean ships and maritime towns. When these were plundered, prisoners, including women and children, were carried away as slaves or into captivity, to North Africa and Spain. The rich could be released by the payment of a large ransom, but there were many prisoners who were too poor for this redemption. The aim of the early Trinitarians was to raise money for the redemption of Christian captives: they would also negotiate terms for the exchange of captives. In Barcelona the Mercedarian Order was founded with the same object in 1218 by James I of Aragon and St. Peter de Nolasco. It was not difficult to raise this money when the Saracens represented the main body of unbelievers to Christians.

The history of the early days of the founding fathers is to some extent aprocryphal but is picturesquely described in 'The Metrical Life of St. Robert of Knaresborough' (Bazire 1968, 74-76), in Dugdale (1730, 498-9), and more critically in Deslandres (1903, 16-19). John de Matha of Provence, a wealthy student at Paris University, is said to have received a vision of an angel, with a cross of red and blue on his breast, resting his hands on the heads of two kneeling slaves. Believing that this vision directed him to deliver prisoners from captivity, he sold his fortune and retired to a hermitage at Cerfroid, near Meaux (Aisne) and spent three years with the hermit, Felix de Valois. This saint is not included in Farmer 1987 and is mentioned in the *Benedictine Book* 1989, 212 as a legendary character. Having together conceived the idea of instituting a new order, they travelled to Rome to receive the approval of Pope Innocent III, who recounted a similar vision, but with a Moor and a Christian on each side of the angel, signifying an exchange of captives. The Pope ratified the order and arranged for a collection of alms for them, the first house being at Cerfroid. The last buildings of this priory are illustrated by Antonin (1925, opp. 54) (pl.IX). The order was also known as the Mathurines, either from the name of their founder or from their Paris House near St. Maturin's Chapel. In Scotland they were known as the Red Friars from the red cross on their garments. Their habit was a soutane with a cross, half red and half blue, on the left side, over a spacular with a similar cross in the centre. This is illustrated by Dugdale (*Mon. Angl.* 1830, vi, 1557). This cross sometimes, especially at the Dissolution, led to their confusion with the Crutched or Crossed Friars, for example at Donnington, Berkshire (*V.C.H. Berks.* 1907, 2, 92), and at Ingham, Norfolk (see 9.5 below).

The constitutions of the Trinitarians were similar to those of the various families of Canons Regular and based, like theirs, on the Rule of St. Augustine. These constitutions are in Dugdale (*Mon. Angl.* 1830, 1558-61). The distinguishing feature was the continual reference made to a threefold principle, arising from their devotion to the Blessed Trinity. There was to be a threefold division of their resources, one part for the redemption of captives, one for the maintenance of the sick and poor in their hospitals and the third for their own maintenance. Each house was to have three clerks and three laymen under the rule of the head of the house, who was called the minister. Such division of their income led to frugality in their way of living, which shows in all aspects of their constitutions. As well as the usual vows of poverty and chastity, they were not allowed the comfort of feather beds, and were only to have pillows. It was forbidden to ride on horses, only on asses which they had to breed themselves or be given, hence their colloquial name of the 'Donkey Brothers" (Deslandres 1903, 23-4). These ideals of self-sufficiency extended to their diet, as they were only allowed to buy such food as they could not produce themselves and could never buy meat, fish or wine. They fasted four days a week from the middle of September until Easter, except at certain festivals, with flesh only to be eaten on certain Sundays. A full diet however could be provided for the sick, the poor and young children. Their communal life included brothers, clerks and laymen sharing the same food, clothing, dormitory, refectory and table, but the sick were to eat and sleep apart with a layman or a clerk infirmarer. If an offence was caused to another person, their pardon must be begged three times. Novices could not be received under the age of twenty. As their life involved much travelling, both to collect alms and to work with captives, there were special rules to cover them when absent from their own houses. All their churches were to be simple and the regular Hours to be chanted in these churches were those of the Canons of St. Victor. As this was a very elaborate liturgy, the following provision is interesting. 'For the regular Hours they shall follow the usage of Blessed Victor, except that they shall omit the pauses or other lengthenings, and the observance of Vigils on account of the work and the small number of servants from the assembly of the pious and of religious men; and indeed, on account of their small numbers, they are not obliged to make such pauses in singing the psalms, or for the same reason to rise so early'. Presumably the 'servants' were the lay members and the 'religious' were the canons. The 'pauses' occur between the two parts of each psalm verse and were an essential part of all psalmody. They were observed for practical as well as spiritual reasons, and could vary in length, on account of the acoustics of the building. Not only was this pause a moment of silence for reflection on the words, but also it gave time for the sound to die away before the recommencement of the chant. The Augustinian church was normally a long, narrow and rather lofty structure which would have had a pronounced echo, whereas the Trinitarians were bound by their constitutions to build small, simple buildings to house the few numbers required in each priory, with consequently no echo. I am grateful to Dr. Mary Berry for her help with the liturgical interpretation of the Rule of St. Victor.

In 1217 Pope Honorius III introduced modifications to the original constitutions and in 1263 Urban IV again reorganised them. The number of brothers in each house could be increased from seven to any number that each individual house required. The rule about riding only on asses was relaxed, as it was noticed that this rule hindered the recruitment to the order of those of noble birth. When there was the gift of a church which was integral to the monastery and which was already dedicated, as that of St. Mathurin in Paris, the name should not be changed, and only those churches which they themselves built should be dedicated to the Holy Trinity. The recitation of the office in the Victorine manner when there were too few canons present to be able to make the pauses in the psalms correctly could be further modified. This modification was indicative of the fact that the Trinitarians had kept to their original intention of building small churches to hold only a few religious. However, by 1368, the Bishop of Salisbury was directing canons of Easton Royal, Wiltshire, to follow the Use of Sarum for their liturgy (Chettle 1947, 371).

That it was possible for women to work for the order is confirmed by Tanner (1787, Warks. XXIX) and by Dugdale (1730, 499); both mention 'sisters' at Thelsford in 1473. There is another mention of them at Thelsford as early as 1300 (see 4.3). Clay (1966, 153) emphasizes that in the 13th century most of the hospitals used women side by side with men for their works of mercy. The sisters usually lodged in a chamber adjoining the hospital and their work was confined to bedside and domestic duties. Clay particularly mentions the Trinitarians (210) and the Canons of the Holy Sepulchre (205) as the most important of the orders for work in infirmaries and pilgrim hostels. The introduction to the Ordnance Survey's map of *Monastic Britain* (1978, 8) mentions that the Augustinian Canons, and principally the Trinitarians, were connected with hospitals more than were the other orders. Although the sisters were attached to the hospitals of the order they did not form an integral part of it until 1612, when they became part of the discalced congregation of the Trinitarians.

The new order spread rapidly throughout Western Europe on a xenophobic tide of hatred against the infidels and pity for their captives. In the first year (1198) John, an Englishman, and William, a Scot, two of the earliest followers of John de Matha, were sent to Morocco, where they negotiated the release of 186 captives. From that time onwards the work continued with great energy, and sometimes with danger and hardship to the brothers. On some occasions it was necessary for them to offer themselves as personal substitutes to prevent the apostasy of the captive under torture, or to go into captivity themselves whilst awaiting the ransom money, as release from captivity could only be effected in one of two ways, either through apostasy or by ransom.

The Trinitarians were the first institution to be specifically concerned with the redemption of Christian captives, although they were soon to be joined by the Mercedarians in Spain, with whom there was a certain amount of rivalry (Clissold, 1977, 107-8). King Louis IX (the saint) favoured the order, as he had himself been a captive, and he is known to have taken Trinitarians with him on Crusades, and to have selected his chaplains from this order and installed them also in his chateaux at Fontainbleu (Clissold 1977, 13-14). Clissold (1977, 110) emphasises the lengthy preparation needed for each redemptive mission, as not only had the money to be raised but also protracted negotiations had to take place. Funds were not only raised in each house of the order from legacies, sale of indulgences, fines and church collections, but also by 'alms quests'. These took the form of elaborately staged processions, sometimes with tableaux or theatrical representations of the miserable plight of the captives. In Southern Europe the released captives were obliged to stay with their redeemers for a period of time, during which they had to take part in the processions, clothed in their prison rags, dirty, and with fetters, even heavier than they had endured in prison. In England there was a procession at Moatenden (Kent) on Trinity Sunday (Furley, 1878, 27), which was 'with cope and canopy, cross and candlestick, flag and banner, light and incense, and chanting and piping'. Special collectors of alms, in England known as proctors, were authorised by letters patent to solicit alms. The proctors from Knaresborough (Yorks.) were licensed in 1286, 1297 and 1303 to beg alms in churches, towns and markets, specifically for the ransom of captives (*V.C.H. Yorks.* 1913, 38). As early as 1228, the Trinitarians had to protect themselves against swindlers posing as collectors by obtaining a papal bull to imprison the fraudulent impostors (Deslandres 1903, 1, 331). Fraternities of lay tertiaries were formed to further the good work, especially in areas where the order had no monastic house. Money was also raised by the issue of certificates called 'letters of confraternity'.

Eventually a house was established in Africa for the brothers to act as agents to the Muslims and pecuniary transactions became a relatively stable tariff (Knowles 1956, 202). Many of the houses which were founded in the 13th and 14th centuries acted as recruitment centres; the eight Scottish monasteries were particularly active in this respect (Gordon 1868, i, 289-90, 301). Patrick Lindsay, James Douglas and James Ogilvie lost their lives in the cause in 1331.

It is impossible to estimate the number of captives who were released. *Encyclopaedia Britannica* (1982, 11, 928) gives an estimate of 140,000 for the years between the first redemption in 1199 until the end of slavery in 1855. The number of those rescued between 1625 and 1855 is estimated as 9,692 by the *New Catholic Encyclopaedia* (Walsh 1967, 293).

When John de Matha died in 1213 there were 35 Houses of Trinitarians, and these increased rapidly in the 13th century in France, Spain and Italy. By the end of the 13th century there were also ten houses in England, eight in Scotland and one in Ireland, and houses in Bohemia, Saxony, Poland and Hungary, to an estimated total of 250 (*V.C.H. Norfolk* 1906, 41). Knowles and Hadcock (1971, 492) give an estimate of the numbers of religious, excluding lay-brothers, in the English houses. These start with 35 in 1216, rising to 68 in 1350, after which year the numbers had fallen because of the Black Death to only 34. Numbers recovered however and stayed between 60 and 65 until a decline to 58 in 1534, with a few lingering on until the Dissolution.

The interest of the English royal family in this newly founded order is shown by their patronage of the houses at Moatenden, Knaresborough, Oxford and Hounslow, mainly through the benefactions of Richard Earl of Cornwall, brother of Hen. III. (See relevant sections of the Gazetteer).

The head of each house was called the 'minister' and this office included the functions of superior and procurator. A number of houses were united to form a 'congregation' under a 'minister general', who held a general chapter for the remedying of faults and discussion of common interests. At the head of each province there was a 'provincial minister'. Chettle (1947, 371) mentions that in 1372 the minister of the house at Moatenden was appointed by the house of Cerfroid as provincial minister and asked to reform abuses, but from 1403 the English province obtained leave from Urban VI to chose their own provincial. With the minister from Knaresborough as the provincial in 1403 they obtained permission to send a fixed quota for the ransom of captives instead of one third of their income, and the reception of novices under the age of twenty was allowed. From 1473 to 1507 the general government of the order was in the hands of a great and energetic ruler Robert Gaguin, whose work is described by Chettle (1947, 373). He resumed the ransoming of captives on a large scale and encouraged the collection of alms, the registers of a number of English bishops bearing witness to the special activity at Thelsford.

Lists of the ministers from the English Houses (Dugdale 1730, 501, and Chettle 1947, 375), indicate that the brethren seem always to have been native Englishmen, and most commonly natives of the counties in which their houses lay. They proceeded to the priesthood in the regular course of ordination, and served as priests in their local parishes. There is evidence for this from Newcastle-upon-Tyne (see 9.8). The more fortunate of the canons could obtain theological training at Oxford (see 9.9).

When the urgency of their work decreased and popular interest lessened, the Trinitarians administered to the poor and needy in their own districts and, as ordained regular canons, they could serve as priests in their local parishes. *V.C.H. Wilts* (1956, 325) points out that until the passing of the Statute of Carlisle in 1307, they would have been able to send one third of their incomes, (which, by their constitutions, was allowed for the redemption of captives), directly to the mother house at Cerfroid, but after this, during the Hundred Years War and the Schism, this would not have been possible, and this portion would have been spent on the local poor and wayfarers. At Easton Royal (Wilts.) some of the work they performed is described by Chettle (1947, 372) from a grant of 1389 in the *Ailesbury MS*, at Savernake (MS. 34), where Sir William Esturmey specified detailed directions as to the distribution of pence and of halfpenny white loaves, washing the feet of the poor, providing candles and celebrating services or prayers for the dead. But they were not unaware of the money that could be made from the rich. Laymen who assisted the order were admitted to its privileges, and were awarded certificates which granted indulgences and the advantages of the prayers of the canons on death. Bate (1924, 14) mentions that the most important person to be admitted to Hounslow was Henry, Prince of Wales, afterwards Henry VIII, in 1508. His certificate, now in the British Library, is richly illuminated (illustrated in Bate 1924, opp. 25). Clark-Maxwell (1926, 19-20) calls these certificates 'letters of confraternity' and states that, in comparison with the larger monastic orders, there are an unusually high number of thirteen surviving Trinitarian documents; whereas, for example, there are only five Cistercian letters. He explains it as an expression of the public wish to support the Trinitarian ideal, and a tribute to their zeal in the collection of funds for their cause. All the letters are after 1483, and issued by the minister of a particular house: the list in Clark-Maxwell (1926, 56-7) shows four from Hounslow, three from Newcastle-upon-Tyne, two from Moatenden, Ingham and Knaresborough respectively, and one from Thelsford. Further work by Clark-Maxwell was published in 1929 (Clark-Maxwell 1929). He had augmented the number of Trinitarian letters to twenty seven, comprising nine from Knaresborough, four from Hounslow, five from Moatenden, two from Ingham, three from Thelsford and four from Newcastle-upon-Tyne. He notes that the Trinitarians, by issuing letters directly from the minister of each individual house, were unlike the other orders who tended to issue them chiefly through their central authority. The dates of issue range from 1412 to 1529.

By the late medieval period many hospitals were in decline, including those of the Trinitarians, owing to the negligence of the descendants of the founders and maladministration (Clay 1966, 212-225).

In spite of accusations levelled against monastic orders at the Dissolution, the Trinitarians seem to have been well respected. Fuller (1811, 2, 43) when writing in 1611 of Robert Hounslow, a provincial minister of the order in 1430, refers to friars as 'locusts' and 'pests of the places they lived in', but comments that with regard to the Trinitarians 'much good did redound from their endeavours ... their alms industriously collected, such collections carefully preserved till they could be securely transmitted, and thereby the liberty of many Christian captives effectively procured'.

Although the order was revised several times, the original constitutions were kept almost intact by a reform in 1597, and an order called the Barefooted (Discalced) Trinitarians was initiated in Spain. This became a distinct order and is now the only surviving branch of the Trinitarians (O.SS.T.) with a mother house at San Grisogno in Rome. Because slavery is no longer an international problem, the Trinitarians now devote themselves to teaching, and serving in parishes, hospitals and prisons. Walsh (1967, XIV, 294) states that in 1964 there were about 800 members in five provinces in Spain, Italy, Canada, and the U.S.A., and a mission station in Madagascar.

Throughout their history the Trinitarians have suffered the misconception of being classed with the mendicant friars. Knowles (1956, 201-2) refers to this confusion and points out that they arrived in England before the friars and followed the Rule of St. Augustine, making them more like the Augustinian Canons. They differed from the friars in that they could receive endowments and own property, and the confusion probably arose because they spent a good deal of their time travelling to collect funds for their redemptive work. This sometimes took them some distance from their house, an example being the Trinitarian from Ingham Priory who was mentioned in the *Paston Letters* as visiting Swaffham, some 38 miles from Ingham. Also, a Hounslow seal matrix was found about a hundred yards above the bridge over the river Peterril, at the foot of Harroby Hill in Cumberland, about a mile from Carlisle; another matrix from Hounslow was found at Oare, near Faversham in Kent (Bate 1924, 10-11). Like the friars they were an international order divided into provinces. However, the head of each Trinitarian house was called 'minister' whereas with the friars that word was reserved for the head of the order, as minister general, or of each province. The friars needed large churches to accommodate as many lay people as possible for preaching purposes, whereas the Trinitarians did not consider this type of evangelism to be part of their mission, and built small churches.

Even Dugdale (*Mon. Angl.* 1830, 1562-3), Tanner (1787, XXIX) and Gasquet (1905, 245-6) include them with the friars, though Dugdale does allude to them as 'canons' in the text. This error is constantly encountered in modern publications, for instance, in several volumes of the *V.C.H.*, including that for Warwickshire (*V.C.H. Warks.* 1908, 10) and Oxfordshire (*V.C.H. Oxon.* 1979, 368); also in Midmer (1979, 2, 14 and each alphabetically listed site); and in Cook 1961 (215). Sometimes, as in Gordon 1868 (296-311) the question even arouses antagonism: 'The Red Friars (who pretend to be Canons Regular, notwithstanding that the name, which they are willing to assume, is strongly controverted by their adversaries) ... '; or complete neglect, as in the publications by Roberts (1949), Little (1979) and Butler and Given-Wilson (1979). Possibly these three do not include the Trinitarians because the only standing building is the church at Ingham (Norfolk), but

Butler and Given-Wilson (1979, 48) do include the short-lived Canons of the Holy Sepulchre, who also are not represented by any standing buildings. Misconceptions arise in Braun (1971, 211), who includes them with the friars and gives them Edington Priory (Wilts.); in Clarke (1984, 103), who states that they followed the Rule of St. Benedict and had houses of both monks and nuns; and in Lawrence (1984, 216), who has one sentence about the order in a chapter entitled 'Other Mendicant Orders'. Only Fosbroke (1843, 73), in the last century, and Knowles and Hadcock (1971, 37 and 205-7), Cowan and Easson (1976, 107-112), and Gwynn and Hadcock (1970, 217) in this century class the Trinitarians correctly with the orders most allied to the Augustinian Canons Regular.

Comparison with other monastic orders is difficult since the Trinitarians were neither an enclosed nor a mendicant order, and were certainly not a military order. They resemble most closely the Augustinian Canons Regular, yet their lasting identification seems to be with the mendicant orders. The conclusion may be drawn that they were highly idiosyncratic, defying the usual categorisations.

4.3 History of Thelsford Priory

4.3.1 The sources

The main secondary sources for the history of Thelsford Priory are Dugdale (1730, 499-501) and V.C.H. Warks. (1908, 106-8). As to primary sources, in particular cartularies, little survives and that only in later, antiquarian, transcriptions. Davies (1958, 110) has two entries for Thelsford. The first (no. 959) mentions part of a 15th to 16th century cartulary which was destroyed in a fire at St. Mary's Church, Warwick, in 1694. Davies says that a list of the contents of this was printed by Bernard (1697, 205-6) (no. 6711), who stated that 'the remainder of the book was reputedly with the Lucy family, Charlecote'. This is presumably the register mentioned in Fairfax-Lucy (1958, 34) as being amongst the family papers at the end of the 18th century, and of which register nothing survives except 'a few disjointed notes copies in an eighteenth century hand'. In the 'Lucy Papers' at the Warwickshire County Record Office (c. 142. 294/75) there is indeed a summary of charters (nos. 8-11) in an 18th century hand, but they add nothing to the information given by Dugdale (1730), and it is therefore probable that Dugdale, who was a friend of the Charlecote Lucys (Fairfax-Lucy 1958, 18-19), saw the original 'Thelsford Register', which he refers to in his footnotes, when he visited the family in the 1630s in order to study their family archives.

The second entry in Davies (1958, 110, no. 560) refers to 'a fragment of the same or another cartulary' which was destroyed by fire at Birmingham Reference Library in 1879. Thomas Phillips borrowed the original from William Staunton and in 1838 made a copy, which is in the Bodleian Library, Oxford (Phillips, MS. 11505).

4.3.2 The early history

In 1205 the site was known as Theulisford (Mawer and Stenton 1912, 240) but during the life of the priory there were many variations, such as Teflesford, Tefelisford, Tevelsford, Tivelsford and Telesford in the 13th and 14th centuries, followed by Thellisford, Thellysford and Thelesford in the 15th century, until finally it was spelt Thellsford in the 16th century.

Thelsford Priory was first occupied by the Canons of the Holy Sepulchre from their house in Warwick (cf 4.1) but there are problems about the date of their arrival at Thelsford and the date when the Trinitarians took over from them. The name of Thelsford is first mentioned in a grant made for a hospital some time between 1200 and 1212 by Henry de Bereford and Isabel his wife to 'the canons of St. Radegunde of Theulisford'. V.C.H. Warks. (1908, 106) states that this grant may have been to the Canons of the Holy Sepulchre as the beneficiaries are referred to as 'canons', as distinct from the Trinitarians which are later referred to as 'friars'. A discussion of the difficulties of confusing the Trinitarians with the mendicant orders is included with 4.2, History of the Trinitarians. Dugdale 1730 (499) does not specifically mention the Canons of the Holy Sepulchre as the recipients of this grant from Henry and Isabel de Bereford when he lists it, together with other grants, to Thelsford Priory, where he names the Trinitarians as 'canons'. Therefore it is not clear if the Canons of the Holy Sepulchre were already established at Thelsford in the opening years of the 13th century before this grant of 1200-12 enabled them to build a church and a hospital there. The dedication to St. John the Baptist (see below) and St. Radegund may indicate that the Canons of the Holy Sepulchre had instituted a church, and possibly a hospital, at Thelsford. Bond (1914, 41) says that St. John the Baptist was the patron saint of the orders whose function it was to guard the Holy Sepulchre at

Jerusalem, and also that it was a dedication especially reserved for hospitals looking after travellers, because of the itinerant life of the saint (Clay 1966, 250). The Canons of the Holy Sepulchre were interested in the provision of hospitals for travellers and the sick (see 4.1) and their Warwick hospital was dedicated to St. John the Baptist. The constitutions of the Trinitarians stipulated that they must dedicate any new church that they built to the Holy Trinity, but revisions of this constitution in 1217 and 1263 allowed them to retain earlier dedications (*cf* 4.2). The retention of an earlier dedication at Thelsford might suggest firstly, that there was already a church on the site at Thelsford, and, secondly, that the Trinitarians arrived there after 1217.

In 1214 Sir William Lucy gave demesne land at Thelsford in order that a church to the honour of 'God, St. John the Baptist and St. Radegunde the Virgin' should be built thereon, and also a hospital 'for the relief of poor people, receipt of pilgrims and sustenance of religious men there serving God for ever'. He also gave the advowson of the church and land at Charlecote. Tanner (1787, XXIX, footnote y) says 'this house was in being in the time of Walter Gray, Bishop of Worcester A.D. 1215 and in the sixth year of Hugh Welles, Bishop of Lincoln, A.D. 1214' and he was of the opinion that Sir William Lucy's grant was to the Canons of the Holy Sepulchre as he understood that the Trinitarians did not arrive in England until 1224, and were to have all their churches dedicated to the Holy Trinity. Both Dugdale (1730, 498) and *V.C.H. Warks.* (1908, 106) say that the grant of 1214 by Sir William Lucy was made to the Trinitarians, which contradicts Tanner, and Dugdale's own footnote (m) (1730, 498), which states that the Bishop of Worcester, Walter Cantilupe, found that 'this Hospital' was in decay in 1240 and at that date brought in the Trinitarians. Both the conflicting entries in Dugdale appear to have been taken from the Thelsford Register which he may have seen at Charlecote; Dugdale does not at any time mention the Canons of the Holy Sepulchre residing at Thelsford. Possibly the 1214 grant was made to these canons and they were already on Lucy property at Thelsford. It is expressly mentioned that the bishop acted with the full consent of the chapter and the patron when he introduced the Trinitarians in 1240. Probably the chapter was that of the Canons of the Holy Sepulchre; the patron, Sir William Lucy, did not die until 1247. It also seems strange that buildings endowed by him in 1214 should already be in a state of decay only 26 years later, if they had continuously belonged to the Trinitarians since 1214. It cannot be known exactly when the Canons of the Holy Sepulchre abandoned Thelsford; their order was in financial difficulties following the fall of Jerusalem in 1188, and they probably found it impossible to maintain Thelsford as well as their hospital in Warwick. Dugdale (1730, 454) does not give a definite date for the demise of the Warwick hospital, but it retained a prior and chapter of the Holy Sepulchre until 1280 when it was indistinguishable from the Augustinian Canons. The Trinitarians were an obvious choice for their successors, as they were also allied to the Augustinian Canons and both orders maintained hospitals. Knowles and Hadcock (1971, 207) place the arrival date of the Trinitarians at Thelsford 'some time after 1224', and Chettle (1947, 366) is probably right with his date of 1240.

Thelsford is the only Trinitarian House with a dedication to St. Radegund, presumably because it was inherited from the Canons of the Holy Sepulchre. She was never the patron saint of the whole order of the Trinitarians (as stated in Bell 1902, ii, 268 and in Jameson 1905, 220) in spite of her association with the release of captives (Brittain 1925, 64-5). Dugdale (1730,498) gives a detailed history of the life of St. Radegund, a Merovingian saint who founded an Augustinian convent in Poitiers and died there in A.D. 587. She had a special regard for prisoners and there is a window in Jesus College Chapel, Cambridge (which is dedicated to her) showing the chains falling from the prisoners. In addition to this former Benedictine nunnery at Cambridge, there are five English parish churches and two monastic houses (Thelsford and the Premonstratensian Bradsole) dedicated to her (Brittain 1925, 62).

4.3.3. The estates of Thelsford Priory (fig. 2)

The grant of 1214 by Sir William Lucy is useful archaeologically as it states the extent of the land given as 'thirteen acres of his demesne land belonging to Cherlcote, and next adjoyning to the way which leads from Cherlcote to Teflesford-bridge, on the west part the torrent called Teflesbroc; with the meadow ground belonging to the said thirteen acres'.

He also gave land to the east of this way as far as the arable land which formerly had belonged to Gerald de Charlecote. His grandson Fulk Lucy, who died in 1301, allowed the canons to enclose the road which at that time lay between their church and their 'habitation'; this shows that the canons had built on both parcels of the land which had previously been granted to them.

16

It was during the lifetime of this Fulk Lucy that a major event took place in the life of the priory. By this date the canons had acquired sufficient resources to build a new church and this was consecrated on the day of the Translation of St. Thomas the Martyr (July 27th 1285) by Bishop Giffard of Worcester. The enclosure of the road made the integration of a small original church with its 'habitation', that is its claustral buildings, possible. Excavation showed that in this period the priory had been enlarged by filling in the original east perimeter ditch and constructing a new church and claustral complex over it. This extension of the perimeter of the priory was further augmented when Fulk's son, Sir William Lucy, who died in 1329, allowed the canons to enclose two more acres of land adjacent to their house to join it to their 'court'. He also gave them 'a certain parcell of ground called the Hay, lying at the head of those two acres along by the brook called Theulisfordbroc' (Dugdale 1730, 499). It may have been at this time that the chancel ('Lady Chapel') was added to the 1285 church. The additional land would have made space for the extension of the church, with its east end very near to the Warwick road (fig. 3 and 61). If the 'Court' was at the site of the present Thelsford Farm (fig. 1), which is at a distance of about 200 metres from this eastern extension of the church, the main road from Warwick to Wellesbourne would have intervened and was possibly the source of tolls mentioned in the 15th century. The 'Hay' could possibly have been land by the Thelsford brook, to the east of this road, but to the north of the court. *V.C.H. Warks.* 1908, 106) says that this Sir William Lucy was 'subsequent' to Fulk Lucy and 'temp. Henry III', that is before 1272. Given the dates of Fulk (d. 1301) and his son William (d. 1329), as quoted in Fairfax-Lucy (1958, 316-7) and mentioned above, this statement in V.C.H. would not seem to be correct. Although there were several William Lucy's Dugdale states that the Sir William who gave the two acres was the son of Fulk (Dugdale 1730, 499). Dugdale (1730, 499) summarises a 1329 inspection grant, which was also a confirmation grant, and he quotes this in full (*Mon. Angl.* 1817, 1564-5, citing Pat. 3, Edw. III, p.2, m.8). By this date the Trinitarians had received not only the lands adjacent to their priory, as mentioned above, but also land in Barford. Included in this list is the original grant of Henry de Bereford, and also lands purchased in Barford from Henry by Philip de Kynton, and 'five yard land' given by Alice, the wife of Walter de Bereford and daughter of Reinbald de Charlecote. There was also a grant from William de Nasford, 'some time Lord of Bereford', of the fishing in the Avon from 'Le Milne to his own Millpool' and leave to make a pound at Barford for cattle trespassing on their lands there, three virgates of land and free entry and exit of their cattle on to the common pasture.

The extent of their other benefactions was fairly local (fig. 2), with the exception of lands and the advowson of churches and chapels at Kirby, Shilton and Packington, all of which were in Leicestershire.

Two hospitals in Stafford are also mentioned in connection with Thelsford Priory. In 1300 a writ to the sheriff of Stafford from Edward I enquires if Edmund, Baron of Stafford, may grant to the minister and brethren of Thelsford the hospital of St. John and the hospital of the Holy Sepulchre, as the brethren and sisters of these two hospitals 'on account of their poverty and indigence are obliged to leave the said hospitals and remove themselves to divers places' (Salt 1911, 269). Clay (1966, 40-1) comments that the leper house of the Holy Sepulchre at Radford, Stafford, would only receive lepers who had goods and chattels and was not bound to support them, and that the prior had been driven away by destitution. Clay also mentions (1966, 108) that St. John's hospital (at Forebridge by the river) is shown on a seal, now at the Society of Antiquaries of London, as having fine transitional-style buildings with triple lancet windows and a delicately pierced trefoil above them. This may not be a true representation of the hospital buildings, not is it certain that the Trinitarians actually administered these two hospitals. The last mention of the leper hospital is in 1320, but the St. John hospital had a longer history, although there were no poor maintained there by 1548.

The estates of Thelsford Priory at the supression are catalogued in a list taken from a minister's account of them (1538-9) (P.R.O. 1964, *sub* Thelsford Priory). In Barford a grange is mentioned 'with its appurtenances and divers messuages, lands, etc'. Also in the list is property in 'Tachebroke and in the suburbs and town of Warwick, Mitton, Longebrugge co. Warw., Solyhill, Wasperton, Assherne co. Warw., Newbolde and Morton'. The site of the priory is described as 'the house or "ministerium" of Thellisford with gardens, stables, and the herbage of a grove called "Thellisford Grove" within the parish of Charlecote'. It also notes tithes in Charlecote and perquisites of Courts.

4.3.4 The later history of Thelsford Priory

During the 14th and 15th centuries the ministers and brethren of St. John the Baptist and St.

Radegund continued to receive small grants, some from their benefactors in the Lucy family, and also permission to continue with their work in the collection of money for their cause. *V.C.H. Warks.* (1908, 107) mentions 'grants in mortmain', made from the acquisition of rents or land. In 1332 these grants were confirmed. Also mentioned is a 1334 licence to continue to collect alms for three years, as they had received in the past special privileges from the pope because of the nature of their work. They would also have received money from the sale of indulgences, and 'letters of confraternity' (*c.f.* 4.2). There is a 'letter of confraternity' of 1486 from a Thelsford minister, named Roger, to Richard Harrys, which is at the British Library (Harl. MS. 43.A.12) (Clark-Maxwell 1926, 57). One of the three surviving Thelsford 'letters of confraternity' (*c.f. 4.2*) consistently refers to Thelsford as a hospital: and the last, dated 1529, is a block of four unused printed impressions (Clark-Maxwell 1929, 213).

Permission to dispense indulgences is mentioned in *V.C.H. Warks.* (1908, 107) as having been received from the Pope in 1411 and 1467. The 1411 licence is interesting as it mentions that there were 'sisters' at Thelsford Priory at this date. 'Sisters' are also mentioned by Tanner (1787, XXIX) when he referred to a lease from the minister of Thelsford in 1413 which described the 'duties and devotions' which the procurators, on a recruiting campaign in Gloucestershire, could collect when they were 'making brethren and sisters for four years at four marks per annum'. Whereas the 'sisters' referred to at Thelsford were possibly nursing the sick in the hospital, the latter were probably women who had received the special privileges of sharing in the prayers and good works of the order, by payment of a sum of money.

The philanthropic zeal of the Lucy family evident in the early years of the priory gave way in the middle of the 14th century to the more personal considerations of family burials and masses for the dead to be said for themselves and their friends. Both Dugdale (1730, 501) and *V.C.H. Warks.* (1908, 107) mention that in 1354 Thomas Lucy gave lands at Charlecote for masses to be celebrated for the souls of William de Clinton, Earl of Huntingdon, and those of himself and his wife Philippa. In 1394/5 there was a gift of forty acres of land and six acres of meadow at Ashorne and Newbold Pacey from Sir William Lucy, Roger Straunge or Strange and John, Vicar of Wellesbourne. In 1492 another Sir William Lucy relinquished all the claims which he and his ancestors had at Thelsford. Dugdale (1730, 501) says that these were 'Toll, Tack, Stallage and Bloodshed'. These may refer to rights the Lucys had to 'tolls' on the road by the priory, to dues for the erection of a stall in a market ('stallage') and for the slaughter of animals ('bloodshed'), 'tack' could refer to the right to take fish from the fishponds or refer to certain pasture lands. This Sir William was not buried at Thelsford, but at Stratford-upon-Avon, although he left forty shillings to the canons of Thelsford 'for the observation of his exequies'. It was his son Edmund, whose will was proved in 1498, who made elaborate provision for his own funeral in the 'Lady Chapel' at the priory. He gave a cross of silver and gilt to the value of ten pounds, and stipulated that his grave should be covered with a marble stone seven feet by four feet with the arms and effigies of himself and his wife. On the day of his burial forty marks were to be 'spent and given ... by the hands of his Executors, to priests, clerks and poor people' (Dugdale 1730, 505). He also willed that at his 'month's mind' twelve poor men should hold torches round his grave, each receiving fourpence in money and a black gown and hood. Furthermore, he stipulated that his 'anniversary' should be kept at Thelsford for twenty years after his death and that forty shillings should be spent 'for Dirige overnight, Masses, and to poor people'. He also asked that 'one priest of the same Order of those at Thelesford' should receive eight marks per annum and sing 'in the said Chappell for his soul, for the souls of Jane his wife, and Sir William Lucy, Knight, his father, and all Christen souls' (Dugdale 1730, 505). It is not known if these 'poor people', for whom he had special concern, were from the hospital at Thelsford, but this is a possibility. The important information in his will related to the archaeology is that he desired to be buried 'on the North side of his mother, Margaret Lucy'. Although Edmund Lucy was only thirty one years old at his death, he had two wives, the first being Jane who predeceased him and with whom he was buried beneath the marble slab, with effigies of both of them upon it. His second wife, Joan, daughter of Sir Richard Ludlow, had remarried after Edmund's death, but asked to be buried by Edmund's side in a will of 1514, leaving forty shillings to the Thelsford House. This is the last recorded burial in the Lady Chapel of the Lucy family.

The son of Edmund and Joan, one Thomas Lucy, did not live at Charlecote, but in London, and was buried at the church of the Grey Friars in Smithfield in 1525 with masses said for his soul in Charlecote church (Dugdale 1730, 505). Fairfax-Lucy (1958, 318) says that Thomas reclaimed the rights which his grandfather, Sir William Lucy, had relinquished at Thelsford and took back the profits from the glebe lands of Charlecote Church and the advowson of the vicarage; he also enclosed the common land which the canons had had the use of for two centuries and withheld the oblations (that is forty shillings) which his mother had left to them in her will. Fairfax-Lucy (1958, 318) gives no dates for these decisions to remove some of their revenue from the canons. Although this may not have meant a great loss of income, it showed a changed attitude on the part of the Lucy family towards their hereditary obligations.

A list of the ministers, the heads of the house, in Dugdale (1730, 501) gives thirteen names between 1247 and 1538, including Robert Bolton who was a provincial minister in 1473. *V.C.H. Warks.* (1908, 108) has fourteen names, as it includes Robert Bowston in 1440, citing Bloom, Gild of Stratford-on-Avon, 186.

4.3.5 The Dissolution of the priory

The *Valor Ecclesiasticus* of 1535 gave a clear annual value of £24.19s for this house (*V.C.H. Warks.* 1908, 107), but *V.C.H. Warks.* says that because it was 'a house of friars' it did not come under the provisions of the 1536 Act. Dugdale, who did not confuse the Trinitarians with the mendicant orders, states that the reason they were not suppressed at that date was that 'through the King's favour (or rather for that it was of so small consequence) the dissolution thereof was forborn in 27.H. when the rest of the lesser Houses went to wrack' (Dugdale 1730, 501). A list of the nett incomes of the other Trinitarian houses is given in the introduction to the gazetteer below (9.1), with Thelsford as the penultimate name in value. With reference to the map of adjacent monastic sites (fig. 65) the hospitals which survived long enough to give Dissolution values were those of Holy Cross, Stratford-on-Avon (£51.19.8^{3}/4d), of St. John the Baptist, Coventry (£83.3.2d), of St. Leonard at Clattercote (£34), of St. Michael, Saltisford, Warwick (£41), of St. Mary at Studley (£117) and of St. Mary, Kenilworth (£538). (*V.C.H. Warks.* 1908, and Knowles and Hadcock 1971).

There is a possibility that the hospital at the priory was still in operation at the time of the surrender, and perhaps afterwards. Bickley (1923, 125) mentions an abstract from the bailiff's account of monastic estates in the County of Warwick under the supervision of the Court of Augmentations for the year ending Michaelmas 1457: 'and for £4.13.4d for rent of tithes of sheaves in Chorleton, late in the special occupation and tillage of the said late house of friars, for the use of the Hospice of the same house, as valued and assessed by the commissioners of our Lord the King, now let to Baldwin Inshawe'.

The information in this abstract would be very useful for future work on the estates of Thelsford Priory as it gives great detail about the exact position, size and values of the lands which had once belonged to the priory at Barford, Tachebroke, Hethcote, Warwick, Solihull, Newbold, Ashorne, 'Chorleton' (?Charlecote) and Wasperton. It also mentions that the lands of Wasperton had been acquired by William Whorwood, as mentioned in Dugdale (1730, 501) but not in *V.C.H. Warks.* (1908, 108), together with 'the annual tithe reserved ... for the site and desmesne lands of the said late house of Friars'.

William Lucy realised that the suppression of this priory would eventually take place and wrote, on the 18th March, 1538, to the bishop of Worcester to ask for possession, as he was the patron. He said that he would like to make an agreement with the head of the house to this effect and continue his tenth yearly due to the king (*V.C.H Warks.* 1908, 107).

However, on 26th October, 1538, the minister and three brothers signed the surrender of their house to Dr. London. *V.C.H. Warks.* 1908, 107) gives the religious there as 'Edmund David, prior and three others', but Dugdale (1730, 501) is probably more correct when he names them as 'Edw. Davie Minister, Frater Jacobus Brown, Will. Lucie, and Nich. Turnar', adding that the only one to receive a pension (of £5 per year) was the minister.

Immediately after the surrender London informed the Chancellor of Augmentations that the house was only worth £18 a year and referred to the canons as 'the crossed friars of Thelisforde' (a mistake of nomenclature which was made at other Trinitarian houses at this period). He also wrote to Cromwell about the fraudulent use of an image called 'Maiden Cutbroghe' and alleged that the sick placed 'a peck of oats' in a trough by her feet, but that the oats ran down under a hollow altar and were collected by 'the friars' at the back of the altar. For the fee of one penny for one pint of 'Maiden Cutbroghe oats' they would be cured of headaches. London said that he had pulled down this image (*V.C.H Warks.* 1908, 107-8).

19

The next stage of the dissolution of the priory differs in the Dugdale and *V.C.H.* accounts. Dugdale (1730, 501) says that on 7th July 35.H.8.(1543) the King 'in consideration of £648.19.2d. sold the site and seven acres of woodland, called 'Thelesford-grove' and lands in Cherlcote and Wasperton to William Whorwood and William Walter, and that the Lucys of Charlecote purchased the estate later from them. However, *V.C.H. Warks.* (1908, 108) says that Cromwell at first told London to accede to William Lucy's original request for possession, but then changed his mind and granted it to Mr. Cheney. But London wrote to Cromwell on 22nd January, 1539, saying that he had given the custody of the Priory to Mr. Lucy and described it 'as in much ruin and the church little and unfinished'. He says that he left the buildings standing, as defacing them 'would not have put £20 in the king's pocket'.

Archaeological evidence suggests that the stones of the church were robbed out in the 16th century, that the smaller ponds and the ditches were filled in, and that the land was probably used for grazing animals in the post-medieval period.

The priory seal was oval, with St. Radegund in the centre and two small figures, carrying ?palms (presumably captives) on each side of her. The inscription is 'S . HOSPITAL . SCE . RADE ....s.DE . VADO . TAVELLI.' This is illustrated in *V.C.H. Warks.* (1908, pl. 1).

Chapter 5
METHODS OF EXCAVATION AND RECORDING; AREAS AND CHRONOLOGY

5.1 Methods of excavations and recording

The choice of method for excavation was dictated by circumstances: neither in 1966 nor in 1972 were the methods used ideal for this type of site. Nevertheless, although the unique opportunities of total excavation of a small priory of a little known order was lost, a good deal of information was recovered.

The aim in 1966 was to investigate as large an area as possible, with limited resources and time, in order to estimate the extent of the land which should be scheduled. There was no alternative to extensive trenching of a ploughed field which showed a homogeneous scatter of medieval finds but no visible surface features. The total length of trenches excavated was 390 m, sampling the area shown in fig. 3. In view of the possibility of more complex excavation at some future date, no walls, hearths or definite levels were removed, making the dating of these structures difficult.

In 1972 the area that was to be destroyed by the new road, and a narrow zone on either side (figs. 3 and 4) were machine-stripped of ploughsoil. Since it was now known that the majority of the priory buildings lay to the east of the line of the new road, the contractors agreed to keep their heavy machinery and any dumping of soil to the west side. The site was cleaned, after the machine stripping, by the use of Dutch hoes. Those areas which showed the most concentration of finds were selected for complete excavation. Some areas proved to be too waterlogged for examination, but these were, fortunately, often those with fewer surface finds. All features were completely excavated with the exception of some of the ditches. After the site had been cleaned by hoeing, a ten metre grid, marked by numbered metal pegs, was laid out over the whole area. This was related to the national grid of the Ordnance Survey (see archive).

In both excavations levels were related to the bench mark (48.19 m above OD) on Thelsford Cottages as shown on the site plan (fig. 3). Section datum lines are recorded on some drawings, and the bottom levels of any feature which do not appear on sections are mentioned in the table of contexts in MF.

As animal bone and building materials were present in most of the features, details of quantities of these, by weight and type, can be consulted in the archive, and are only mentioned in this text where their significance is relevant to discussion.

In the 1966 excavation, features were originally prefixed by the letter F (e.g. F1, F2, F3 etc.) and layers by trench number, peg number and layer. For example II/12/E would indicate Trench II, peg 12 and layer E, the peg number being the peg to the right of the layer in question. In the compilation of this report, however, these have all been given a context serial number, 1-273 for features and 300-373 for layers. In 1972 a serial number for all contexts 400 onwards, was used, and these have been retained unaltered. New contexts added during the compilation of this report in 1988-9 are numbered 600 onwards. Details of all contexts will be found in MF Tables A and C.

In general, where a feature is shown with edges in broken outline, or extensions shown in dotted outline, the lines are assumed, but not proved by excavation; where ditches are shown with hachures, that part has been excavated fully.

5.2 Areas and chronology

In the following text, the site is discussed in seven areas designated A-G, as follows (fig. 3):

A   south end of the 1972 area - principally ditches (6.4)
B   north end of the 1972 area - ?mill platform and water channels (6.5)
C   south central part of the 1972 area - ancillary features west of the priory (6.6 and 6.7)
D   north central part of the 1972 area - culvert and ditches (6.6 and 6.8)
E   church and cloister (6.10 - 6.13)
F   west range of claustral complex (6.10 and 6.14)
G   gardens and ploughlands north of the church and cloister (6.15). SE end of Trench II/part of eastern perimeter (6.9)

Within these divisions each area is described chronologically within the following periods:

Period I   pre-13th century (prehistoric and pre-priory)
Period II   c. 1200 to c. 1285
Period III   late 13th century to late 14th centuries
Period IV   15th and 16th centuries
Period V   post-medieval

The discussion of the sequence in each area or cutting is in the form of a commentary on the figures, which leads the reader through the sequence of contexts and their stratigraphic relationships. Some indication will be given of the principal reasons for periodisation of structures or other features, and of layers. Detailed justification must however be sought in the plans and sections; in the tables of contexts and graves (MF Tables A and C) and from the associated finds sections in chapter 7. While the structural and stratigraphic data normally provide the sequence, it is in some cases only the finds (or their absence) which suggest assignation to periods, notably the presence or absence of certain building materials, or the dating of coins, metal objects, pottery and other artefacts.

Three layers occurred over many parts of the site, and are referred to in the text in the shorthand of: *A* modern ploughsoil; *E* the general layer of Dissolution-period debris; *Q* pre-priory soil - a yellow sandy soil, mottled with brown flecks; and *Z* undisturbed 'natural' glacial sands, clays and gravels.

Chapter 6
THE EXCAVATIONS

The full version of the text of this chapter will be found in the microfiche, MF-2 to MF-95, to which the reader is referred for detailed arguments and evidence, together with Tables A and D, which have details of individual layers, features, and graves. The numbering of the sections that follow are the same as those in the microfiche, for ease of reference.

6.1 Introduction

The site plan (fig. 3) shows the 1966 trenches, the course of the gas pipe-line, and the area of the new road of 1972. This includes also the outlines of the plans of areas A, B, C/D, and E/F/G; the latter comprises the area of the claustral complex. Fig. 4 shows the 1972 excavation area, with outlines of all important features, and details of a few which do not figure in subsequent plans, such as the part of 461 observed between areas A and C.

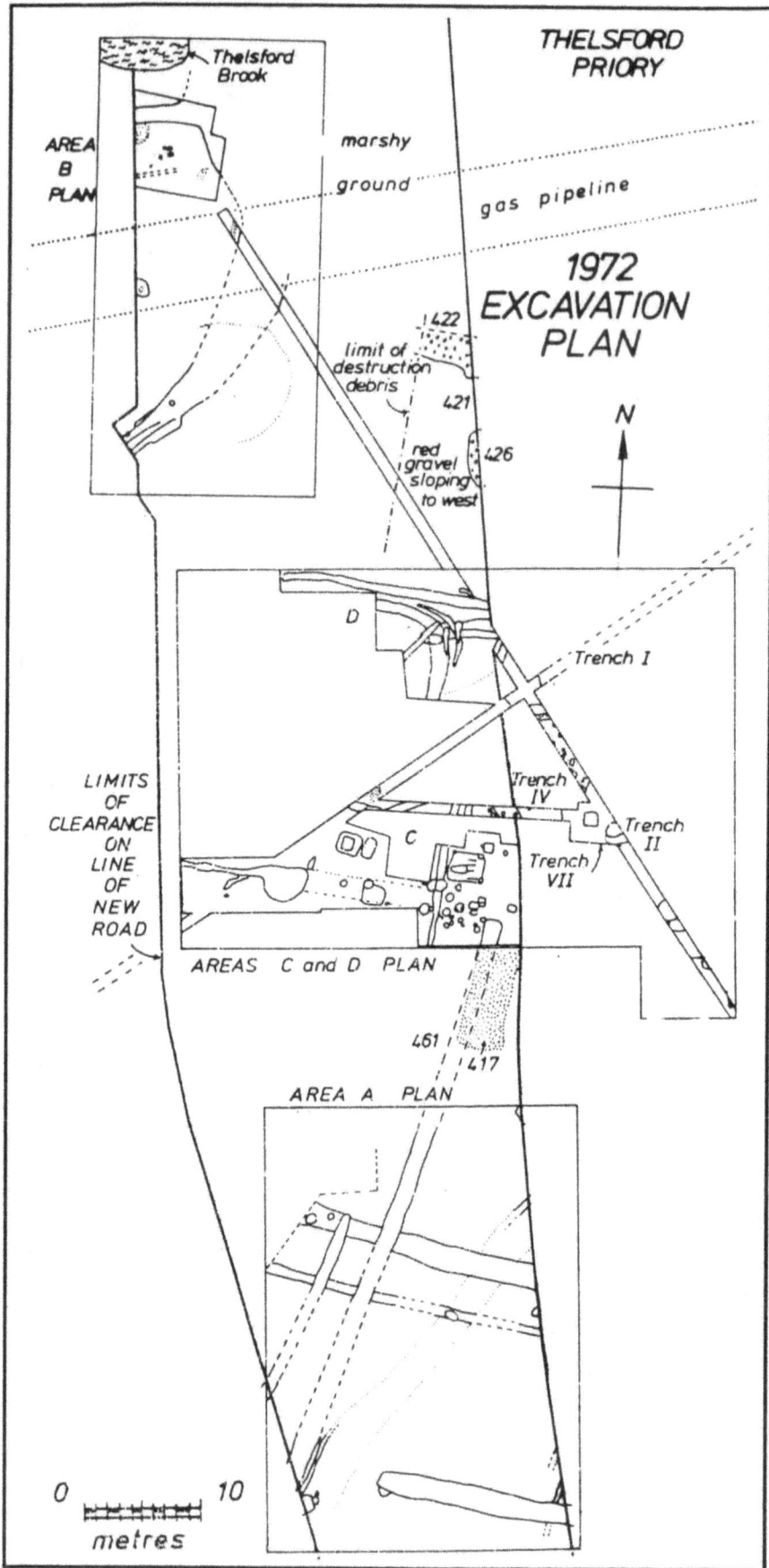

THELSFORD
PRIORY

Thelsford
Brook

AREA
B
PLAN

marshy

ground

gas pipeline

1972
EXCAVATION
PLAN

422

limit of
destruction
debris

421

N

red
gravel
sloping
to west

426

D

Trench I

LIMITS
OF
CLEARANCE
ON
LINE
OF
NEW
ROAD

Trench
IV

C

Trench
II

Trench
VII

AREAS C and D PLAN

461

417

AREA A PLAN

0   10

metres

Fig 4

24

6.3 The SW end of Trench 1 (figs. 5-7)

This lay west of the area stripped in 1972. 22 may be a prehistoric gulley; 28 and 29 are components of the western boundaries of the priory; 28 is a trench for a fence or hedge outside a wide ditch of period II; somewhere in the area of the southern arm of the fishponds; 29 is a ditch of period III; these are discussed further below. The date of the fishponds is not known, but they are most plausibly associated with period III; some version could be earlier, including the southern arm here cut by Trench I.

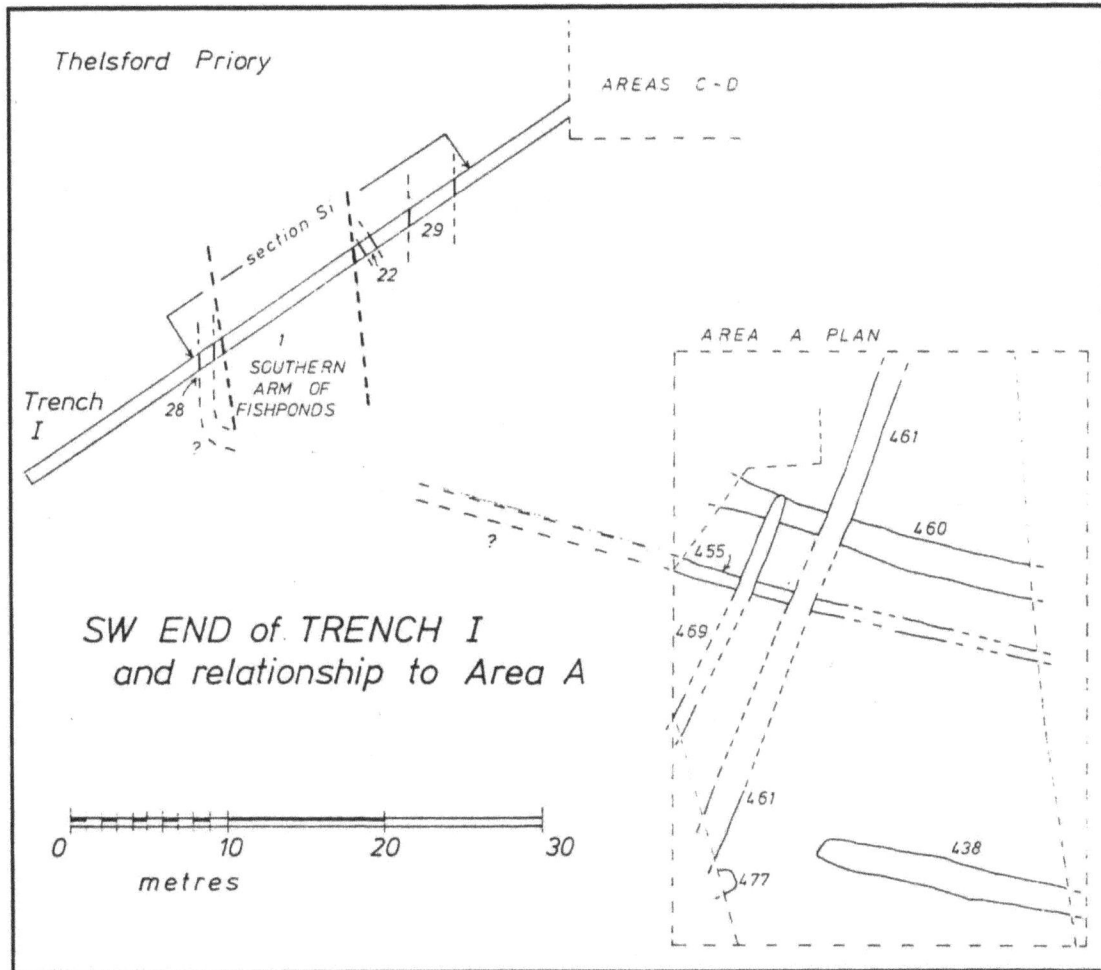

Fig 5

6.4 Area A (figs. 6-7)

6.4a Introduction

In this area elements of the southern perimeter boundary in periods II-III and other ditches draining north were found.

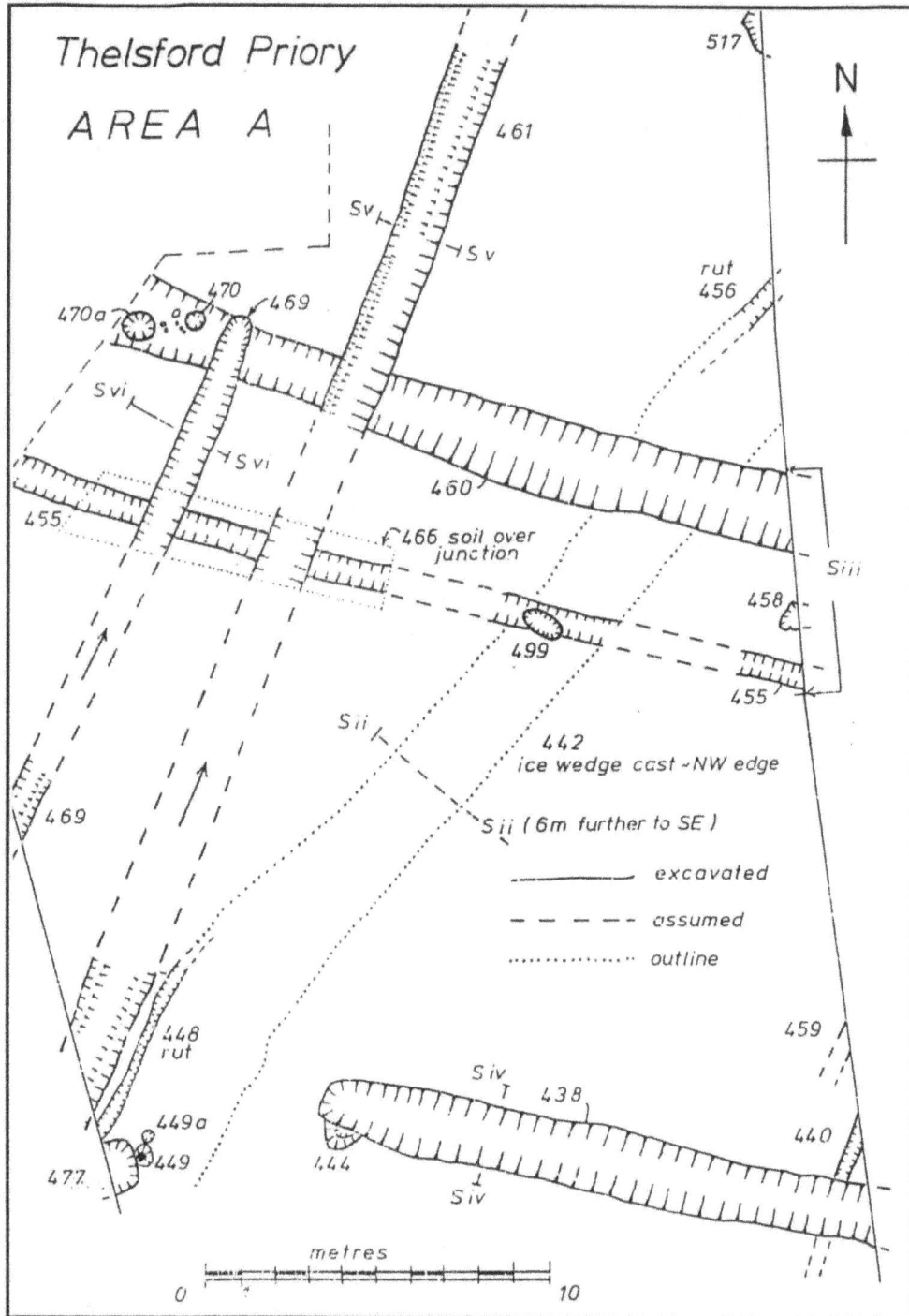

Thelsford Priory
AREA A

461
Sv
Sv
470a 470 469
Svi
Svi
455
466 soil over junction
460
Siii
458
499
455
Sii
442 ice wedge cast ~NW edge
Sii (6m further to SE)
469
―――――――― excavated
― ― ― ― ― assumed
·············· outline
459
448 rut
Siv
438
449a
440
477 449
144
Siv
517
rut 456
N

metres
0   10

Fig 6

6.4b Period I

The NW edge of the periglacial ice-wedge cast (442) provided a hard surface which may have been used as a road; ruts were defined on its western edge. 440 and 459 may represent pre-priory hedge or ditch boundaries; 517 could be prehistoric.

6.4c Period II

460 is the principal ditch of the southern perimeter, with 455 as a fence or hedge outside it, equated with 28 in 6.3 above. This double boundary was also located in its eastern arm (6.9, 6.12a); the western perimeter was probably somewhere in the area of the fishponds, as suggested in 6.3 above; and Thelsford Brook would have formed the northern boundary (*c.f.* fig. 3).

26

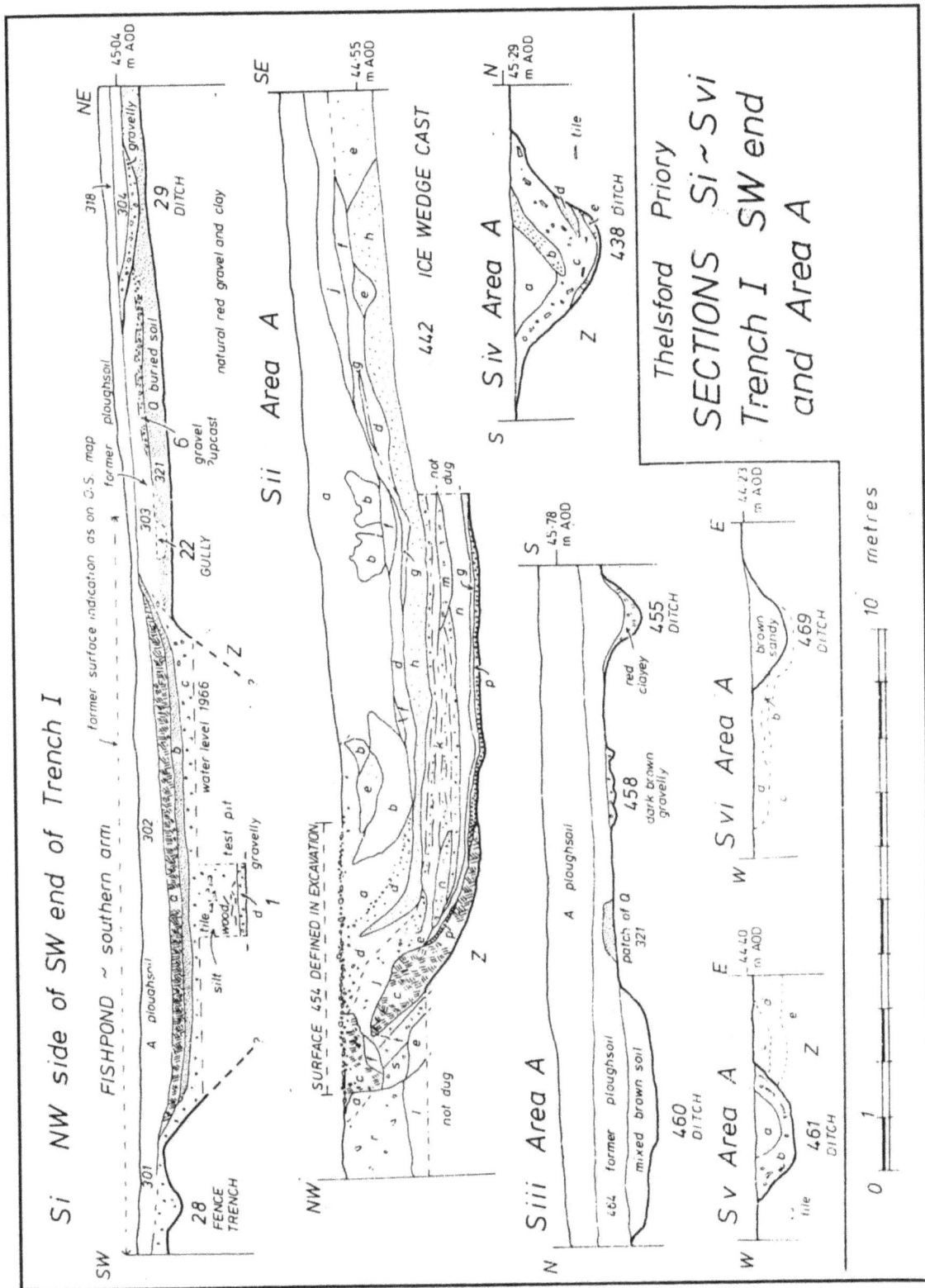

Si NW side of SW end of Trench I

FISHPOND ~ southern arm

Sii Area A

ICE WEDGE CAST

Siii Area A

Siv Area A

Sv Area A

Svi Area A

Thelsford Priory
SECTIONS Si~Svi
Trench I SW end
and Area A

metres

Fig 7

27

6.4d Period III

The priory enclosure was extended to the south in period III, 438 being the new southern perimeter ditch; the length noted ended within area A; there may have been an entrance here with some features within it, including 449 with a 25 cm square post. 477 could conceivably be the end of a continuation of the southern boundary. 461 and 469 drained the area northwards, cutting through the period II perimeter; they may have also inhibited flooding by storm-water. 499 was cut into the period II fill.

6.4e Period IV

Pits or postholes 470 and 470a were cut into the period II fills.

6.5 Area B (figs. 8-11)

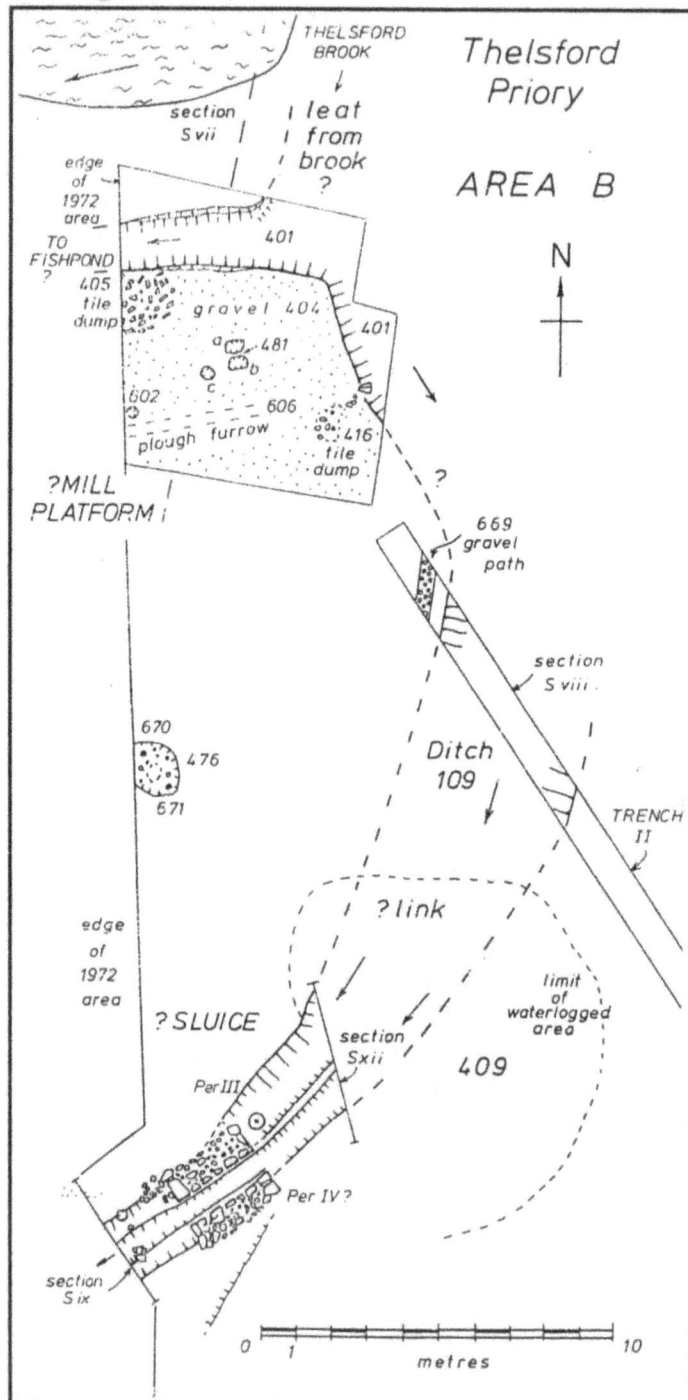

Fig 8

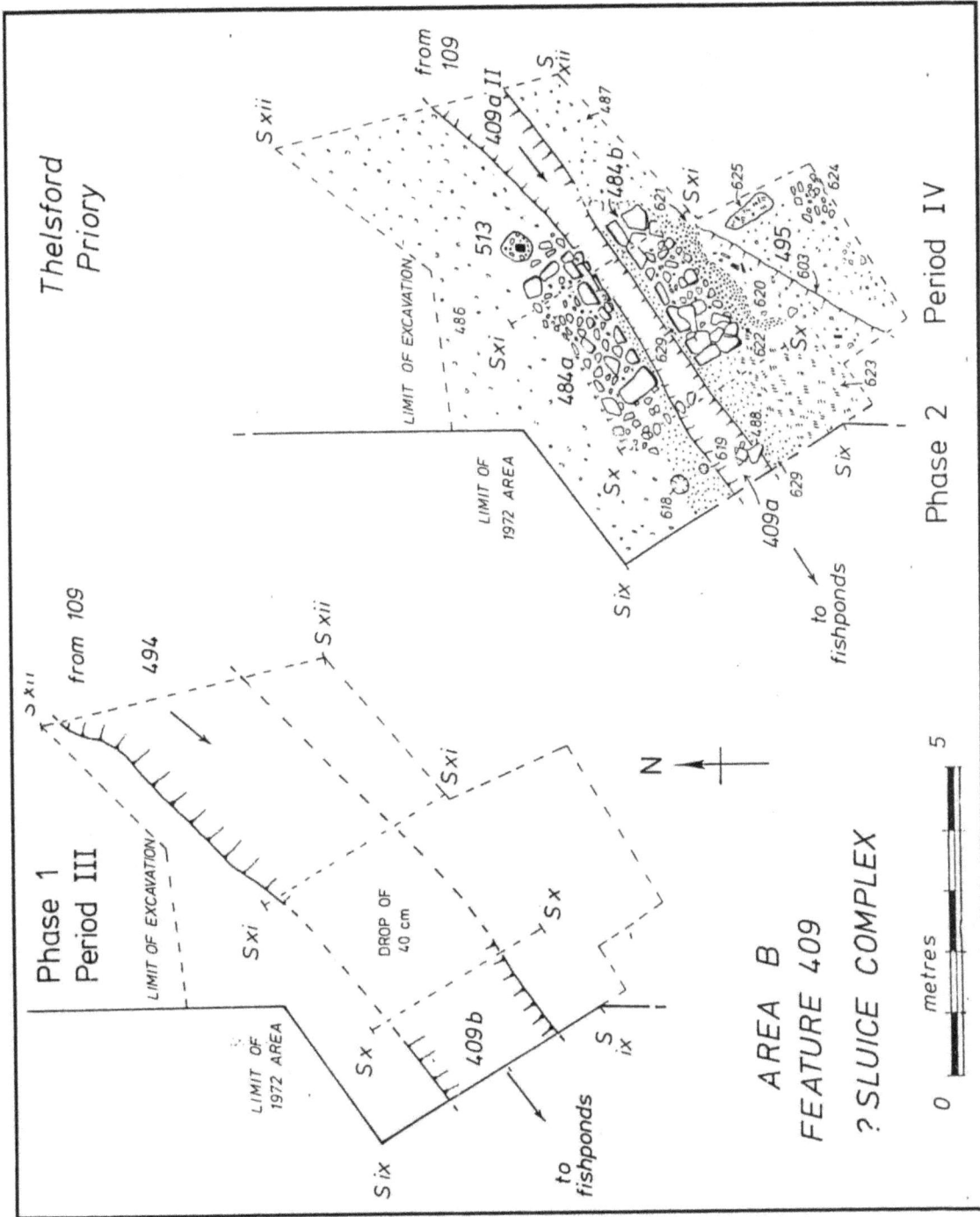

Thelsford Priory

Phase 1 Period III

Phase 2 Period IV

AREA B
FEATURE 409
? SLUICE COMPLEX

Fig 9

6.5a Introduction

At the north end of the 1972 area were two complexes associated with the water system; a possible mill area and a ?sluice complex, linked by a ditch. An isolated pit with postholes (476 - only on fig. 8) may also be associated

6.5b The north end of area B and the NW end of Trench II

Close to Thelsford Brook was a raised area or platform, with a ditch or water channel to its north and east. This was at the southern end of a straight section of the brook (fig. 3). It is suggested that a leat was drawn off this, bifurcating as 401; the upper arm took water to the upper part of the fishponds, the other to the ?sluice complex 409, via ditch 109, and then on to the fishponds.

Building materials and other features on the metalled platform suggest the possibility that here or in the vicinity was a substantial building, possibly a watermill. Dating evidence is poor, but it is suggested to be of period III, as is the first ?sluice.

6.5d ?Sluice complex 409 (Plate I)

The first feature here, of period III, was ditch 494/409b, bringing water from the brook via 109. There may have been some sluice structure at this time, as there is a sharp drop of c. 40 cm from the base of 494 into 409b (sections Six-xii fig. 11). Subsequently, in period IV, there was a more definite structure of substantial foundations (484a, b), with a sharply-dropping channel between; a major post (513); and possibly some timber structure to the SE (fig. 9, stage 2). Was the possible watermill in this area, perhaps secondary? The ?sluice went out of use before the Dissolution.

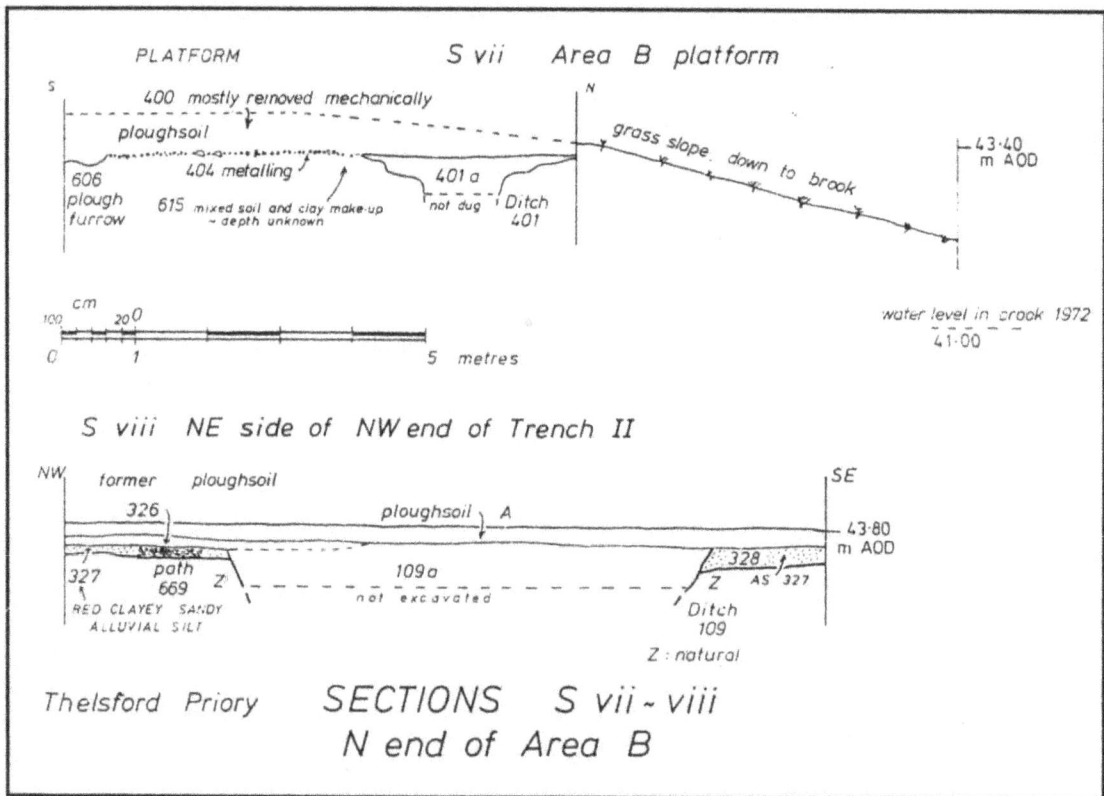

Thelsford Priory   SECTIONS   S vii ~ viii
N end of Area B

Fig 10

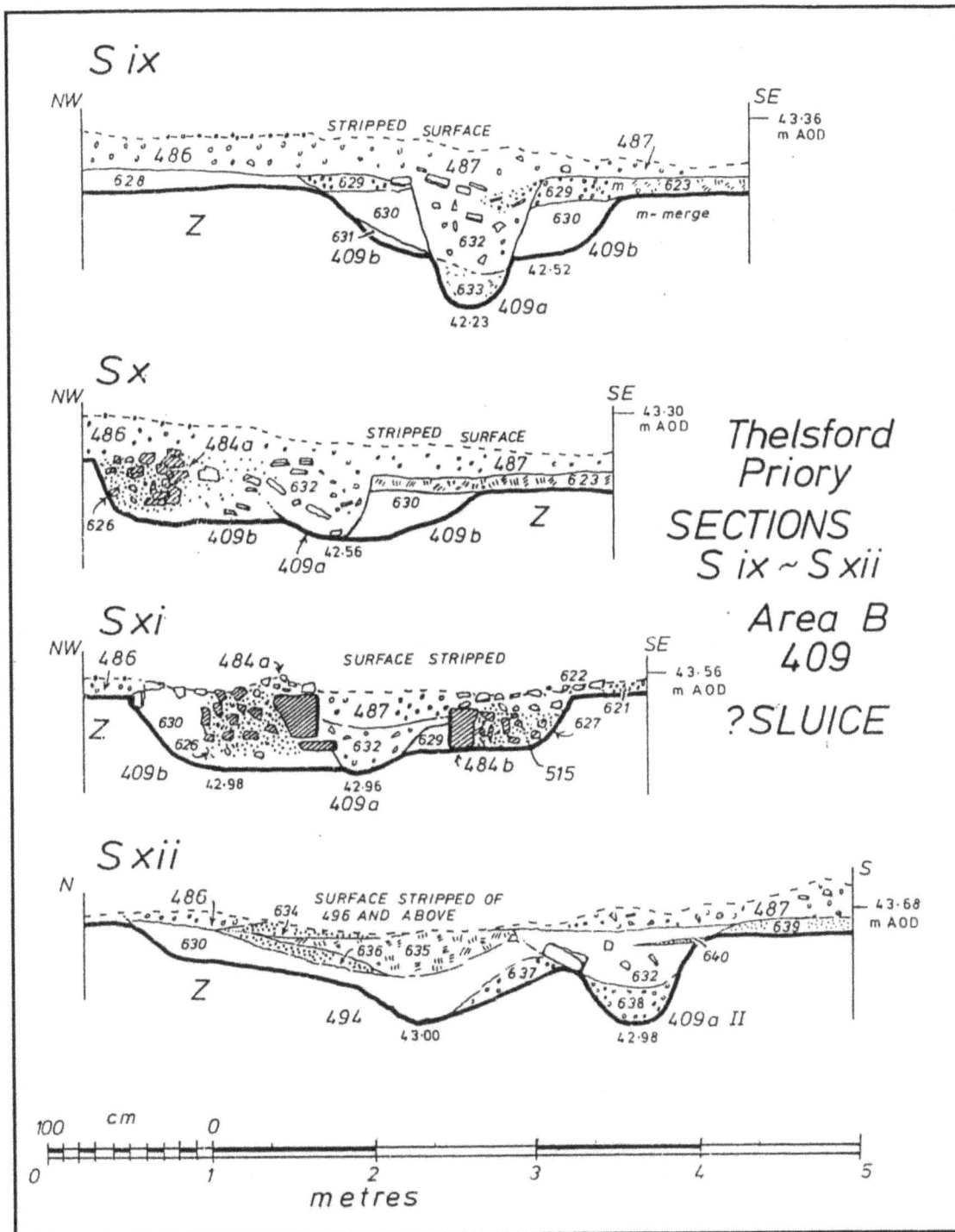

Fig 11

6.6 Areas C and D - introduction
(figs. 12-22, sections Sxiii-xxi)

These areas lay west of the claustral complex; within them was a series of ancillary buildings and structures, with associated ditches, a culvert and other features.

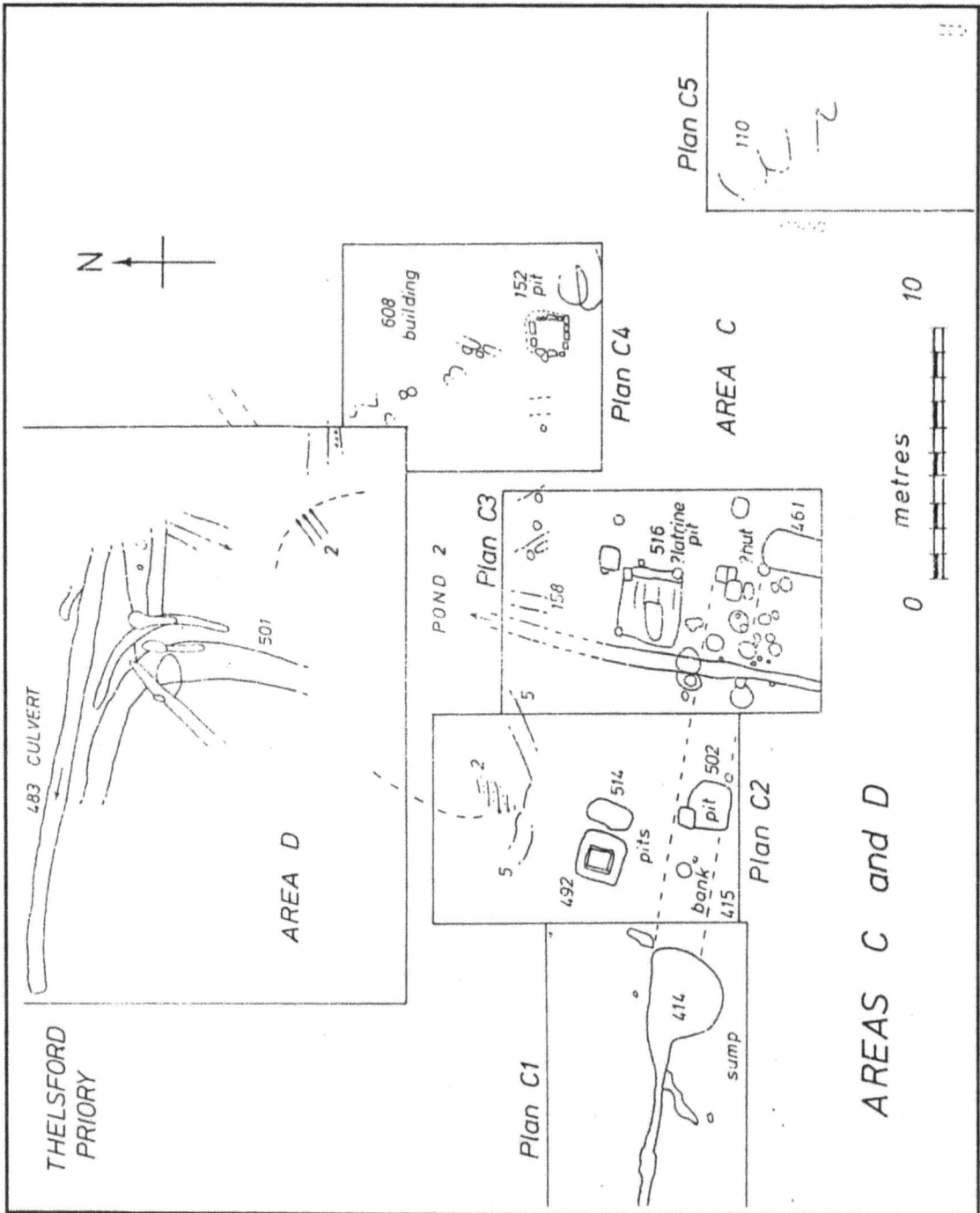

THELSFORD PRIORY

AREA D

483 CULVERT

501

2

608 building

152 pit

Plan C4

POND 2

Plan C3

158

516 Latrine pit

461

?nut

N

AREA C

492

514

pits

5

2

502 pit

bank

415

5

Plan C2

414

sump

Plan C1

AREAS C and D

110

Plan C5

0   metres   10

Fig 12

32

6.7 Area C

6.7a Area C - plan 1, pond 414 (fig. 13)

The posthole 25, and gulley 492, area pre-priory, of period I, possibly prehistoric. In period II, a ditch (407) led from the fishpond area, draining into a sump or pond (414); a large hook in its base (7, 10, IR 44) would be suitable for net-retrieval and suggests that this was a small fishpond. 415/480 comprise a later bank, discussed further below.

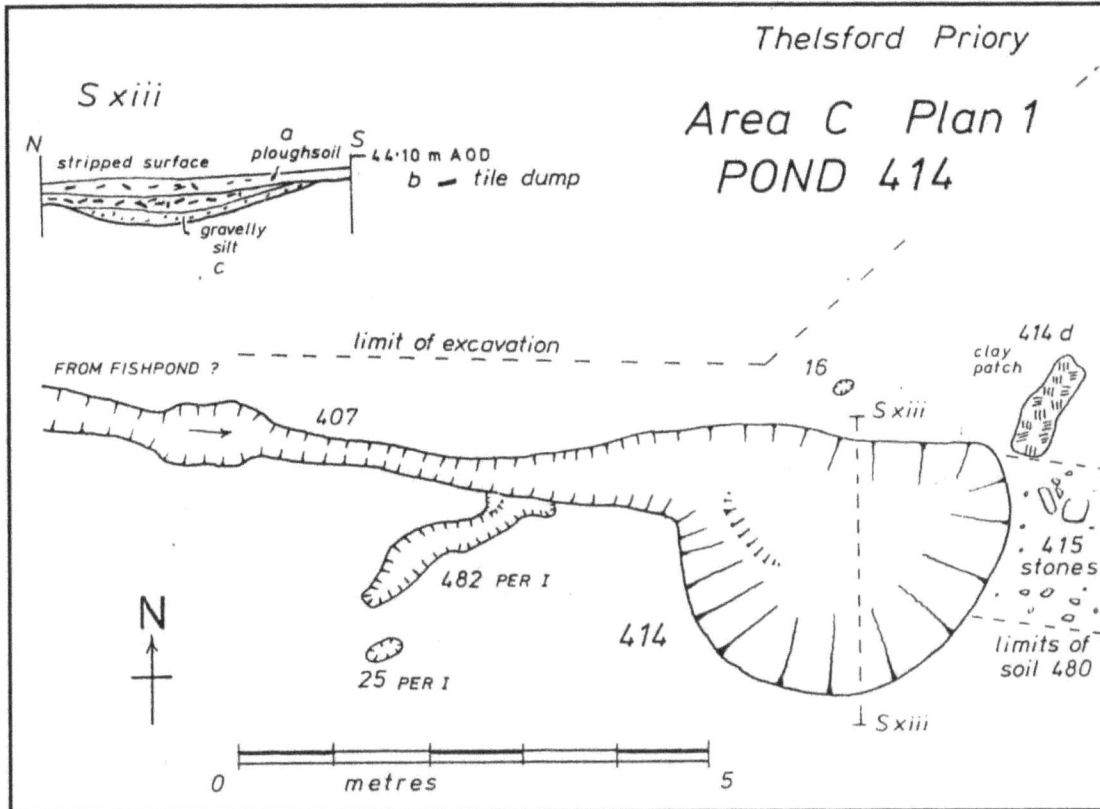

Fig 13

6.7b Area C - plan 2, features 492, 502, 514, etc. (fig. 14)

The earliest feature here, of period II, was a pond (2), into which several ditches drained. In period III, two pits were dug (492 and 514). The former was complex, with slots around a central prepared platform (Sxiv, fig. 22). This and 514 both contained burnt material; they may have been associated with metal-working, though there was no evidence of metallic residues.

Further south, another pit (502) also contained charcoal and building material, but is more likely to have been a cesspit, with two associated postholes (a and b), and two more to the west (468, 468a).

The latter were overlaid in period IV by the bank feature 415/480. This may have been merely a boundary between the area sloping up to the south and the wetter areas to the north, sloping down towards the Thelsford Brook; or may have acted as a flood bank or barrier.

6.7c Area C - plan 3, ?hut, ?latrine 516 etc. (figs. 15-19)

Fig 15 shows all features; in figs. 16-19 they are separated by period. In period I (fig. 16), there were several complex postholes and the end of a gulley (157b). In period II, in Trench IV, were two postholes (153-4) and a ditch 158, possibly later, but ending close to the trench. Further south the concentration of postholes may indicate a squarish hut, c. 3m. in each dimension (corner posts 423, 511, 446, 506), with other features to the west; there was no evidence of the possible hut's function.

In period III (fig. 18) a ditch (505) traversed this area, draining northwards into pond 2. The major ditch 461 ended here (see 6.4d above). Between the two were several substantial postholes and a deep rectangular pit (516 - see also Sxv on fig. 22). This had an unmortared line of stone foundation and

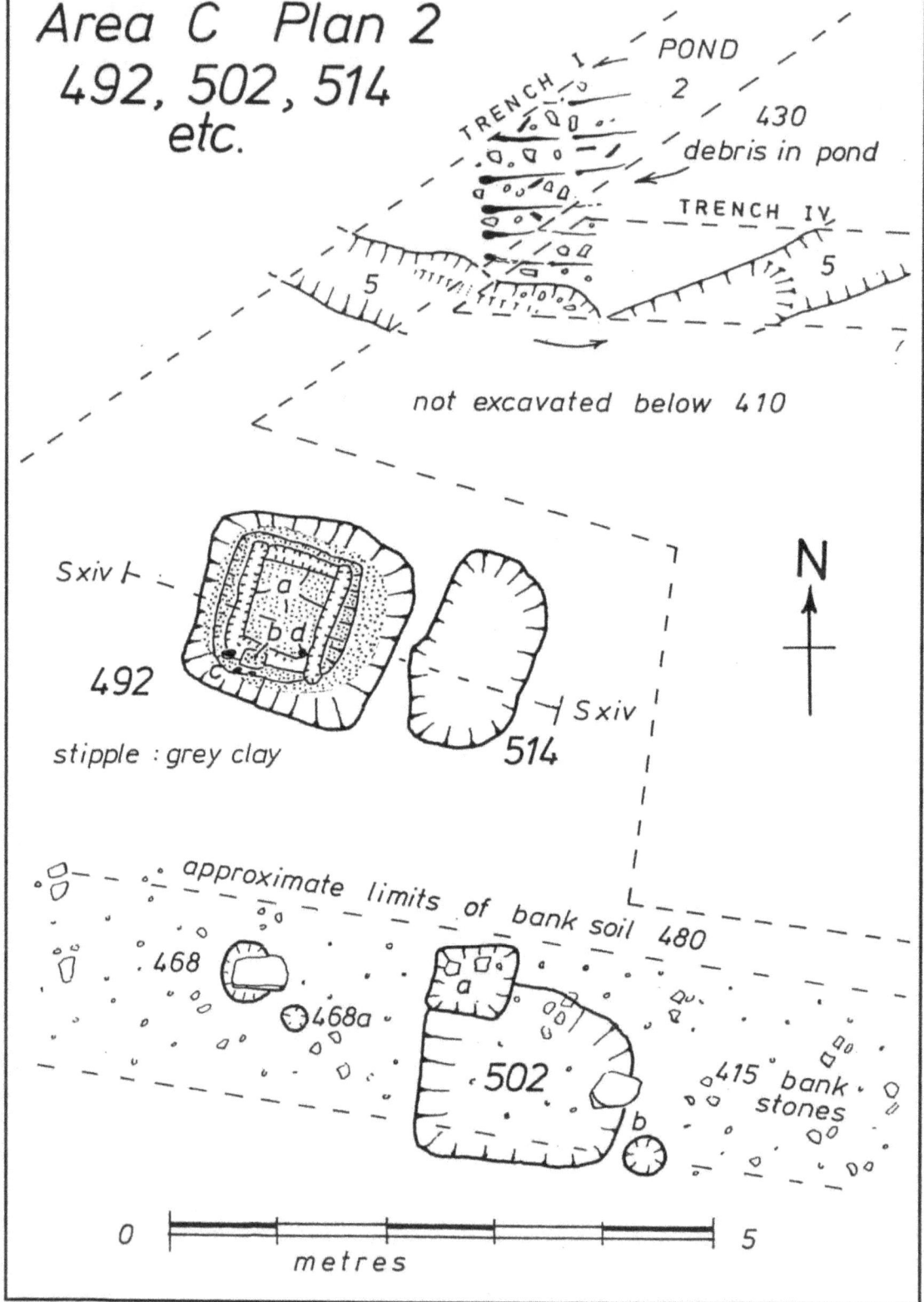

Thelsford Priory
Area C Plan 2
492, 502, 514
etc.

POND
2

430
debris in pond

TRENCH I

TRENCH IV

5

5

5

not excavated below 410

N

Sxiv

a

b d

c

492

stipple : grey clay

Sxiv

514

approximate limits of bank soil 480

468

468a

a

502

b

415 bank stones

0   5

metres

Fig 14

34

postholes in its base (a); from this extended two channels (d and e) and a hollow with stones (c). The whole complex is interpreted as a latrine structure with a pit and the supports for seating structures.

In period IV this area was traversed by the bank 415/180 discussed above, ending here in an area of metalling (417) overlying the filled-in ditch 416. A ?path (644) traversed the NE corner of the area on this plan.

6.7d Area C - plan 4, 608, 152 etc. (fig 20 and sections Sxvi-xviii on fig. 22)

Of period I was a posthole (117) with a post-ghost, possibly prehistoric; 119 may be of period I or II; and also 155, in Trench IV, which is in line with the period II postholes 153-4 on plan 3 (fig. 17).

In period III there was a timber and stone building, of which burnt residues survived. It is difficult to interpret this satisfactorily on the basis of evidence from a narrow trench; but 107 may be part of a west wall; and ?wall-trenches 115 the east wall, perhaps with 121-2. Within the building was a destruction layer (337) of dark soil, charcoal, charred wood, and some large blocks of limestone

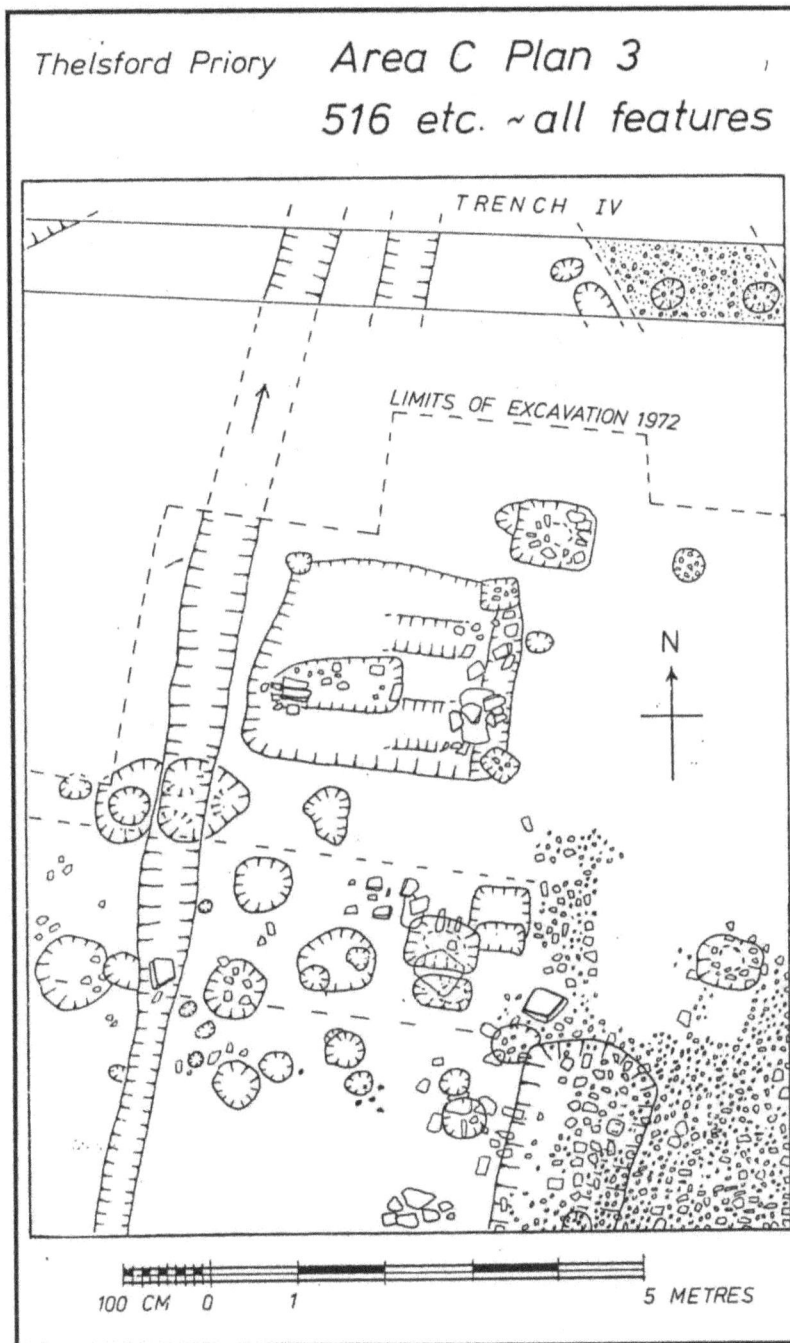

Thelsford Priory Area C Plan 3 516 etc. ~ all features

TRENCH IV

LIMITS OF EXCAVATION 1972

N

100 CM 0 1 5 METRES

Fig 15

35

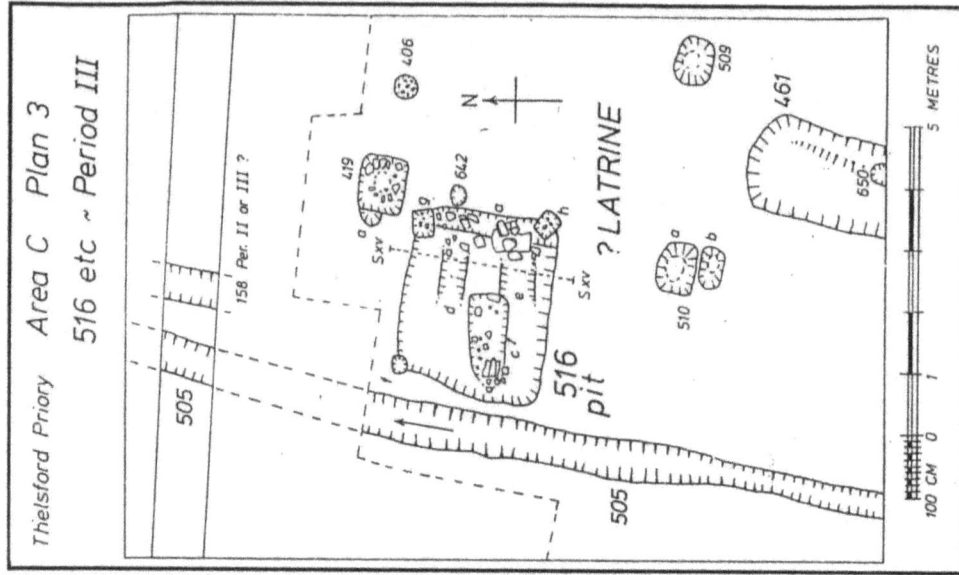

Thelsford Priory   Area C   Plan 3

516 etc ~ Period III

?LATRINE

516 pit

Fig 18

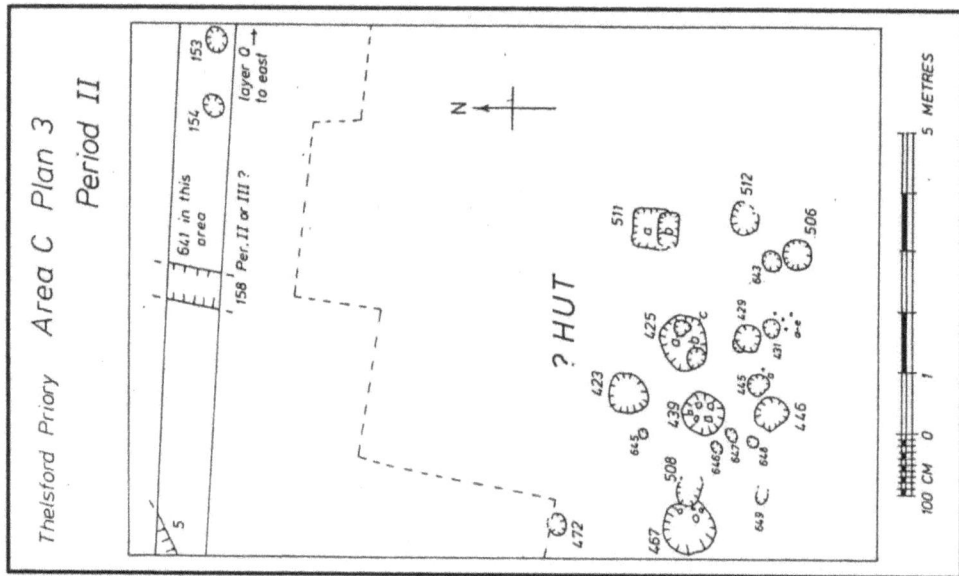

Thelsford Priory   Area C   Plan 3

Period II

? HUT

Fig 17

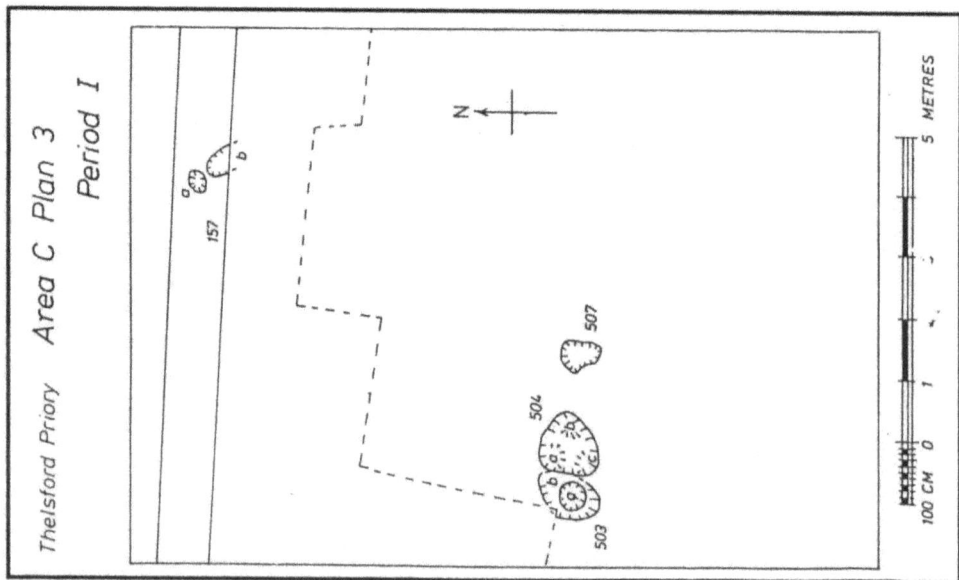

Thelsford Priory   Area C   Plan 3

Period I

Fig 16

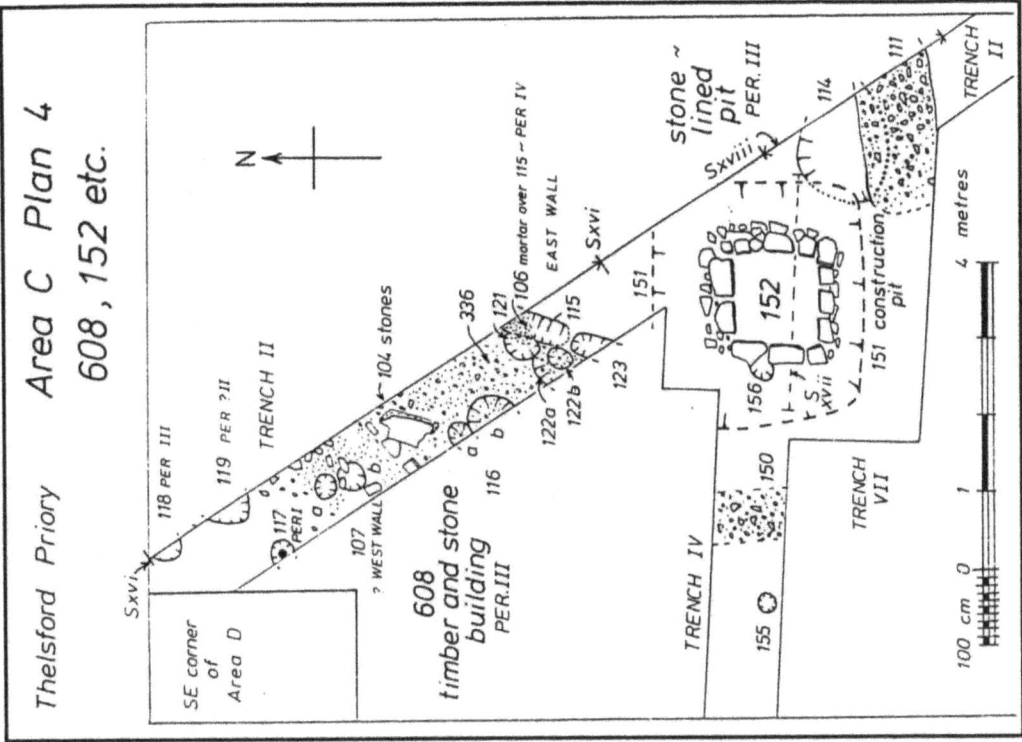

Thelsford Priory   Area C   Plan 4

608, 152 etc.

608 timber and stone building PER.III

Fig 20

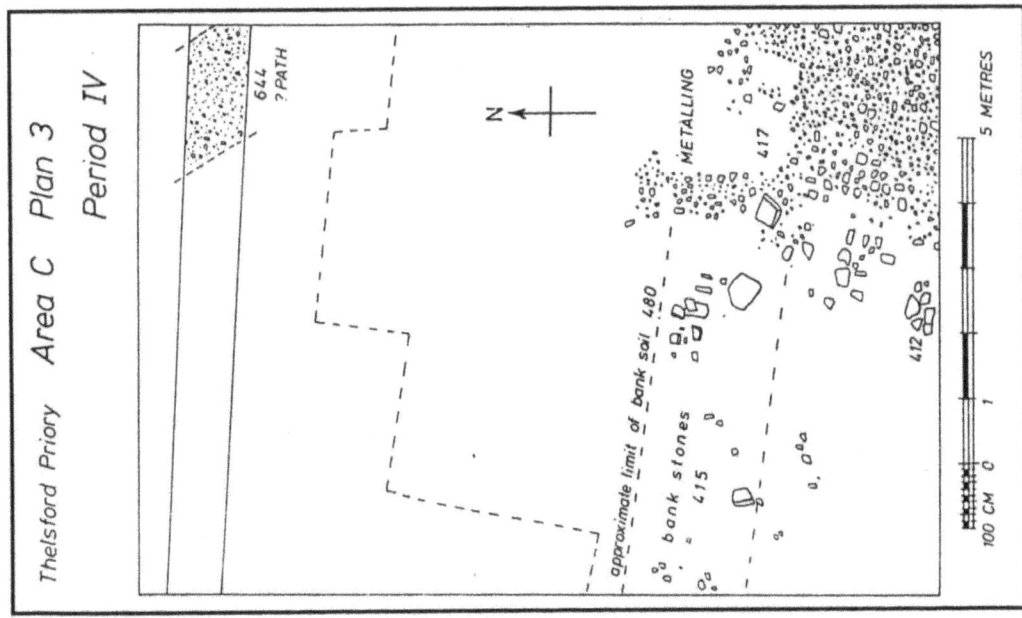

Thelsford Priory   Area C   Plan 3

Period IV

Fig 19

37

(104). The building may have thus been *c*. 3m wide from west to east, and at least 5m. long.

South of this was a ?cesspit (114), later replaced by a major stone-lined pit, similarly interpreted, with a ?boundary wall (111) to its south; there were many finds in its filling layers. This complex may have been intimately associated with the building to the north (Plate II).

6.7e Area C - plan 5, 110 etc. (figs 21 and Sxix on fig. 22)

In this area, 601 was the edge of a cut in the natural, filled with the buried soil layer Q (Sxix), and interpreted as the edge of a terrace, or a negative lynchet, of pre-priory date. Of the priory period III were a path or tiles (100), and a ?cesspit (110a); and of IV a replacement pit (110b), and the end of another feature (112). 108 could just be the eastern end of the bank 415/480, discussed above.

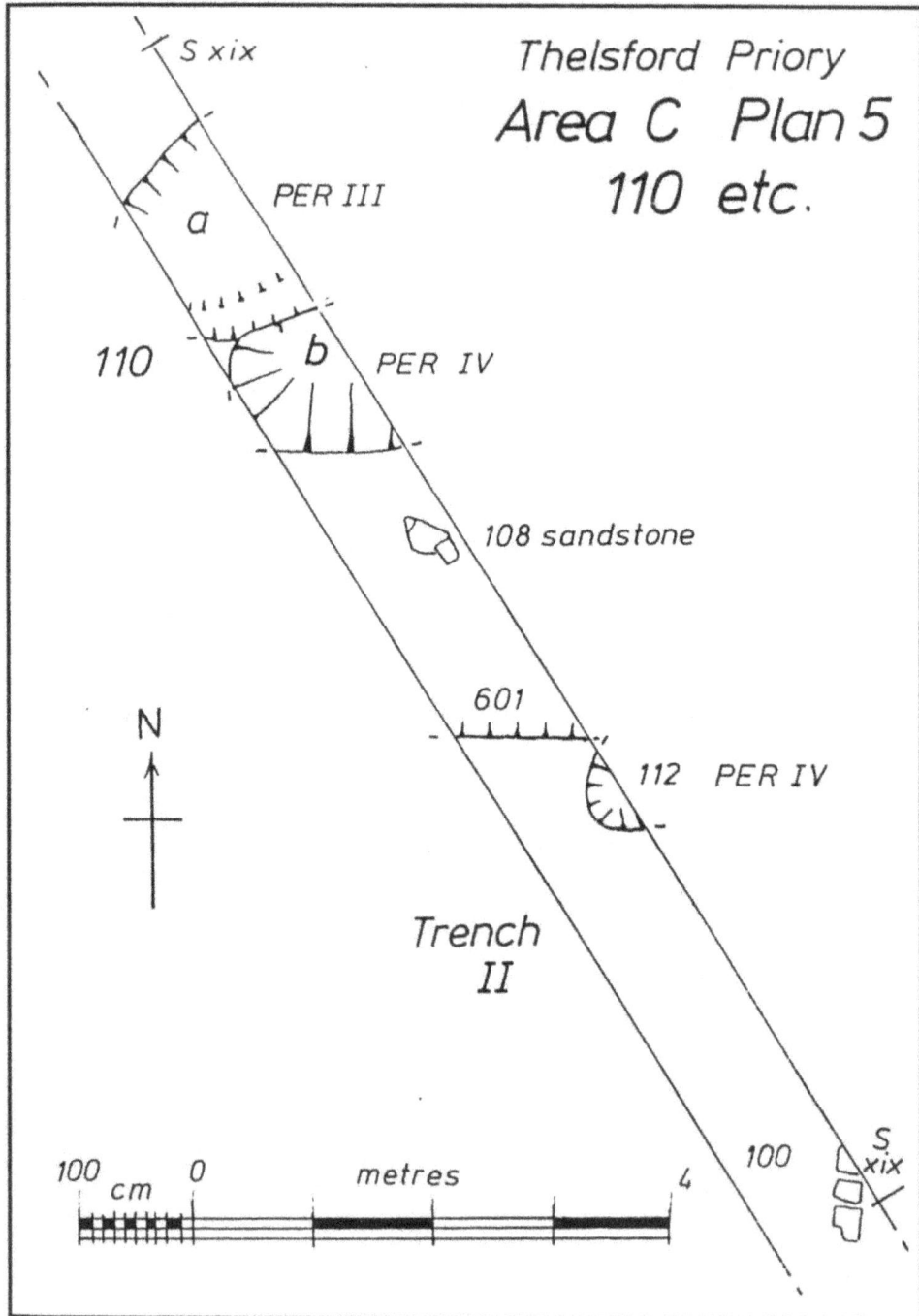

Fig 21

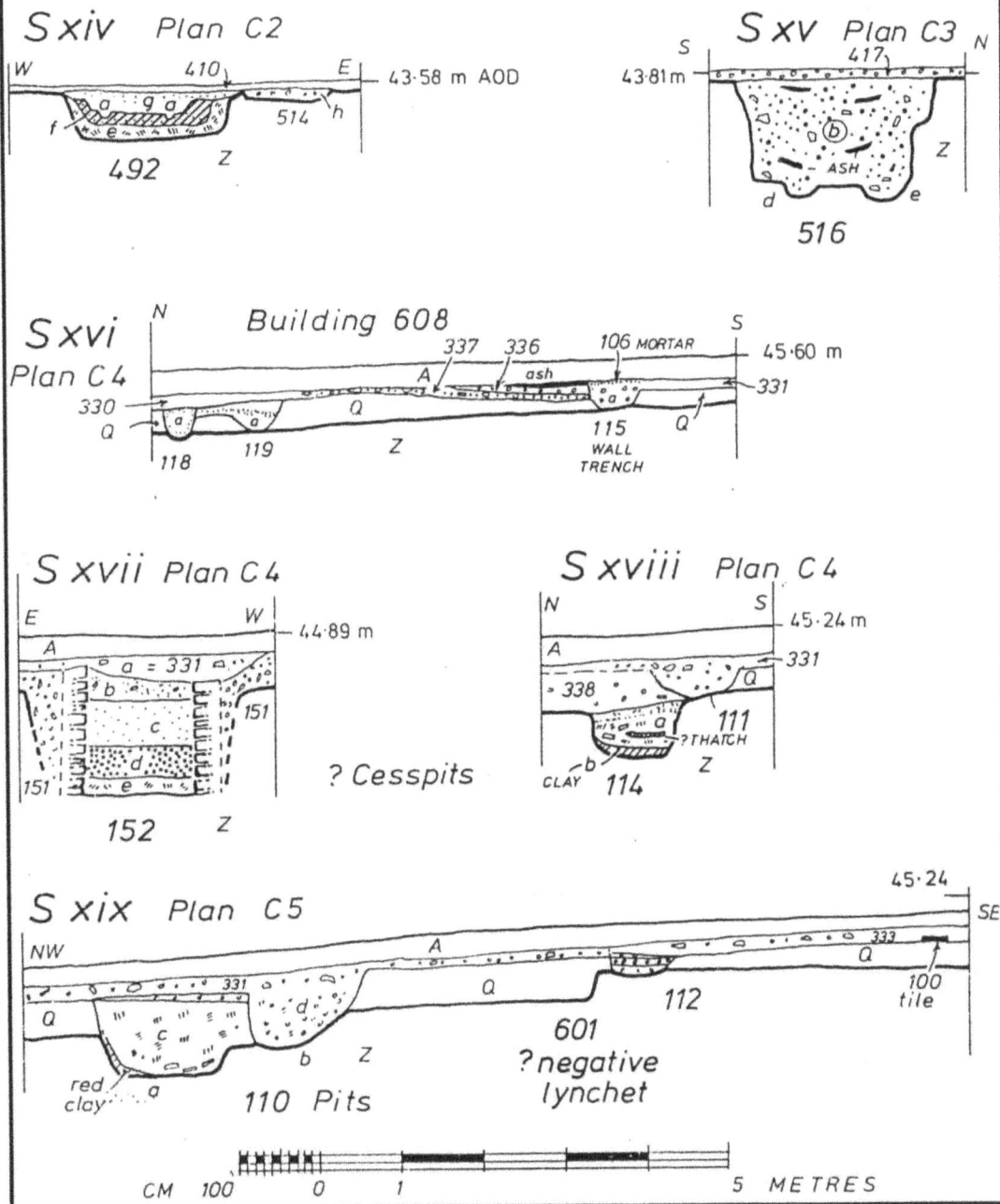

Fig 22

6.8 AREA D (figs. 23-27)

6.8a Introduction

Fig. 23 shows all features; figs. 24 and 26 (plans 2 and 4) isolate features of periods III and IV; fig. 25 gives detail of culvert 483; sections in the area are on fig. 27.

6.8b Periods I-II (fig. 23)

The shallow gulley 103 was the only pre-priory feature, probably prehistoric. Of period II, the NE side of pond 2 was encountered here, with ditches 120 and 127 draining into it.

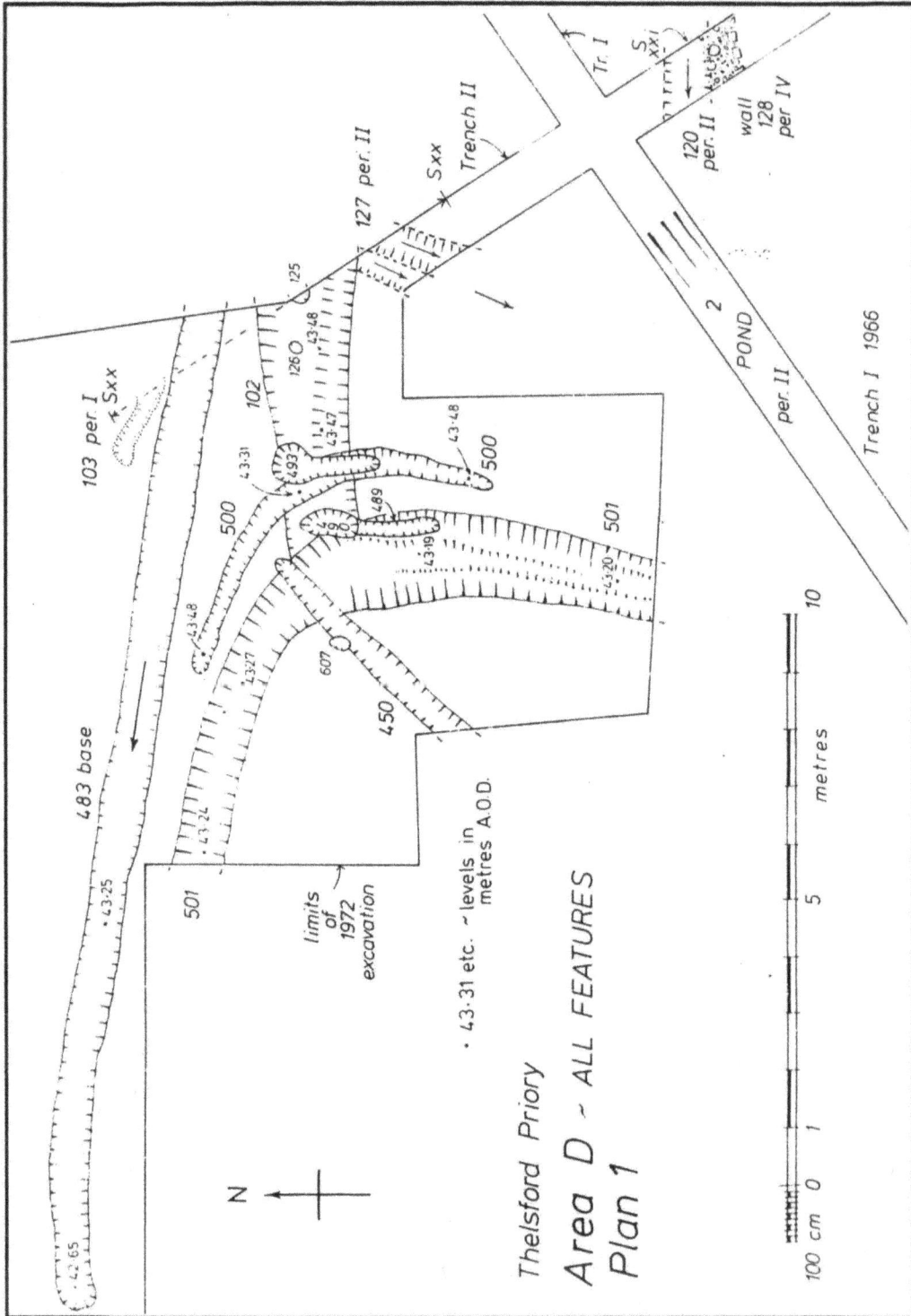

Thelsford Priory

Area D ~ ALL FEATURES
Plan 1

Fig 23

40

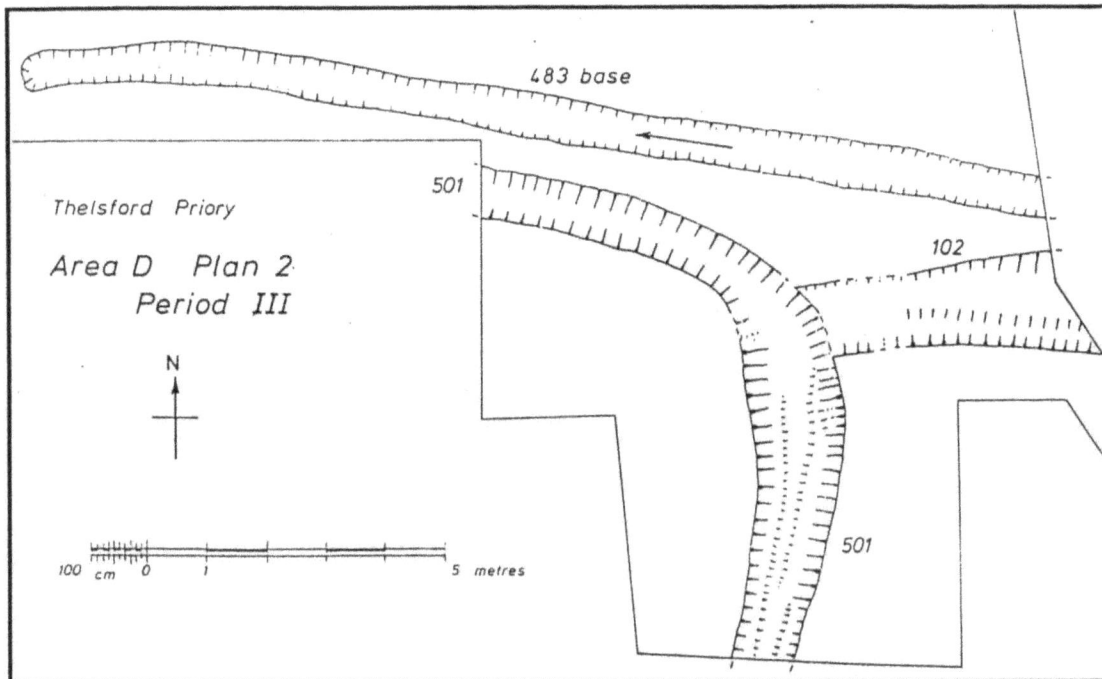

Thelsford Priory

Area D   Plan 2
Period III

N

100 cm 0   1   5 metres

483 base

501

102

501

Fig 24

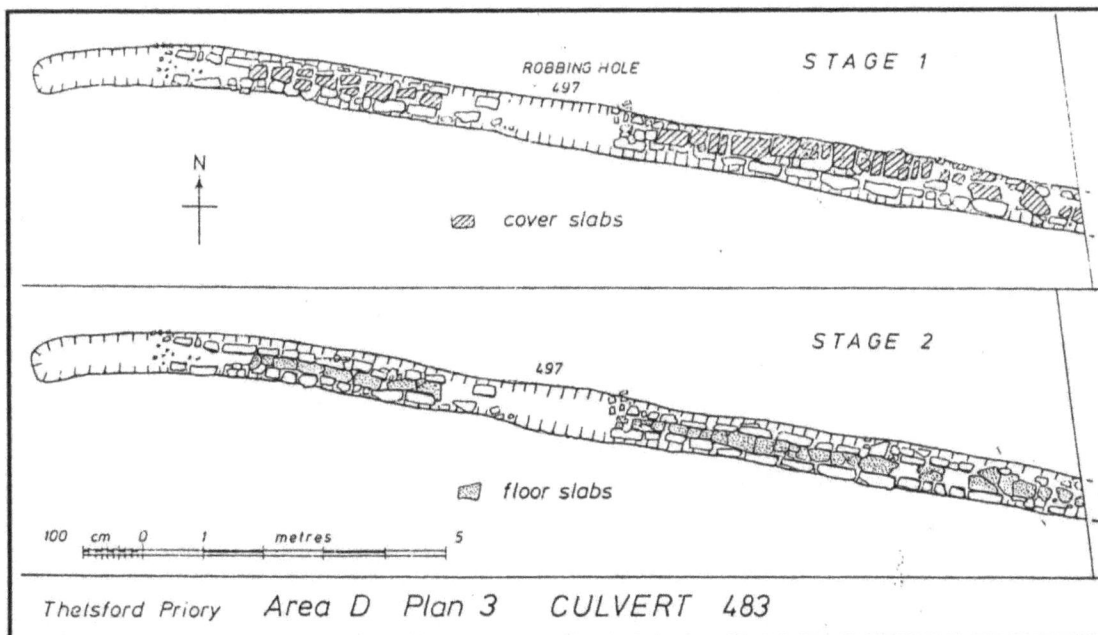

STAGE 1

ROBBING HOLE
497

N

cover slabs

STAGE 2

497

floor slabs

100 cm 0   1   metres   5

Thelsford Priory   Area D   Plan 3   CULVERT   483

Fig 25

41

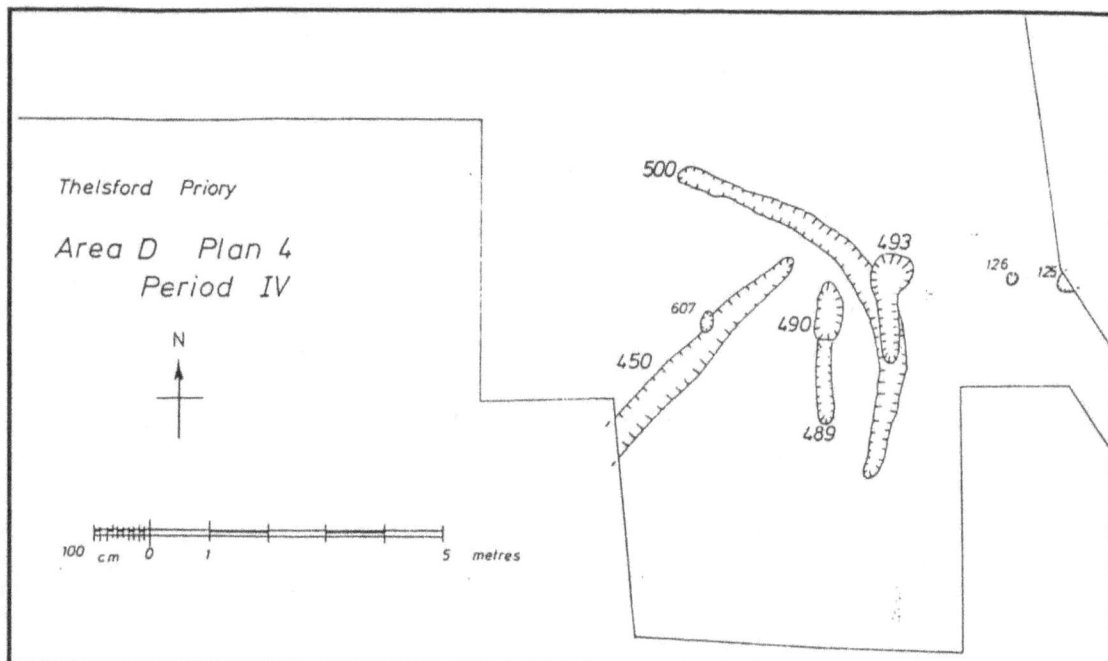

Fig 26

6.8c Period III (figs. 24-25)

Ditches here appear to have been for local drainage, 501 being a sump. Culvert 483 was well-constructed (see also Sxx on fig. 27) and represents a more systematic attempt to drain water away westwards from the claustral complex to the east (Plate III).

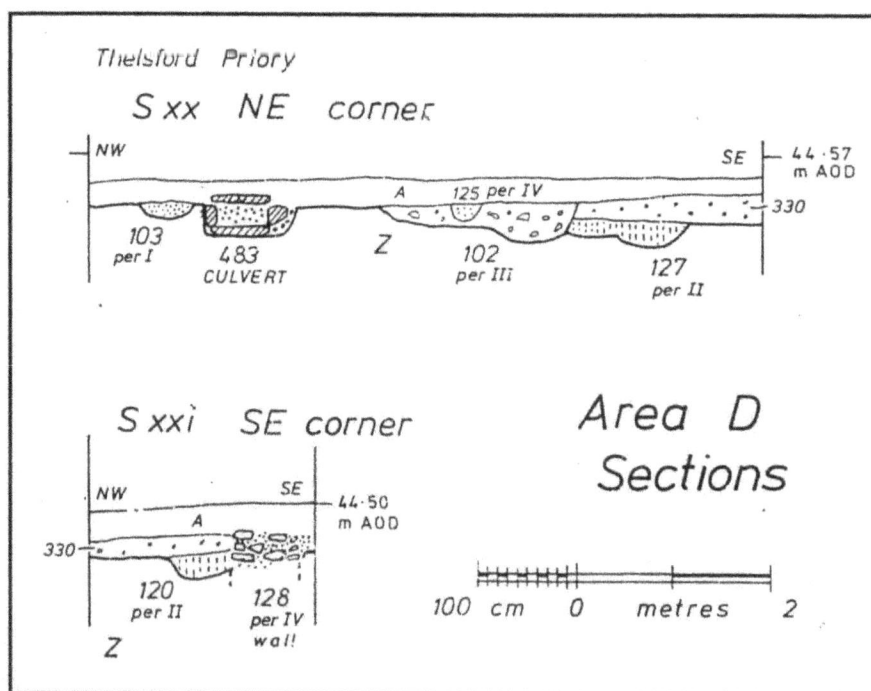

Fig 27

6.8d Period IV (figs. 23 and 26)

The ditches shown here are secondary to those of period III, and represent further attempts at drainage. There were also three postholes here, and (only on fig. 23) a substantial east-west wall foundation (128), which does not appear to link with any other defined structure, lying as it does well south of the cloister (*c.f.* fig. 28).

6.9 The SE end of Trench II (fig. 28)

Fig. 28 shows in plan and section the best (albeit oblique) section through the period II perimeter; the main ditch 101, and the subsidiary ditch, fence or hedge 455. Here the buried soil Q is seen only on the left of section Sxxii; in the rest of the trench it had been stripped off, and a ?terrace, ?road or field cut into the natural (664) either in period II or later; but it was filled in period III or later, the layer 101e not only filling the cut-away area, but spreading over the filled-in main ditch, preceding later cultivation (335). 113a and b may represent a further hedge inside the ditch 101. The period II perimeter in its eastern arm will be discussed in 6.12a and b below (*c.f.* also fig. 61).

6.10 Area E, F, G - introduction (fig. 36)

These areas comprise the church and cloister (E), the west range of the claustral area (F), and gardens and ploughlands north of the buildings (G); under these were elements of structures of period II and its

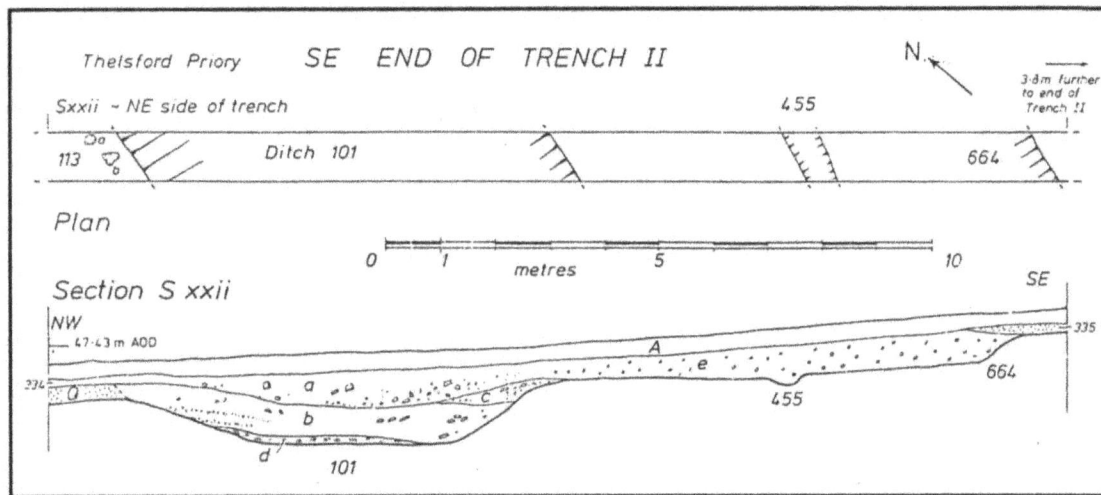

Fig 28

eastern perimeter. The claustral complex to be described next is of course the heart of the whole priory complex, but it must be emphasized that the plan reconstructed from diverse elements encountered in narrow trenches is highly conjectural and represents only the 'best fit' of the available evidence.

6.11 Area E - introduction (the church and cloister)

The features to be discussed were located in Trenches I and VI, and examined in a small area in Trench III.

6.12 Area E - the cloister (figs 29-30 and sections Sxiii-xxv)

6.12a Trench I (fig. 29 and section Sxxiii)

PERIOD I

The buried soil (Q) survived here in part and sealed four prehistoric features, filled with blue-grey sandy soil and set in a slight natural hollow. These were postholes 12, 50 and 51, and a pit (45) which yielded an important group of flints of Mesolithic or Early Neolithic date (7.1).

PERIOD II

The eastern arm of the period II perimeter (101 and 455) was again encountered here in a rather shallower form; the single fill (612) was probably levelling for the period III complex.

On the left of fig. 29 three north-south features (37, 54, 57) cut into layer Q are interpreted as the settings for timber walls, possibly part of the cloister of this period, of more than one phase. On the right of fig. 29 layer Q has been cut away (609) or absorbed by a ploughsoil (323) of period II (outside its perimeter), under the later cloister.

43

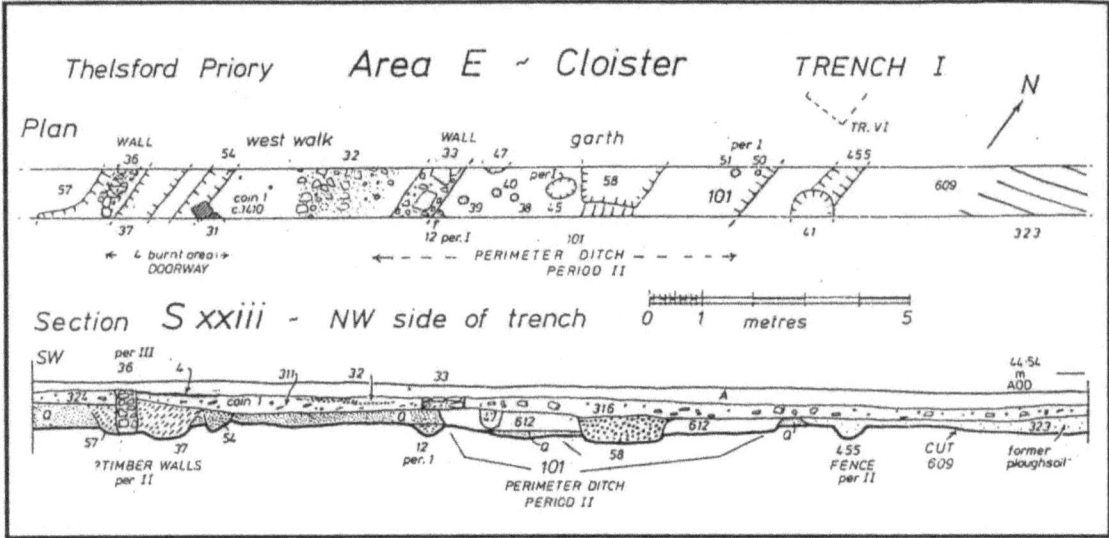

Thelsford Priory   Area E ~ Cloister   TRENCH I

N

Plan   WALL 36   west walk   WALL 33   47   garth   per 1   51 50   455   609

57   37   31   54   32   coin 1 c.1410   39   40   38   45   per.I   58   101   41   323

12 per.I   101
← ↳ burnt area →
DOORWAY   ← — PERIMETER DITCH — — — →
PERIOD II

Section S xxiii ~ NW side of trench   0   1   metres   5

SW   per III 36   4   31n   32   33   44.54 m AOD

32n   coin 1   316   A   323

57   37   54   12 per.1   612   58   612   455 FENCE per II   CUT 609   former ploughsoil
?TIMBER WALLS per II   101   PERIMETER DITCH PERIOD II

Fig 29

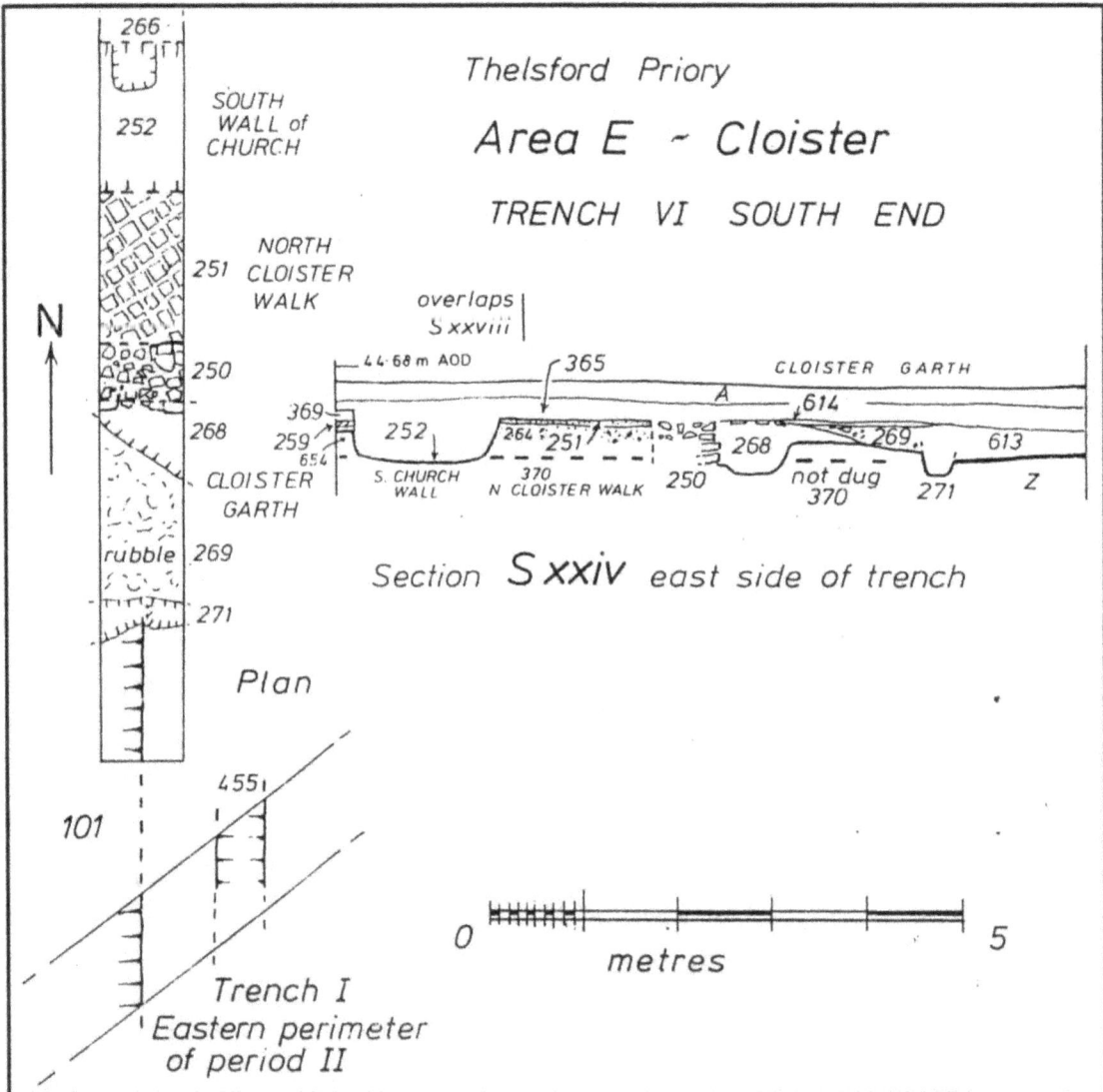

Thelsford Priory

Area E ~ Cloister

TRENCH VI SOUTH END

266
252   SOUTH WALL of CHURCH

NORTH CLOISTER WALK
251

N   250

268
CLOISTER GARTH

rubble 269

271

Plan

455

101

Trench I
Eastern perimeter
of period II

overlaps S xxviii

44.68 m AOD   365   CLOISTER GARTH

369   A   614
259   252   264   251   268   269   613
654   370   250   not dug   271   Z
S. CHURCH WALL   N CLOISTER WALK   370

Section S xxiv east side of trench

0   metres   5

Fig 30

44

PERIODS III-IV

36 and 31 are tentatively interpreted as the foundations of the SW corner of the cloister; there appears to have been a doorway here, witnessed by iron door fittings and a key (7, 10a, nos. 17, 31 and 38) and a burnt area (4). The line of the inner side of the west walk is given by the lightly founded wall 33; the significance of the apparently greater width of this walk, by comparison with the others, is discussed below in 8.5. It is possible however that the evidence of 31 is too tenuous, and that the southern wall of the cloister is further south, giving a wider south walk.

The surface of the west walk does not appear to have been tiled, at least in its latest life, but of progressively-replaced organic material (311). Dirt accumulation in or on the floor is witnessed not only by building debris and animal bone, but by the finding at one point of a pile of a dozen oyster shells; there was a jetton of c. 1410 (7.13c, coin 1) in this layer; mortar 32 may represent a late attempt at floor patching.

Within the garth was a group of deep post- and stake- holes (38-40 and 47), and parts of two ?pits (41 and 58); a function for one of these (41) is discussed in 8.5.

6.12b Trench VI - southern end (fig 30)

The period II perimeter ditch (101) extended along the western edge of this trench, backfilled with gravel (370) for the period III structures.

252 is interpreted as the robbed south wall of the church. The adjacent north cloister walk retained impressions of a tiled floor (251); 250 was its south wall (the north side of the garth).

In the garth itself, 271 could have held a wooden waterpipe.

6.12c Trench III (fig 32 and SW part of Sxxv on fig. 31)

Further tile impressions (205) of the north walk were defined here; its southern wall (250) extended to the NE corner of the garth (206); this was constructed of large sandstone blocks, and incorporated reused carved stone (see 7.3a, nos. 11 and 12, and pls. VI-VII), surviving to a height of 46 cm above the floor.

In the east cloister walk, the tiled floor had covered a ?grave (207), but south of this the surface of the walk was only hard mortar (27). The west wall (17) was apparently slightly set out from 206; there was clearly rebuilding here. The east wall of the east walk (and of the whole cloister) (26) was massive. The part adjoining the church consisted of a squarish platform (204) incorporating more massive stone; this was possibly a buttress.

South of this was another doorway (672) with a ?column base (208) on its south side; the cloister wall resumed beyond this as 26; again (like 17) possibly set out to give a narrower east walk.

Beyond the cloister to the east was a posthole (42) of period I, and a further ?wall foundation (209); the latter is in line with the east wall of the first phase of the church, as discussed below.

6.12d Interpretation of the cloister (figs. 29, 32 and 36)

The only features of period II that could form part of a cloister are the possible timber features in Trench I, some 3 m inside the eastern perimeter.

The remaining features of periods III and IV were diverse in character and spatial relationships, and must represent several phases of construction and rebuilding. The only dating evidence is that of the tracery fragments built into 206 (earlier 14th century), the jetton of c. 1410 in the west walk floor and pottery of 15th century date from similar contexts. It is not possible to separate the features recovered as between periods III and IV, but it is assumed that much of the layout originated in period III, in the late 13th century; and that the features observed were those at the time of the Dissolution.

6.13 Area E - the church (figs. 31, 32 and 36)

6.13a Introduction

Any church of period II must have been west of that defined in the excavation, well inside the perimeter ditch. Elements of the period III/IV church in two phases were recovered, but not its west end, which must be in unexcavated ground between Trenches V and VI; this allows the length to be determined only within certain limits.

45

6.13b Trench VI (fig. 32 and section Sxxvi on fig. 31)

The north wall of what is interpreted as the nave of the church was represented by the large robbing trench 273, similar in depth to the south wall trench 252.

Between these walls were mortar floors (253, 259), relaid at one point over a grave (254); and with a few tile impressions by 260; the latter could have been the base of a column, about one-third of the distance between the two walls. This is the basis for the suggestion that there had been a north aisle of half the width of the nave. The graves in this area are discussed in 8.7 below.

6.13c Trench III (fig 32 and Sxxv on fig. 31, Plate IV)

The south wall of the church (252), as seen in its robbed state, was erratic in width towards the east, implying reconstruction. This must be at least partly associated with the later eastward extension as a chancel.

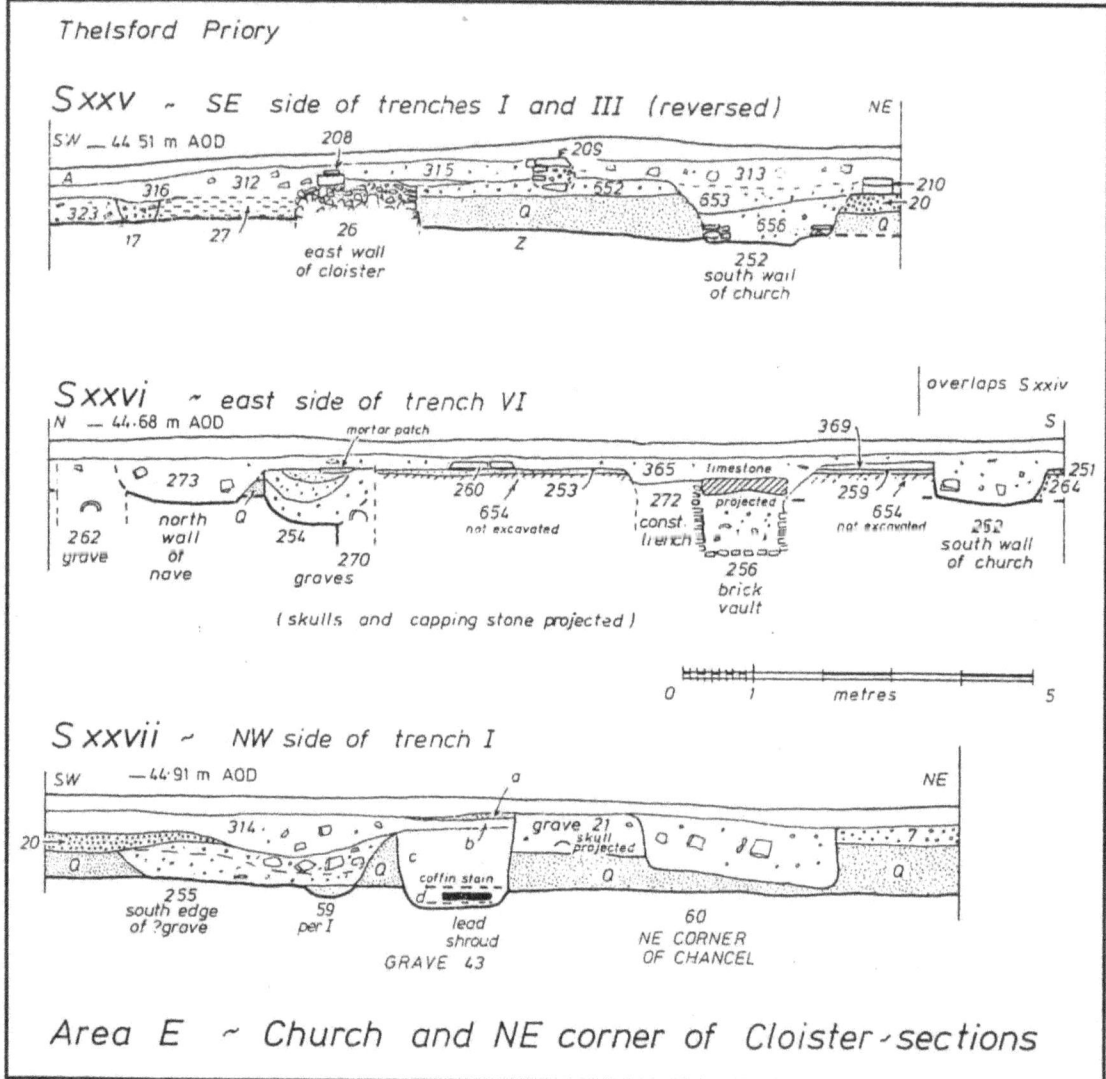

Fig 31

On the north side of 252, two north-south foundations were defined. 201 appears to have been the earlier, cutting to the depth of the natural gravel (not on section). The trench for this was not filled with robbing spoil, but consolidated with large blocks of green sandstone, with some other material including ceramic tile. This is suggested to have been a wall foundation which had been robbed of its ?squared stones and then deliberately back-filled in medieval times; and that this was formerly the east wall of a single-celled church of period III, itself perhaps with an internal eastern sanctuary and a western nave.

The other foundation (202) appeared to be *in situ*; this is interpreted as the east wall of a nave defined as such when the church was extended by the addition of a new chancel.

46

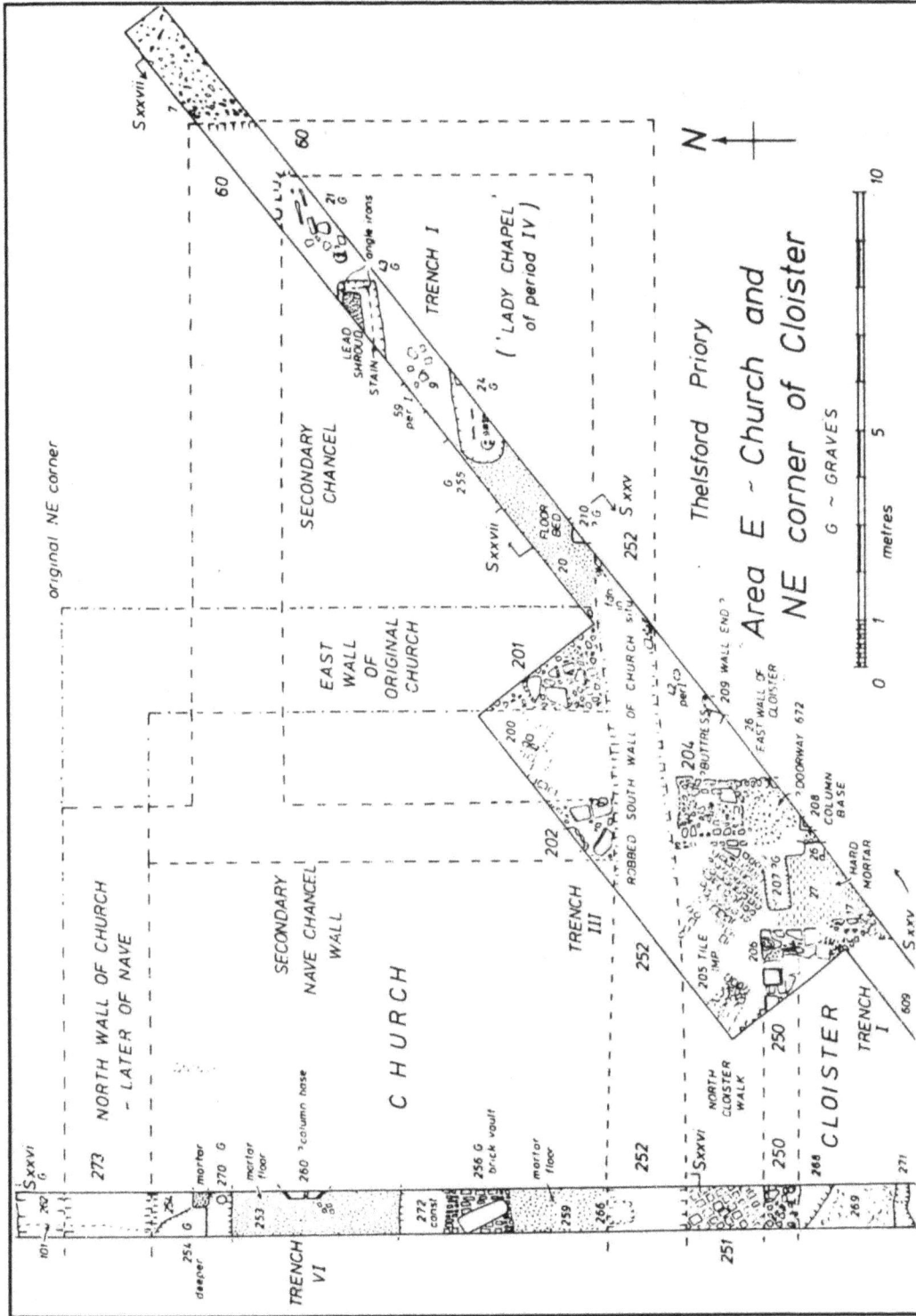

original NE corner

NORTH WALL OF CHURCH
- LATER OF NAVE

SECONDARY
CHANCEL
WALL

EAST
WALL
OF
ORIGINAL
CHURCH

C H U R C H

SECONDARY
NAVE CHANCEL
WALL

S xxvii

273

Sxxvii
G

272
const

260 ?column base

256 G
brick vault

mortar floor

270 G
mortar

253

251

259

mortar floor

256

252

TRENCH
VI

101

252

Sxxvi

271

269

250

268

CLOISTER

NORTH
CLOISTER
WALK

TRENCH
I

509

250

S xxv

S xxv

201

202

200

TRENCH
III

ROBBED SOUTH WALL OF CHURCH

205 TILE
IMP

206

207 G

17

204

BUTTRESS

209 WALL END ?

EAST WALL OF
CLOISTER

DOORWAY

COLUMN
BASE

HARD
MORTAR

208

26

42
per I.G.

G 255

G
255

FLOOR
BED

20

252

252
G

210
G

59
per I.G.

9
G

24
G

G

LEAD
SHROUD
STAIN

angle irons

21
G

60

60

7

SECONDARY CHANCEL

TRENCH I

('LADY CHAPEL
of period IV)

N

Thelsford Priory

Area E ~ Church and
NE corner of Cloister

G ~ GRAVES

metres

0 1 5 10

Fig 32

Between these two wall trenches was a mortar bed (200) with some tile impressions. This could be either in the east end of the original church; or in the later chancel. Since it did not spread over the consolidated backfill of 201 (and indeed appears to have respected the edge of this wall), the former hypothesis is more likely - that 200 may have belonged only to the single-celled church.

In any case, 201 and 202 cannot have co-existed; and the hypothesis put forward is that adhered to in the rest of this report.

6.13d Trench I - the chancel ('Lady Chapel' in period IV) (fig. 32, section Sxxv right-hand end, and Sxxvii, NW side of trench)

In this part of Trench I, the buried soil Q survived extensively with one period I feature (59).

The south wall of the church in its robbed form (252), extended eastwards beyond 201, with a few stone *in situ* at its base. In this area, it is interpreted as the south wall of the new chancel. In the latter were disturbed graves and floor levels (7 and 20), the former identified as those of the Lucy family (8.7 below). The trench finally cut across the robbed NE corner of the chancel(60); the return westwards as defined here is nearly 3 m south of the north wall of the original church as previously described. The new chancel is thus seen as narrower than what now became only the nave of the church, but continuing the facade of its south side.

6.13e Interpretation of the church (figs. 32 and 36)

If the arguments outlined above are accepted, the church was originally a single-celled rectangular building between c. 16 and c.25 m long and c. 13 m wide externally (c. 19 m long and c. 9 m wide internally). A length of over 20 m seems likely, to extend as far as the west side of the cloister. The width of 9 m internally is considerable, and supports the suggestion of a nave-aisle division.

This building was shortened by c. 3 m and became the nave of a longer church, a chancel being added, c. 14 m x 9.5 m externally, c. 13 x 6.4 m internally, with its south wall in line with that of the original church; and possibly involving a partial rebuild of the latter. The whole extended church would then have been c. 33 m long externally, if it extended to the side of the cloister (possibly 100 feet?) (for the latter see 6.16 below).

The foundations were variable but fairly substantial, of green sandstone facing, infilled with limestone. The historical context of the church is discussed in 8.5 below.

6.14 Area F - the west range (figs. 33-34)

6.14a Trench I (fig. 33, and section Sxxviii)

The buried soil (Q) appeared to have been truncated or disturbed in this area; the layer of crushed green sandstone (56) lying directly on it is attributed to period II (it is cut by period III ditch 152). If this is building or robbing debris, it suggests stone buildings hereabouts and is the only evidence for a possible period II church in this area (c.f. also 172 and 183 on fig. 34 below).

Of period III, the SW corner of the west range was represented by 49, with floor residues of mortar (605) and stone slabs (55) inside, also a pit (35).

6.14b Trench V, - southern part (figs 33-34, plan; and sections Sxxviii-xxx)

Further features assigned to period II were defined here; a linear pile of green sandstone (183) and a ?wall-trench (172); both of these are on an alignment quite different from that of the buildings of period III; but are still candidates for features of the period II claustral complex, of stone or timber based on smaller stone pads.

Trench V cut through the rooms or buildings of more than one phase of the west range from south to north; Trench I also cut obliquely across the southern room. The total length of the west range was up to 23 m. There appear to have been up to four rooms with partitions, with a major tiled hearth (171) in the centre of the largest and an entrance way through the northern ?lobby into the cloister walk.

The evidence for the west range is fragmentary, but the buildings appear to have been timber-framed, on dwarf walls or footings of limestone. Floors may have been of organic material, except in the hearth area; roofs may originally have been of thatch, replaced in the mid 14th century by red ceramic tile. To the SW was an area of ?garden soil (309 in Sxxviii). The function of the west range is discussed in 8.5 below.

48

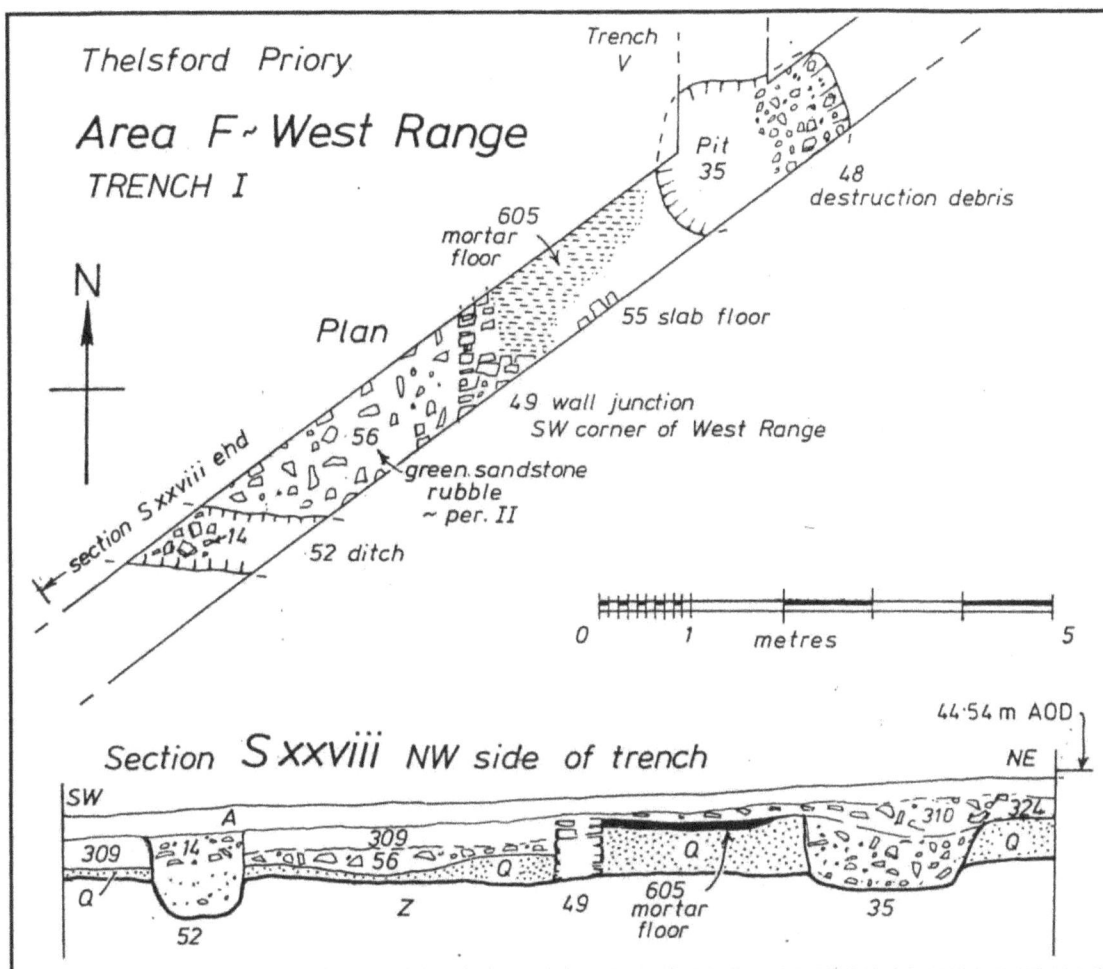

Fig 33

6.15 Area G - gardens, ploughlands and graves north of the church (figs. 34-35 and sections Sxxix, xxxi and xxxii)

6.15a Introduction (fig. 35)

Features comprising Area G were located in the northern ends of Trenches V and VI, north of the church; these sealed layers and features of period II inside its eastern perimeter.

6.15b Trench V (fig. 35, including section Sxxxi)

The buried soil (Q) appears to have been wholly stripped off in this trench, or absorbed into later layers. Numerous post- and stake-holes of period II survived, cutting into the natural, representing temporary structures. There were also two ?drainage features of this period; the end of a pit or ditch 211, and 175, the latter draining NE.

These features were truncated in period III by the digging of two large scoops (195 and 198), interpreted as shallow gravel-quarrying at the inception of period III, for its constructional works. These were back-filled; the material (351, 363) used for this was limited by a wall (174). To the south of this was ?garden soil (349), extending to another wall (168) (fig. 34 and Sxxix).

In the north part of the trench were further layers of make-up and crushed stone (350) of building activities. North again the only layer on the natural was a mixed ?medieval ?ploughsoil (352) (not on these figs.); a road (673) crossed this, heading for a ?ford on the Thelsford Brook (only on figs. 62-3).

49

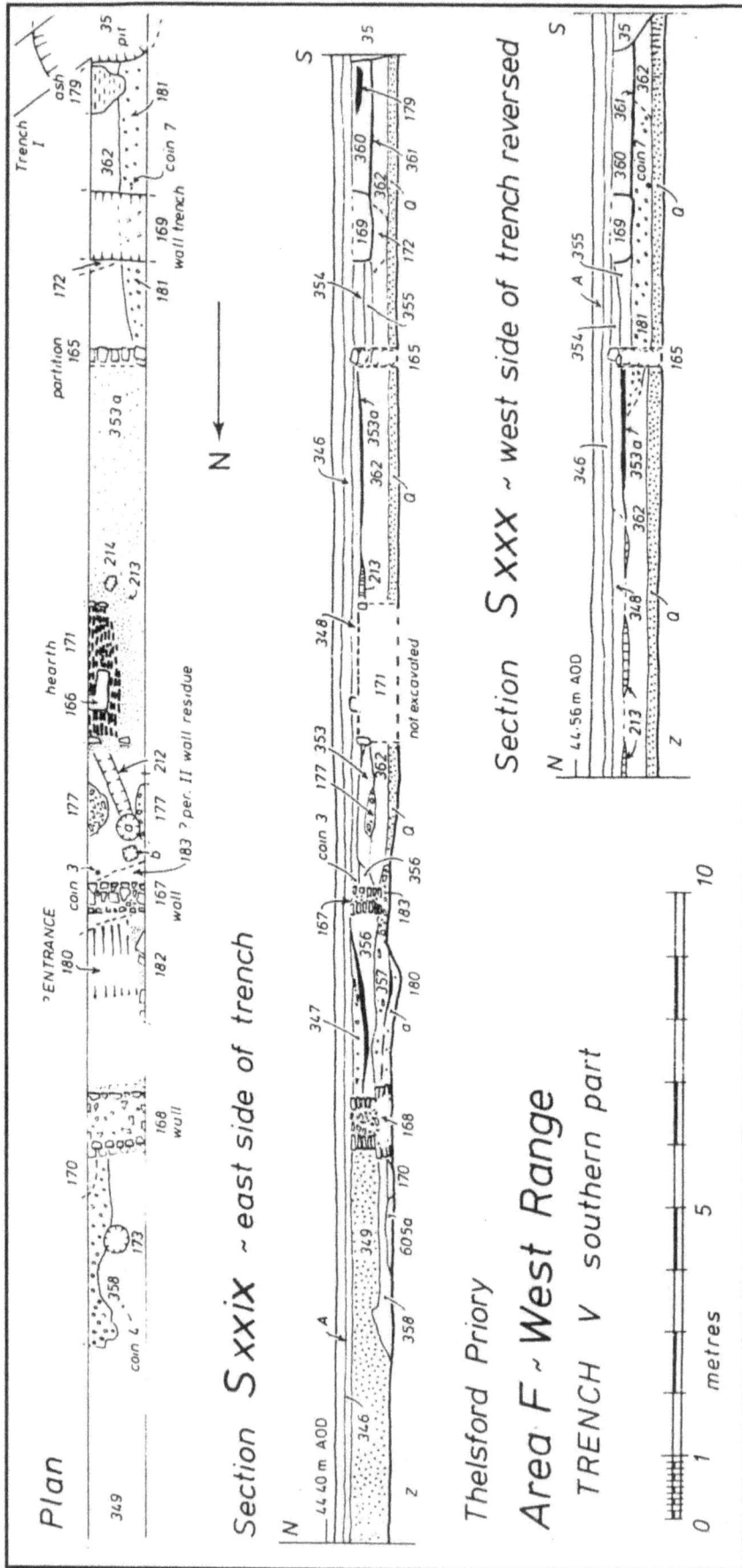

Plan

Section S xxix ~ east side of trench

Section S xxx ~ west side of trench reversed

Thelsford Priory
Area F ~ West Range
TRENCH V southern part

Fig 34

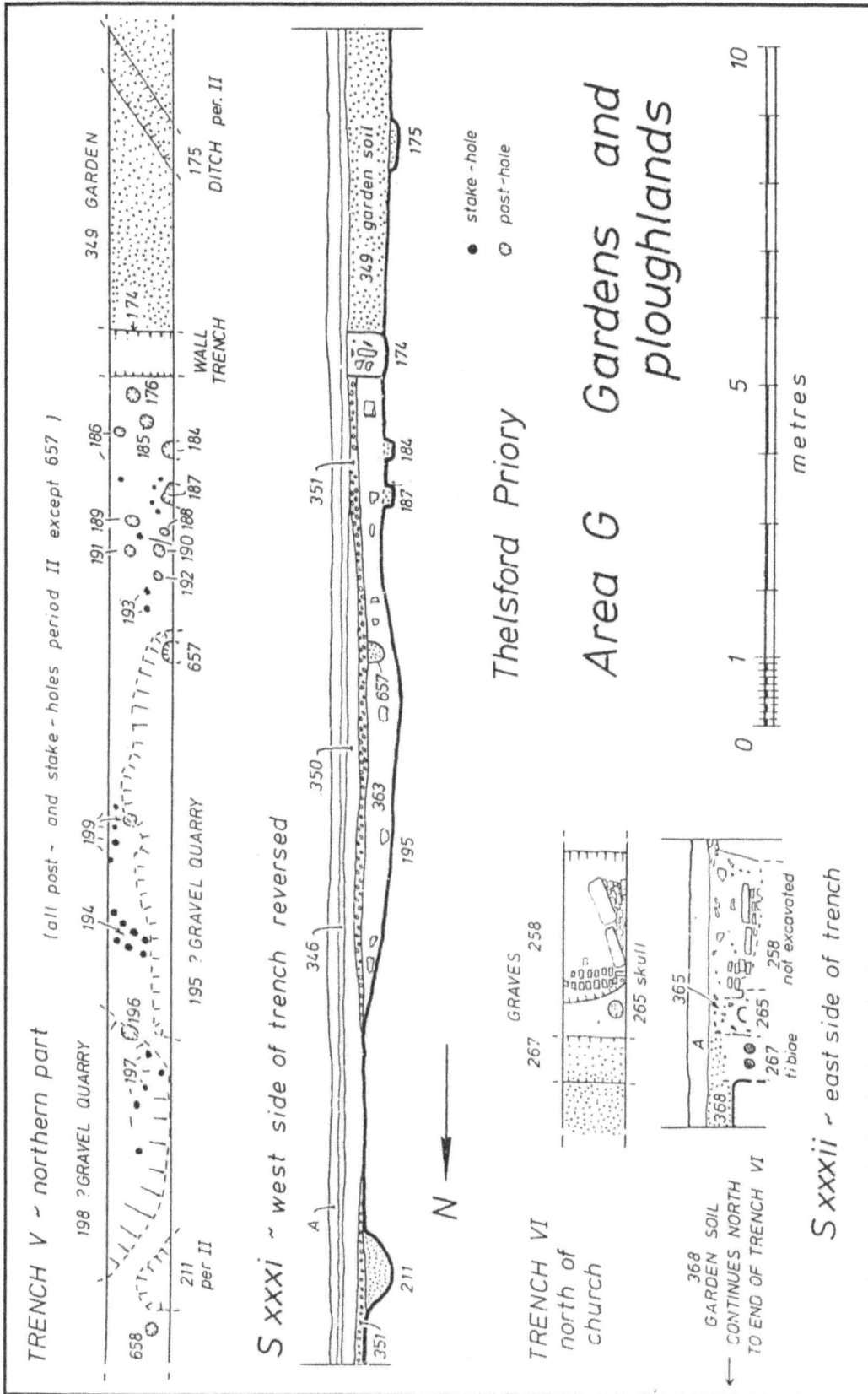

TRENCH V ~ northern part (all post ~ and stake ~ holes period II except 657)

349 GARDEN

175
DITCH per. II

349 GARDEN

174

WALL
TRENCH

176

186
185 184

191 189
192 190 188 187

193

657

199

198 ?GRAVEL QUARRY

195 ?GRAVEL QUARRY

658

211
per. II

196
197

194

● stake ~ hole
○ post ~ hole

S xxxi ~ west side of trench reversed

349 garden soil

175

174

184

187

351

350

363

195

346

657

211

351

N

Thelsford Priory

Area G   Gardens and
ploughlands

0   1   5   10

metres

TRENCH VI
north of
church

GRAVES

267   258

265 skull

S xxxii ~ east side of trench

365
A

368

368
GARDEN SOIL

CONTINUES NORTH
TO END OF TRENCH VI

267 265 258
tibiae   not excavated

Fig 35

51

6.15c Trench VI (fig. 35, including Sxxxii)

Immediately north of the church were three graves, part of what was presumably a narrow northern cemetery; the garden already discussed lay north of these.

6.15d Interpretation of gardens and ploughlands

Somewhere in the area of Trench VI the period II perimeter ditch 101 seemed to be veering westwards; the features found in Trench V would however have been well inside this, to the west.

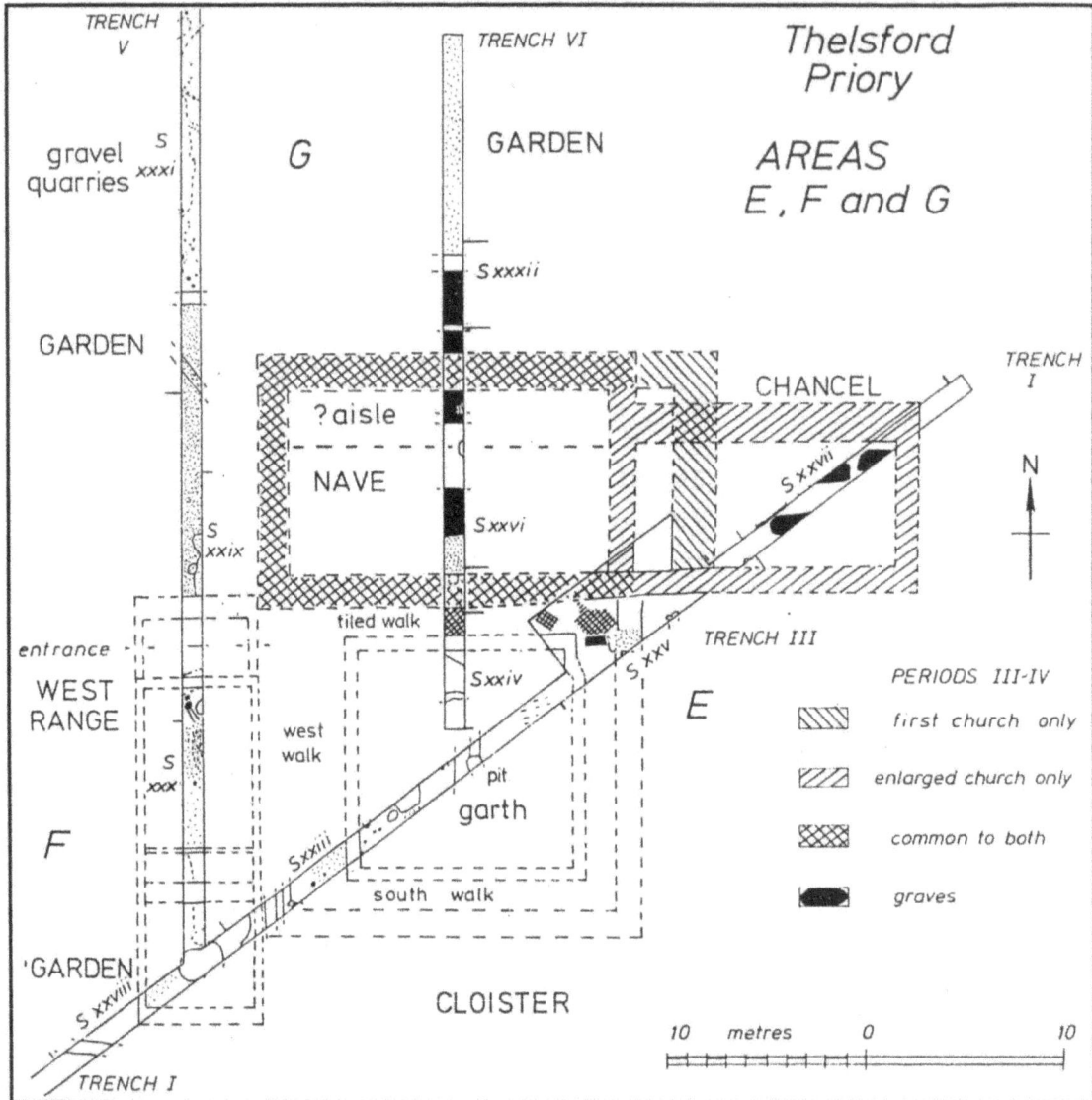

Fig 36

There seem to have been two areas of garden, one contained between walls north of the west range, ?another (or the same?) north of the church itself, in which there were some graves close to the church.

North of the western of these ?two gardens was an area of gravel-digging and building activity, giving way to a ploughsoil between this and the Thelsford Brook, traversed by a road on the south side of the brook (figs. 62-63).

6.16 Area E, F and G - discussion (fig. 36)

Fig. 36 incorporates all the evidence from Trenches I, III, V, and VI, the basis of the hypotheses advanced above; it also includes the outlines of features of periods I and II.

Little attempt has been made to suggest the width of walls as they would have been above the ground. The lines shown are a combination of foundations, wall-trenches or robber-trenches.

The west range is shown here with a total external length of 21.6 m, with four rooms, of which the largest yielded the principal 'internal' evidence of a major hearth. North of this, and west of the church, is a garden, bounded by a wall on the north wide, beyond which are shallow gravel quarries. There is likely to have been some boundary between the garden and the cemetery area north of the church, which has its own boundary wall to the north, and beyond it ?another garden, encroaching on the cemetery (Sxxxii).

The cloister is shown as *c.* 18 m from west to east and *c.* 15.5 m internally from north to south with a central garth of *c.* 11 m square internally, with a possible central feature. The west walk was 4.3 m wide, but the north (tiled) walk was only 1.6 m at maximum. The position of the south wall of the garth and the cloister itself are conjectural. The east walk appears to have been only 1.6 m wide, like the north one; the south walk may have been even narrower; but there are problems here at its north end, where the extant NE corner does not accord with the wall-line going south.

The church is shown in the two suggested phases; the western wall is conjectural, but it is assumed to extend the full length of the north cloister walk, as far as the NE corner of the west range. This gives a first phase single-celled church of c. 23 x 13 m externally, and a second phase enlarged church with a nave of c. 19 x 13 m externally and an asymmetrical chancel *c.* 14 x 9.5 m externally - a total length of c. 33 m (?100 ft). There may have been a north aisle for the single cell/church/nave in either or both phases, dividing it into two areas of 3 and 6 m wide. The inner side of the north wall of the new chancel is approximately in line with this nave/aisle division.

The first church is dated to the inception of period III after 1285, the second to some time after 1301, possibly entirely within period III. In period IV what is presumably the eastern extension is referred to as the Lady Chapel; the graves here are argued to be of similar date (6.17 below). The datings given are historically based, but are not contradicted by the archaeological evidence.

The dating of the church is discussed further in chapter 8.

Plate I
Sluice 409 from west, showing second stage of excavation (scale in 50 cm intervals).

Plate II
Stone lined pit 152, from north (scale in centimetres and decimetres)

54

Plate III
Stone lined culvert 483, from east (scale in 50cm intervals).

Plate IV
Trench III from south-west, showing tile impressions (scale in 50 cm intervals).

55

Chapter 7
FINDS

In each class of find, the first bracketed reference is to the context letter or number combination. The second (or only) bracketed reference following this is the Roman numeral designation to periods, dated as follows:

I	pre-13th century
II	c. 1200 to c. 1285
III	late 13th to 14th centuries
IV	15th and 16th centuries
V	post-medieval

(U/S = unstratified)

e.g. Glass no. 24. Part of opaque, blue? rosary bead (166) [III] means that this is from context 166, which is assigned to period III.

In the table of contexts (layers and features) (Table A in microfiche) the finds are listed in the following order, using abbreviated prefixes:

FL	Flint	IR	Iron
COAL	Coal	CA	Copper alloy
ST	Stone	OM	Other metals (silver and lead)
RT	Roof tile (ceramic)	CP	Clay pipes
BR	Brick	WO	Wood
DFT	Decorated floor tiles	POT	Pottery types
PFT	Plain (undecorated) floor tiles	CHAR	Charcoal
MOR	Mortar	FI	Fibre
BD	Burnt daub	HB	Human bones
SL	Slag	AB	Animal bones
GLW	Window glass	BO	Bone objects
GLV	Vessel glass		

References in finds sections of report (including microfiche)
(places underlined in text)

Ascot Doilly	Jope and Threlfall 1959
Basing House, Hants.	Moorhouse 1972
Bayham Abbey	Streeten 1983
Bedford	Baker et al 1979

Bolingbroke Castle, Lincs.	Drewett 1976
Bordesley Abbey	Hirst *et al* 1983
Bramber Castle	Barton and Holden 1978
Denny Abbey	Christie and Coad 1981
Dominican Priory, Oxford	Lambrick and Woods 1976
Fishpool, Notts.	Cherry 1973
Goltho, Lincs.	Beresford 1975
Hadleigh Castle	Drewett 1975
Humberstone, Leics.	Rahtz 1959
Kenilworth Castle	Rahtz 1966
LLMC	London Museum Medieval Catalogue 1940 and 1954
Lydford Castle, Devon	Saunders 1980
Lyveden, Northants.	Bryant and Steane 1971 and 1975
Manor of the More, Rickmansworth	Biddle *et al* 1961
Naesholm Castle, Denmark	La Cour 1961
Nuneaton	Mayes and Scott 1984
Old Sarum, Wilts.	Musty 1959
Potterspury, Northants.	Mynard 1970
St. Aldates, Oxford	Durham 1978
St. Mary's, Coventry	Hobley 1971
St. Peter's Street, Northampton	Williams 1979
Tiddington	Barfield forthcoming
Upton, Glos.	Hilton and Rahtz 1967
Waltham Abbey	Musty 1978
Warwick, Barrack Street	Klingelhofer 1978
Weoley Castle	Oswald 1962-3
Wintringham, Hunts.	Beresford 1978
Wisby	Thordeman 1939
Wythemail, Northants.	Hurst and Hurst 1971
V.C.H. Warks.	V.C.H. Warks 1908

7.1 Worked Flints (Plate VIII)

A total of 24 worked flints were recovered; 12 in 1966 and 12 in 1972. Those residual in medieval contexts were from 102, 105, 410 (4 flints), 418, 438, 441, 461 (2 flints), 469 (3 flints)._____ One was found in layer 321, the soil present before the priory, and nine were from the prehistoric pit 45.

The 1972 flints were unfortunately lost in transit; those from 1966 were submitted to Dr. Lawrence Barfield of the Department of Archaeology and Ancient History, University of Birmingham, who reports as follows:

'Twelve flints were recovered in 1966, comprising eleven struck flakes or blades and one core. The raw material in all cases is black with a brownish hue, while preserved cortex shows that the original nodules included rolled pebbles, presumably from Midland boulder clay deposits, as well as some pieces with a less abraded cortex.

Eight of the flakes and blades are from pit 45. Of these, two are conjoining cortical flakes struck in sequence from the same core, and two other flakes in all probability come from the same core as well, but do not conjoin. The cortex surface of one of the conjoining flakes is partly covered by a series of deep scratch marks, all aligned in the same direction before the flake had been detached from its core (pl. VIII). The explanation of these marks remains unclear. One possible explanation is that they result from the removal of attached chalk from the nodule prior to knapping (note1).

Two other pieces, from the same pit, are crested flakes which are characteristic of discard associated with the preparation of cores for the production of blades. Another blade has been struck from a bipolar core.

Also from 45 is a core worked from a small pebble. This has been prepared for bladelet production by trimming on one face and a striking platform has been struck following trimming. It

58

was not however subsequently used.

The other three flints examined were all recovered in medieval contexts and are discard flakes, apart from one broken blade.

The flints from 45 are clearly *in situ* finds, showing that this is a prehistoric feature close to an area where flint knapping was being carried on. The emphasis on blade production seen in the finds from this pit suggests that the assemblage is either Mesolithic or Early Neolithic in date, as the manufacture of blades is not usual in later Neolithic or Early Bronze Age industries (Pitts 1978, 179-197). Although bipolar blade production is usually taken to be a Mesolithic trait we have too little evidence to decide conclusively between these two periods.

Since their dating remains uncertain, the Thelsford flints cannot be accurately related to the background of either Neolithic or Mesolithic settlement in the Avon. However, it can be noted that the flint scatters so far reported from the middle Avon valley are predominantly Neolithic and Early Bronze Age in date and Mesolithic finds are rare (Barfield forthcoming).'

Note 1
I am grateful to Dr. M. Newcomer for this suggestion.

7.2 Coal

Coal was in general use in later periods, available from the North Warwickshire coalfields; details of contexts in MF.

7.3 Stone

7.3a Architectural fragments (Plates VI & VII)_

Fig. 37 shows some of the 14 architectural fragments, most from destruction levels; details in MF. 10 and 11 are fragments *in situ* which were reused in the construction of the cloister wall 206 (IV) and are dated by Professor D.A. Walsh to not earlier than the end of the 13th century, and possibly slightly later. He thinks that the scale of the fragments suggest a use within a building rather than as part of the main fabric.

Fig. 37   10.   (pl. VI) Green sandstone fragment from the corner of structure 206. The top surface of the left side measures 30cm and the facing side measures 60cm. Both surfaces have a small niche 7.5 cm long and 4 cm wide with pointed trefoil arches at a distance of 7.5 cm from the corner. Each side has a traceried niche with a prominent ogee arch, which measures 66 cm in length and 10 cm in width. On the corner side of each of these two larger niches there is an oak-leaf design. The facing side has an arch, decorated on the underside with foliage, which D.A. Walsh considers to have some of the naturalistic quality found towards the end of the 13th century (206)(V).

            11.   (pl. VII) Green sandstone fragment, 50 cm on the side which was used as a facing stone for wall 206, 38 cm on side with foliated arch, and 30 cm on third side (top measurements). The stone is pierced by a long-lobed trefoil decoration, and the arch is decorated on the underside with formal, rather static foliage, indicating a later date than no. 10, probably in the early 14th century (206) (IV).

Both stones could have come from structures which were dismantled when the 1285 church was extended at the beginning of the 14th century by the demolition of the east wall, 201 of period III. They could however have been incorporated into wall 206, the inner wall of the cloister at a later date.

I am grateful to Professor D.A. Walsh, of the College of Arts and Sciences, University of Rochester, New York, for examining drawings and photographs of these fragments.

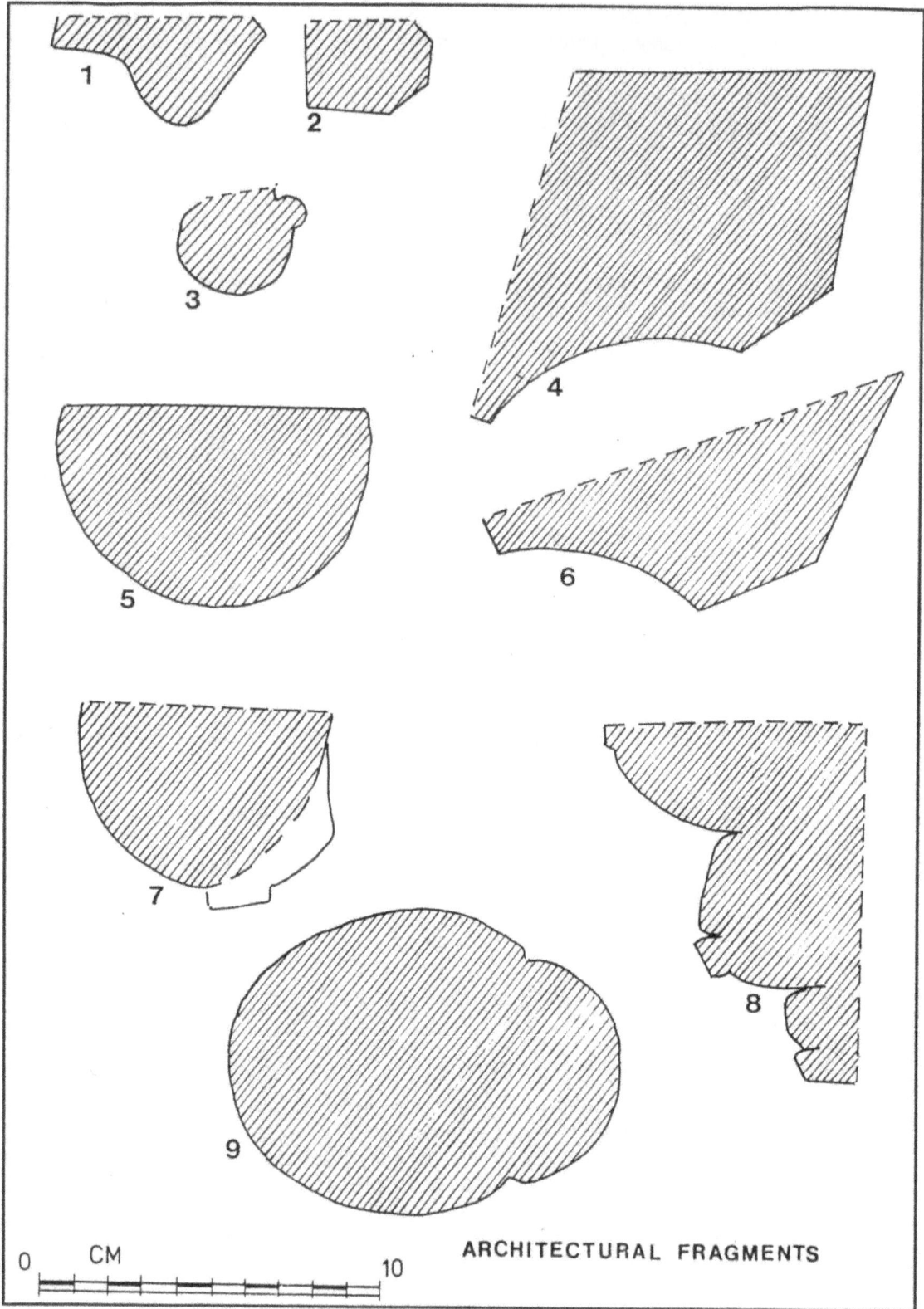

ARCHITECTURAL FRAGMENTS

0   CM   10

Fig 37

7.3b Roof slates

These are of yellow-white lias limestones, close grained, with no visible fossils; they are of various sizes, from 11 x 10 cm to 48 x 25 cm, average 1.5 cm thick; details in MF.

7.3c Flagstones

Similar stone to the roof slates, with worn surfaces, and traces of mortar on the underside. All come from area B (II-IV); they are 14 cm square and 3.5 cm thick; details in MF.

7.3d Building stone

Lumps of limestone were used as core for walls and foundation; details in MF.

7.3e Stone objects

These include fragments of hones, rubbing stones, a pounding stone, a 'wedge', and three fragments of rotary querns; details in MF.

7.4 Structural ceramics (fig. 38)

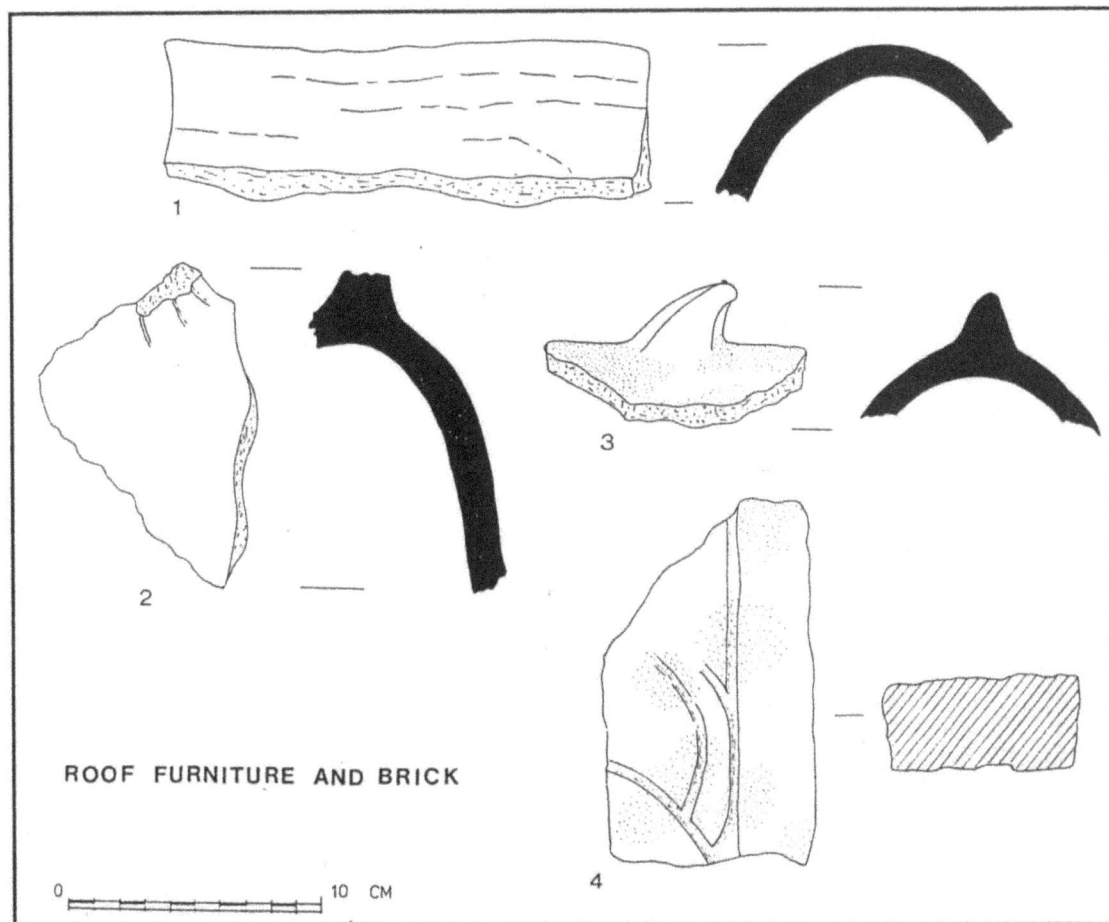

ROOF FURNITURE AND BRICK

0 ⊢——————⊣ 10 CM

Fig: 38

7.4a Roof tiles

These are glazed and unglazed, of various sizes, with ribs or pegholes. Ridge tiles include those in fig. 38; details and types in MF.

7.4b Brick

Many of these were incorporated into structures such as tombs. Some bricks were kept and typed. An example with relief glaze, possibly from a fire-back, is shown as no. 4 in fig. 38; details in MF.

7.5 Floor tiles (fig. 39)

7.5a Decorated floor tiles

These include examples of counter-relief and relief tiles (nos. 1 and 15) and inlaid/slip decorated tiles (2-14); details in MF.

DECORATED FLOOR TILES

Fig: 39

62

7.5b Undecorated floor tiles

These are square or triangular, of two types; details in MF.

7.6, 7.7, 7.8 Mortar, burnt daub and iron slag as described in MF.

7.9 Glass (fig. 40)

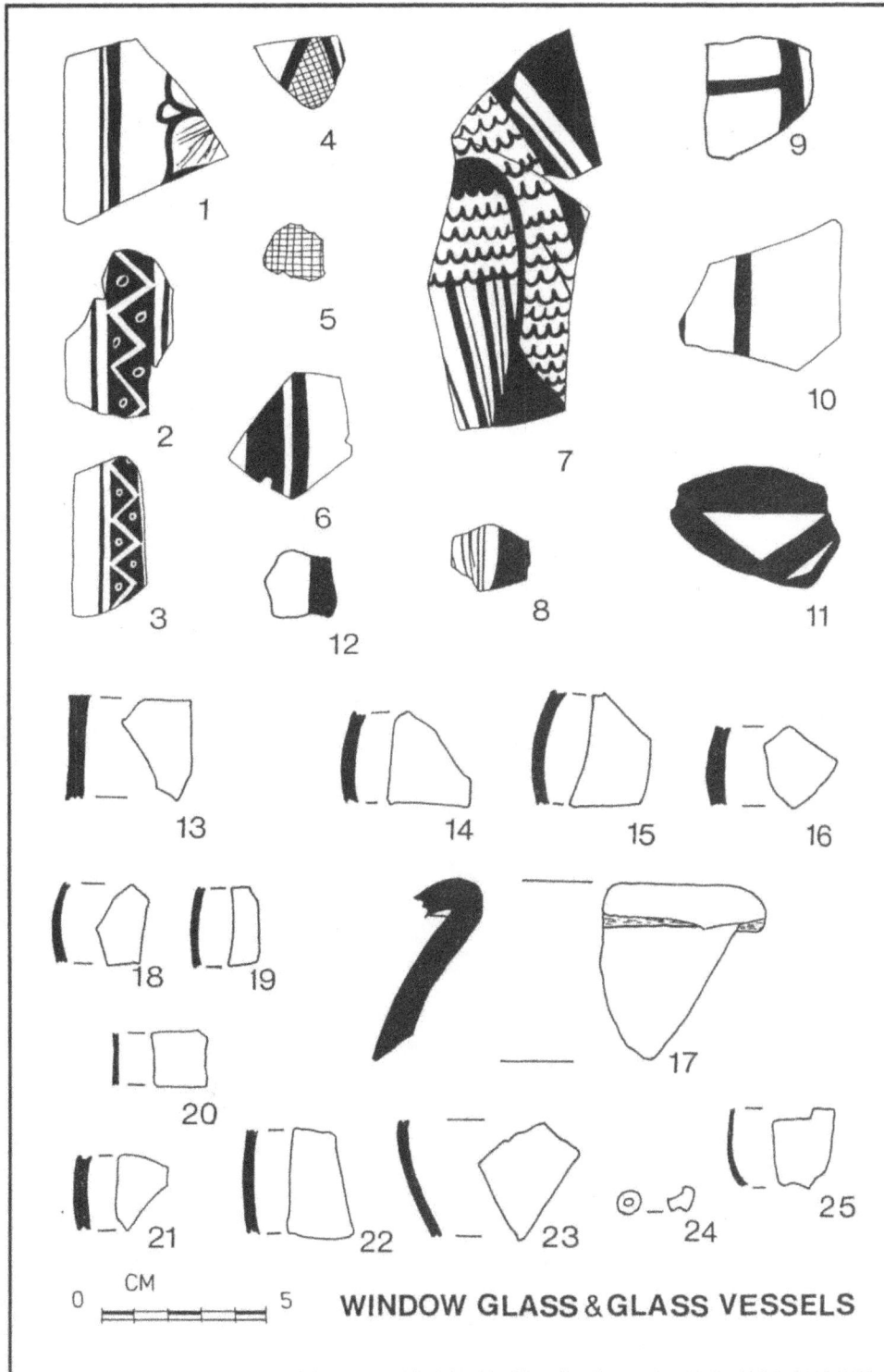

WINDOW GLASS & GLASS VESSELS

Fig: 40

7.9a Window glass (fig. 40, 1-12)

Window glass was found mainly in the church in poor condition. It is usually *c.* 3 mm thick and is now black and opaque; fresh fractures show a clear greenish-white or yellow; the design is painted in red-brown.

1, 4, 5	Floral design with cross-hatching.
2, 3	Border design.
6, 7, 8	Angel or eagle.
9-12	Possibly parts of letters in Lombardic script.

All the glass could be contemporary with the rebuilding of the church in 1285. Other window glass was found without any design. Details of all pieces in MF.

7.9b Glass vessels (fig. 40, 13-25)

13.	Clear pale blue with one straight edge.
14-17	Probably originally green and from distilling apparatus, especially 17, which has a regressive fold.
	This form of alembic is discussed in Moorhouse 1972, 91-5. Detail and comparanda in MF.
18, 21	Clear, light brown, with positive curvature.
19, 20, 22, 23	Clear pale green, with positive curvature.
24.	Bead, opaque, azure, possibly from rosary.
25.	Base of flask, pale green. Detail in MF.

7.10 Iron objects (figs. 41-42)

7.10a Objects other than nails, by Ian H. Goodall, Royal Commission Historical Monuments England; spurs, by Blanche Ellis
FIG. 41

Fig. 41		
	1*	Carpenter's gouge bit with lanceolate terminal (301) (V).
	2*	Nailed terminal and part of one side of grooved blade of spade-iron, probably originally triangular in shape with a rounded mouth. Spade-irons of this shape, which include one from Lydford Castle, Devon (165, Fig. 18.3), are known from 13th to 15th century contexts, although none has a terminal (304) (III+).
	3*, 4*	Whittle tang knives with broken blades and tangs. The tang of 4 retains wood-graining from the former handle (451, 516) (V, III).
	5*, 6	Scale tang knives with broken blades and tangs, both with non-ferrous shoulder plates (152b, 152d) (III).
	7*, 8*, 9, 10	Knife blade fragments, 8 with an inlaid cutler's mark. 9 is 70 mm long, 18 mm maximum depth, 10 is 62 mm long, 10 mm maximum depth (451, 451, 35, 430) (V, V, III + IV, V).
	11.	Disc, 35 mm diameter, 1.8 mm thick, with hole near edge. Possibly the end-cap from a knife handle (347) (IV).
	12*	Blade from a pair of shears (152b) (III).
	13*	Arm from pair of shears, broken across base of bow. Short, broad blade with cusp on arm (311) (III).
	14*	Incomplete rectangular staple (451) (V).
	15*	Eyed spike with broken shank (414) (II-V).
	16*-19*	Studs with rectangular heads (401a, 31, 365, 410) (III-IV, IV-V, V, U/S).
	20*	Wedge with ridged body and L-shaped head (493) (IV).
	21*-23*	Hinge pivots, 21 with a tall, slender guide arm; the others shorter, stouter and with broken shanks (152, 329, 410) (III, V, U/S).
	24*	Hinge with spiked U-shaped eye and tapering; broken strap (307) (V).

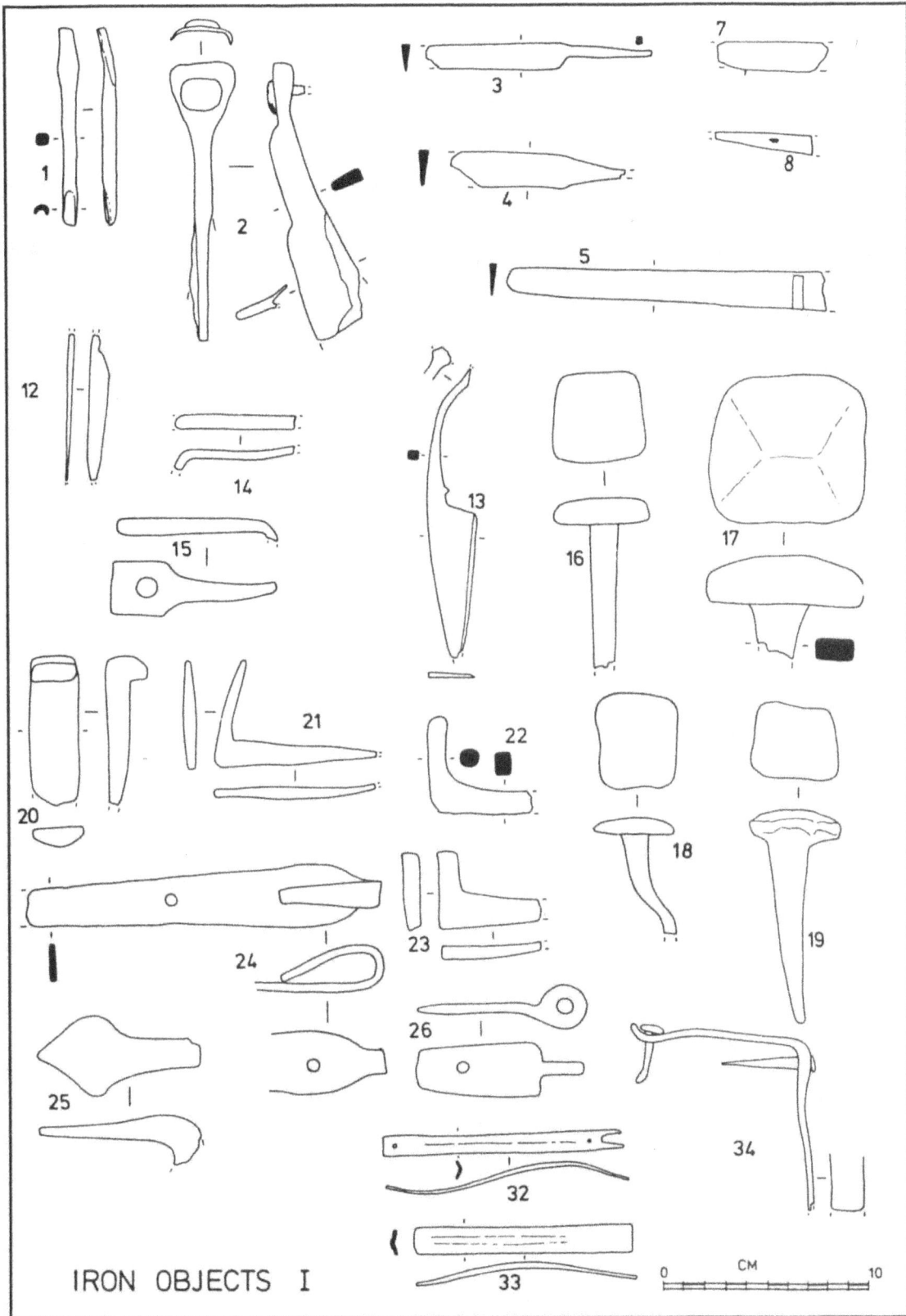

IRON OBJECTS I

Fig: 41

65

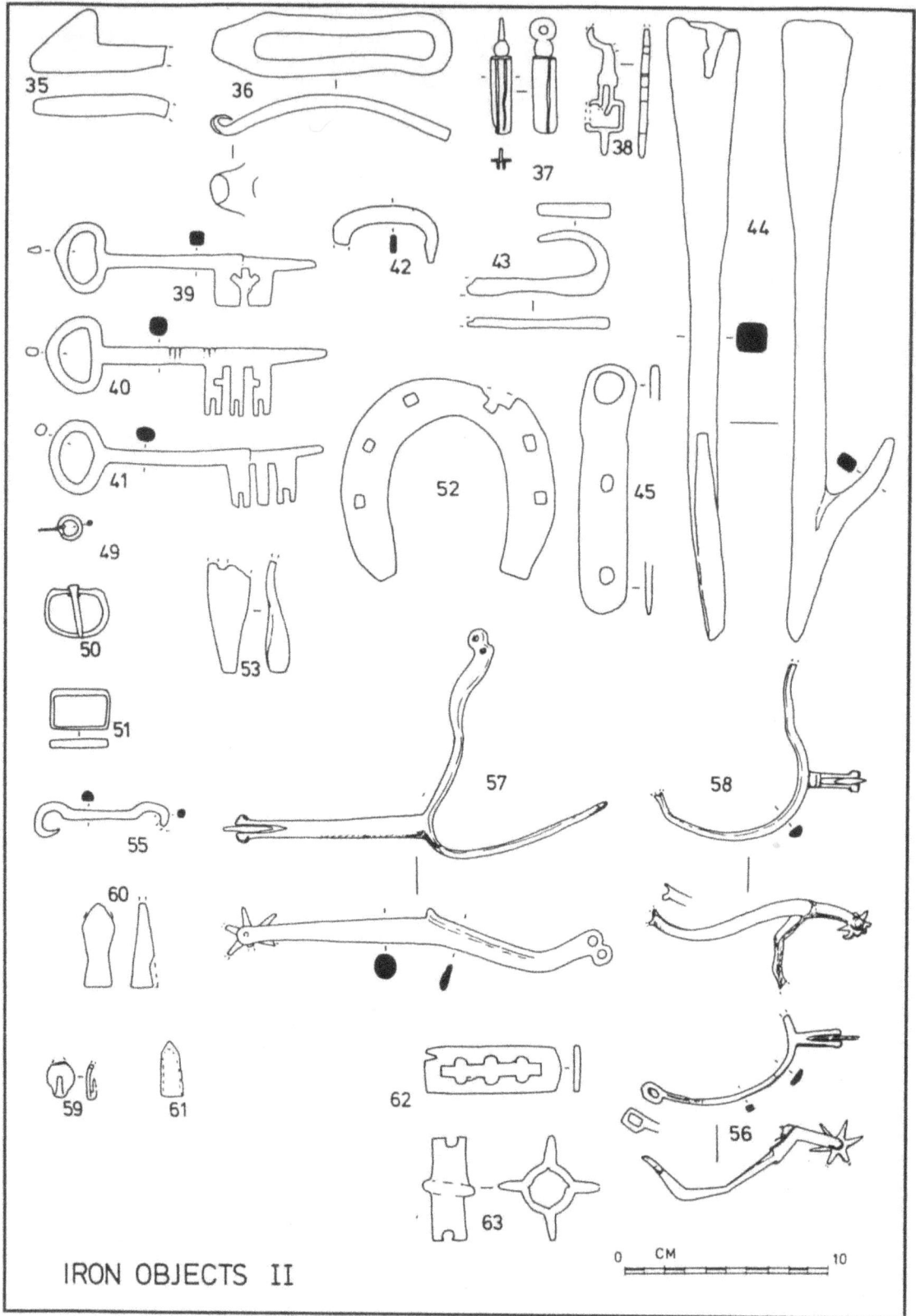

IRON OBJECTS II

Fig: 42

66

25*	Rear terminal from nailed, U-shaped eye of strap hinge (31) (III-IV).
26*	Leaf from pinned hinge (313) (V).
27-29	Incomplete lengths of strap, perhaps from hinges or used to strengthen chests or coffins (see no. 34). 27 with two nailholes, is 119 mm long and tapers from 25 mm to 18 mm; 28 is 65 mm long, 20 mm wide; 29, in five pieces, is 17 mm wide (151, 324, 324) (III, III-IV, III-IV).
30,31,32*,33*	Incomplete lengths of binding strip, probably from caskets. 30 is 140 mm long, 5mm wide and 2 mm thick; 31 curved and with one rivet in place, is 60 mm long, 15 mm wide (300, 304, 410, 410) (V, III, U/S, U/S).
34*	Angle iron from coffin (43) (IV).

Illustrated objects are marked*

FIG. 42

Fig. 42	35*	Latch rest with broken shank (335) (III-IV).
	36*	Hasp, curved in side view, the hooked terminal acting as a fingerhold. Similar hasps were used in conjunction with staples and padlocks to secure doors and chests (329) (V).
	37*	Padlock key with a looped terminal and bulbous moulding above an elongated sheet metal bit. It is of an uncommon form, continental iron examples including one from Naesholm Castle, Denmark (132, fig. 49.N.806), occupied c. 1240-1340-46, and three from the mass graves at Wisby, Sweden, of 1361 (129-30, fig. 149. 1-3). A gold example, 15 mm long and attached to its padlock, comes from a hoard of jewellery deposited at Fishpool, Notts., probably in 1464 (312-3, pl. LXXXVId) (438) (III + IV).
	38*	Latch key with broken bow and incomplete distorted bit, and probably of late medieval date like others from Bedford (281, fig. 176. 1425) and Waltham Abbey (157, fig. 21.2) (31) (III-IV).
	39*-41*	Keys with variously-shaped bows and solid stems which project beyond the bit (374, 438, 430) (III+, III + IV, V).
	42*	Hinged shackle from padlock of a type probably introduced during the 15th century and common throughout the post-medieval period. Medieval examples include one from the 1507 fire deposit at Pottergate, Norwich (Atkin et al 1988, 62, fig. 44, no. 70) (410) (U/S).
	43*	Fire-steel, originally D-shaped, but now missing one hand-hold. The striking-edge is partly worn away (316) (III-V).
	44*	Substantial socketed hook originally hafted on a wooden handle. Its context, the bottom filling of a fishpond, suggests a use connected with the retrieval of nets (414) (II-V).
	45*	Eyed strap, either part of a hinge or from a bucket where it supported the handle (see G.C. Dunning in Butler 1974, 100-1, fig. 10, pl XXIV (490) (III).
	46.	Collar 49 mm diameter, 9 mm thick, 20 mm deep (401a) (III-IV).
	47.	Ring, grooved, 25 mm diameter (341) (V).
	48.	U-shaped fragments of two chain links (307) (V).
	49*	Circular buckle with iron pin, a type used on shoes and hose (Russell-Smith 1956) (465) (III).
	50*,51*	D-shaped and rectangular buckles (451, 451) (V).
	52*,53*,54	Horseshoes, 52 complete with slightly thickened tips and rectangular nailholes, 53 an arm tip with calkin, 54 an arm fragment 65 mm long (514, 451, 300) (III, V, V).
	55*	Mouthpiece link from bridle bit (451) (V).
	56*	Rowel spur of unusually slender proportions. The complete side and stump of the other area of flat section behind the wearer's heel, but 25 mm from its junction with

67

the neck the depth of the complete side is reduced by a small step on its upper and lower edges, beyond which it continues with an extremely slender squared section. The whole side plunges to curve under the ankle, its front end rising to the terminal which is a single rectangular loop pierced vertically with a slot for the passage of the spur leather. The short straight round neck is only long enough for the proportionately large star rowel of six widely separated rounded points, two of them now broken. Iron spurs were often protected and enhanced by tinning (Jope 1956), and there are possible traces of non-ferrous plating. The spur, typologically 13th to early 14th century, is the earliest type of rowel spur and is unusual in featuring the change of depth and section of its side. It would have been worn on the right foot. A single spur leather would have encircled the foot, passing through the remaining terminal on the inner side of the foot while being attached to and buckled near to the missing outer terminal which, on this type of spur, was usually of single-ring form. It may be compared with a complete spur in the Museum of London (LMMC 1940, fig.30.6). Overall length 115 mm, length of neck 25 mm, diameter of rowel about 28 mm (341) (V).

57*   Long-necked rowel spur. The sides are of flattened D-section formed with a small ridge along their top edge around the back of the wearer's heel, and coming to a slight point above the junction with the spur neck. The sides, now distorted and broken, project gently downwards to bend under the ankles and rise towards plain figure-of-eight terminals. The relatively heavy round neck tapers to become less thick at the rowel box, and has bold conical rowel bosses. Small star rowel originally of six separated points, two now missing. Traces of non-ferrous plating, visible on x-radiograph, are probably tin plating (Jope 1956). Typologically late 15th to early 16th century. Overall length now 190 mm, length of neck 95 mm, diameter of rowel originally about 33 mm (U/S).

58*   Rowel spur of fairly slender proportions, with D-section sides, now distorted, the front end of one and terminal of the other missing. The most complete side slopes into a curve under the wearer's ankle; only an indentation of one ring of the terminal remains. Short tapered neck with rounded sides. The rowel box divides two-thirds of the neck and curves evenly downwards, swelling into prominent conical rowel bosses. Star rowel of eight points, only two still complete. All surfaces are damaged by rust so that the moulding encircling the neck at its junction with the sides is unclear. Typologically 16th century. Length overall 107 mm, length of neck 30 mm, original diameter of rowel about 22 mm (35) (III-IV).

59*   Part of an attachment for a spur leather. The leather was originally clasped by a flat hook, the stump of which remains and swells into the disc-shaped body of the attachment. The ring at the other end, by which it was attached to the spur terminal, is missing. This is part of the most common type of attachment for the leathers of late medieval and post-medieval spurs (the Towton Battlefield spur, in the possession of the Society of Antiquaries of London, has two larger disc-shaped attachments. See LMMC 1940, 112, fig. 35.1) (451) (V).

60*,61* Socketed arrowheads (441, 461) (I + III).

62*   Plate with shaped central slot (314) (V).

63*   Collar with four projecting, shaped fins (451) (V).

7.10b Nails (fig. 43)

Fifteen main types have been identified; B are from coffins, C1 may be door studs, L are from horseshoes. Details in MF, including Table A showing types and provenances.

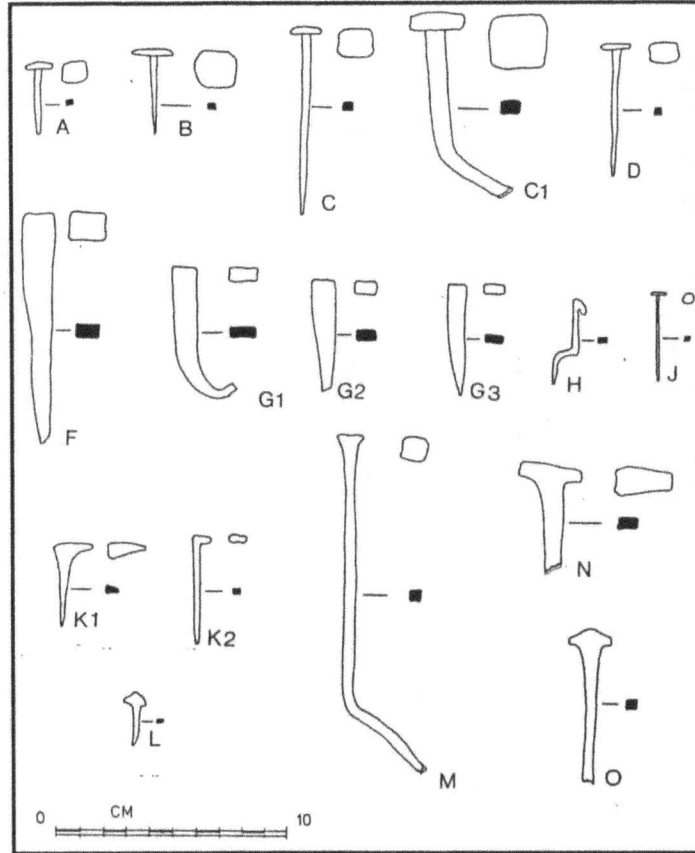

Fig: 43

7.11 Copper alloy objects

7.11a Illustrated (fig. 44)

1. Hinged strap-end, or book-clasp; the three separate parts consist of two plates and one hinged terminal, held together by three rivets. The top plate is decorated with an incised edge and the reverse plain; there are remains of leather between the two plates. The hinged terminal is decorated by punched ornament and pierced, the acorn knop also being pierced. The object is complete and has an excellent patina; no exact parallel has been found, but is similar, though more complete, than the one from Upton, Glos. fig. 15, no. 3; there is another example from Bordesley Abbey, fig. 76 (438) (III + IV).

2. Thimble, similar to St. Peter's Street, Northampton, fig. III, no. 87, and to those discussed in finds from Basing House, Hants, 60 (52) (III-IV).

3. Stem of candlestick, turned brass, similar to Upton, Glos. fig. 51, no. 118; the knop mouldings are similar to LMMC (1954), fig. 55, no. 4, which is 16th century (345) (V).

4. Object with inserted ring, broken below a punched depression which does not pierce through the metal; possible one arm of a balance beam; similar to Old Sarum, Wilts, fig. 5, and Goltho, Lincs. fig. 44, no. 37 (438) (III + IV).

5,6 & 7 Three rings, with flattened surfaces. No. 5 may be a ring from a snaffle-bit, *cf.* LMMC 1954, fig. 19a, A. No. 6 is similar to St. Peter's Street, Northampton, fig. 113, no. 112 (465, 300 and 514) (III, V, III).

8. Bronze wire, twisted into two loops. *cf.* Bolingbroke Castle, Lincs. fig. 16, no. 78 and St. Peter's Street, Northampton, fig. 113, no. 115 (473) (III).

9. Pin, twisted into hook; wire is coiled twice round head (461) (III).

10-13 Pins, all with coiled wire heads (255, 166, 347, 348) (III or IV, III-IV, III-IV, V).

14. Rectangular buckle, broken and pin missing; similar to examples from St. Aldate's, Oxford, fig. 30, nos. 9-11, and Lyveden, Northants, fig. 11b.2 (480) (IV).

15. Rim of vessel, or part of bell, the outer surface being heavily burnt. If vessel, similar to Wintringham, Hunts., fig. 49, no. 32. If bell, similar to Dominican Priory, Oxford, fig. 11, no. 3 (110) (III).

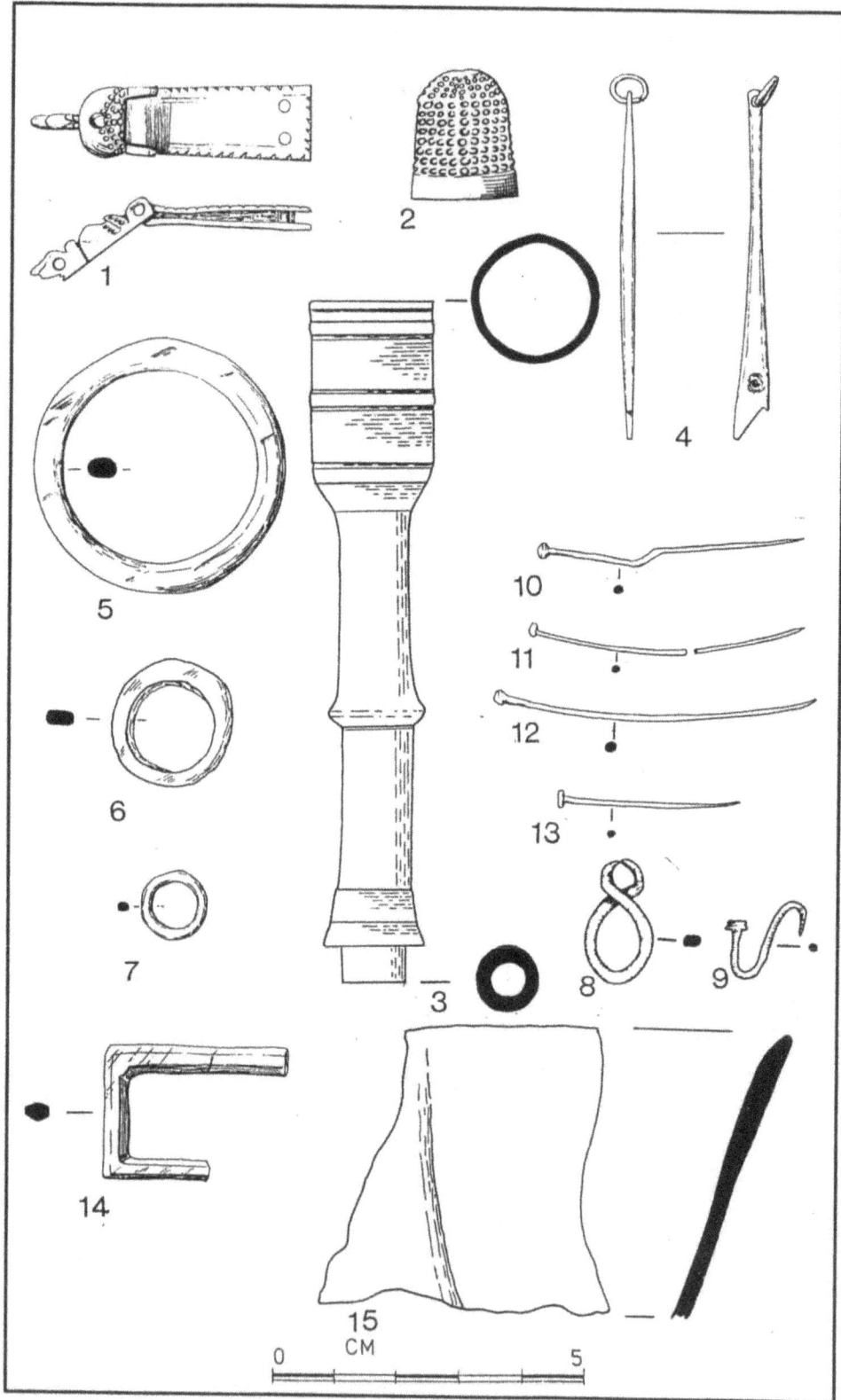

Fig: 44

7.11b Not illustrated

Non-illustrated pieces include pin shanks, lace-end tags, wire, cauldron feet fragments, a small vessel fragment, a strip, and part of a thimble; details in MF.

7.11c Seal-matrix (fig. 45)

English type of small, conical, pendent seal-matrix; height 2 cm, diameter of face 1.7 cm. The six-facetted cone has a terminal of 'pointed arch' form, not trilobate but with a single piercing. The surface of the casting is well preserved.

Fig: 45

Design: Central *fleur de lys* within an incised circle, surrounded by legend.

Legend: VOX DE LUCIS in Lombardic letters. This legend provides not only a motto in Latin, but is also allusive to the name of the Lucy family of Charlecote, patrons of Thelsford Priory. Additionally, the central *fleur de lys* was known in English as *fleur de luce*, and provides another allusion to the Lucy family. The X of VOX also serves as the central cross (usual in these designs), see *P.R.O. Seals* 1968, 27. The probable date is 13th century. LMMC 1954, 295 comments that later seal matrices are more elaborate, and that Lombardic script was used only before 1345 (see also 6.9 above). A seal-matrix of similar form was found at Wintringham, Hunts., fig. 42 (see also chapter 8, for discussion of heraldic aspects of this piece) (415) (IV).

7.12 Other metals

7.12a Lead objects (not illustrated)

These include five pieces of H-section 'came', with inner grooves for holding the glass. One piece was welded at the corners into a triangle with fragments of glass remaining in the grooves. There are also a circular weight, a flat piece, a casting, a lump, a disc, and a triangular strip; details in MF.

7.12b Lead shroud by Philip Rahtz, University of York, (fig. 46 and pl. V).

The lead from this coffin was 2 cm thick and all joints were soldered, with butted welds. Basically, it consisted of six pieces of lead which were encased round the body in the following manner:

To a basal piece (1) was added a further piece (2), which made the base wider, and was also folded up to form side A. Side B (3) overlapped the edge of 1, and was soldered onto it, to form the other side.

To the head end of the sides and base thus formed were added piece 4, which was overlapped around the upper parts of sides A and B but was butt-welded to the base pieces 1 and 2. It was cut at the corners, leaving a vertical flap. The sides A and B meanwhile had also been left standing vertically. The body was then inserted and sides 2 and 3 were folded over the body. The foot piece (5) was then fitted. Next the central gusset (6) was welded on. Finally the flap of piece 4 was folded over pieces 2, 3 and 6 to seal the body completely. A hold was drilled in the base to allow the body fluids to escape (43) (IV).

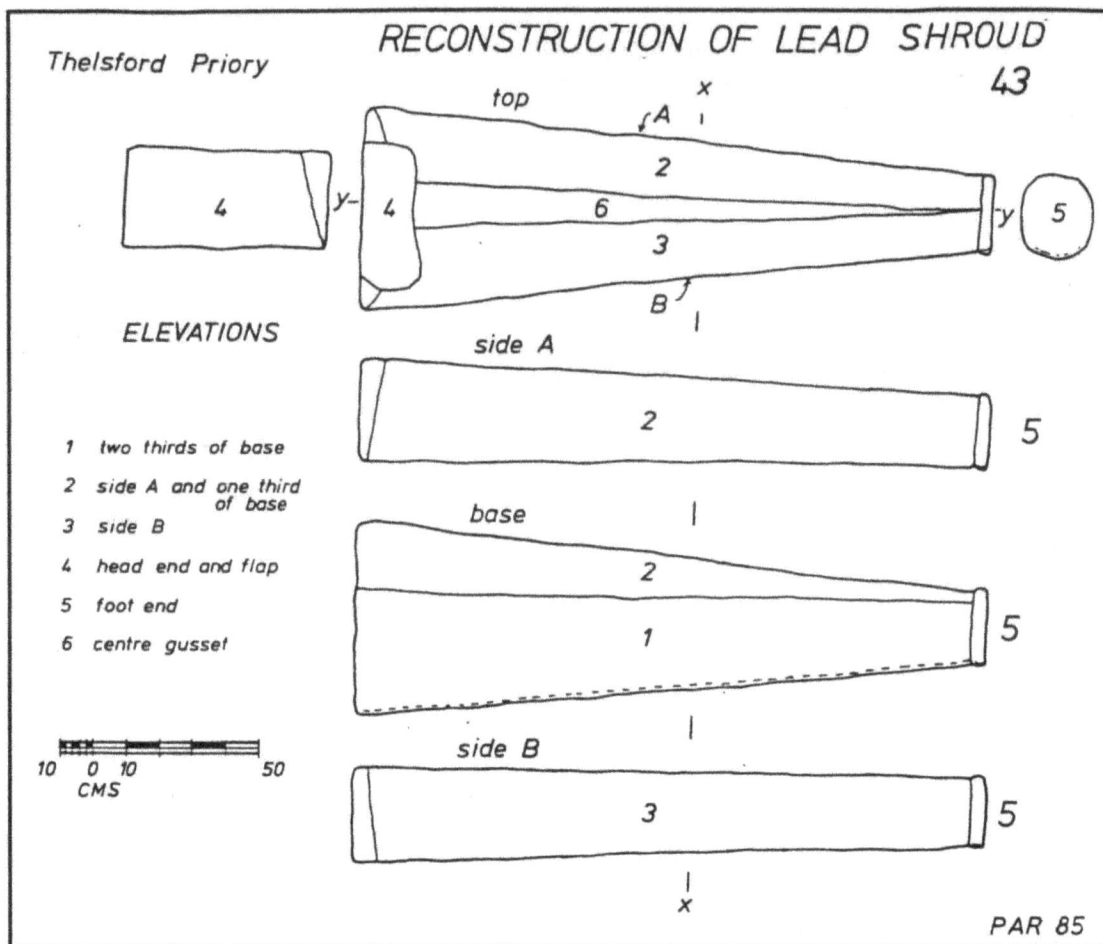

Fig: 46

7.12c Silver Objects (fig. 47)

A silver belt buckle and plate, a silver chape and a silver eyelet stud, all being part of the same belt fitting, were found on the skeleton within the lead coffin described above. All, except the stud, bear traces of gilt on the silver, and the buckle plate bears traces of red enamel. Both the buckle plate and the chape have fragments of leather surviving, held in position by one rivet in the case of the chape, and two in the case of the buckle plate. The two loops which hold the buckle rivet are part of the reverse side of the buckle plate, and the decorated obverse seems to have been added to it. The ring on the buckle is broken, and the fork is not intact. The decoration on the buckle plate is of a lion *rampant argent*. The chape is decorated on both sides and the terminal knob is small and pointed; this may have been a pendent type of belt fitting. The decoration is of the same style as the buckle, with three lions *passant gardant* on one side and four *fleur de lys* on the other (set in lozenge-shaped frames). The buckle and plate is similar to, but smaller than, the bronze one from Lyveden, fig. 42, no. 19. It is more closely paralleled by those from LMMC, 1954 pl. LXXV, no. 8 (which is bronze), and fig. 63, no. 7 (which is shown with its leather belt). No parallels can be found for the form of the chape, though it would seem from the London Museum collection that the use of belt with metal buckle and pendent tag was most common in the 13th century and again in the 15th century, when they were much smaller, (LMMC 1954, 265). No parallels can be found where both buckle and chape are made of silver and decorated with heraldic designs (see also discussions in chapter 8 concerning the heraldic aspects of these pieces) (43) (IV).

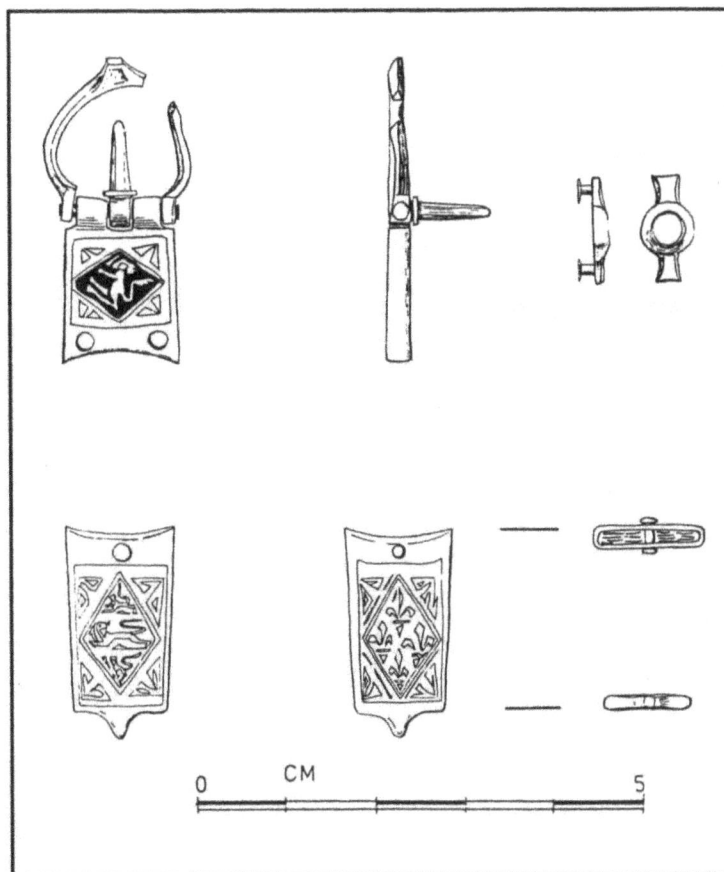

Fig: 47

7.13 Coins and Jettons, by the late Stuart Rigold and W.A. Seaby, Warwickshire County Museum

Coins, by the late Stuart Rigold

Illustrated items are marked *

4. Silver, diam. 14 mm broken and corroded; not English, possibly some sort of Hanseatic Sechsling, with an eagle. If so, late 15th or early 16th century? (349) (III-IV). Location on fig. 34. W.A. Seaby adds: Halfpenny size. Possibly imitation half sterling from Flanders or Brabant, the so-called black money of the late 13th to 14th centuries.

5. Edward I, London halfpenny, class IIIc (1280-1): shows some wear, but can hardly have been lost much after 1300 (374) (?III).

JETTONS 1 AND 6

Fig: 48

73

W.A. Seaby adds:
> *Obv.* + EDW R ANGL 'DNS hYB. Crowned facing bust, drapery as two wedges.
> *Rev.* CIVI TAS LON DON. Long cross pattee, etc.

8.   Small fragment of silver coin; lettering indecipherable (460) (II).

W.A. Seaby adds:
> England. Farthing, a cut quarter of a Long Cross Penny of Henry III (1216-72) and almost certainly struck at Gloucester (*c.* 1248-50).
> *Obv.* henRI]cv[s REX III] Crowned facing head.
> *Rev.* ..... [GLO]..VCEI. Long Cross.

Note by M.G

The earlier dating of coin 4 to late 13th-14th rather than late 15th - early 16th century is quite compatible with context 349 as this is a period III feature. The identification of coin 8, as dating to *c.* 1248-50 is relevant to the stratigraphical information from ditch 460, the dating of the pottery and the absence of ceramic tiles.

Jettons by Stuart Rigold, fig. 48

1*   French official (Tours?), of normal late 14th century type, but rather more delicate, though shallower fabric. Diam. 26 mm. *Obv. chastel tournais* surmounted by *fleur-de-lis* (*cf.* but presumably subsequent to, the gros *fleur de lise* of 1356) + AVE. MARIA. GRASIA. PLENA, pellet stops, lettering of Charles V type. *Rev.* Cross flory, with simple *lis* terminals instead of the typically elaborate ones, in quatrefoil; trefoils and pellets flanking crown in spandrels. Certain details, e.g. the spelling of GRASIA, the cross-terminals and the long-serified L, suggest it is subsequent to the normal fabric pieces, and closer to the later derivatives, and perhaps *c.* 1410 (311) (III-IV).

6*   Late French official, possibly an imitation. Diam. 26 mm. Such things seem to occur about the second quarter of the 15th century, but were being ousted by Tournai jettons. *Obv.* Four lis in field, central star and two (four?) smaller stars. Star initial mark, rather garbled 'Ave Maria' legend, with letters sideways - AVMAIA..GA IA? *Rev.* Cross Flory with pierced sexfoil in central quadrilateral *lis* and A cusp terminals, stars in spandrels. Charles VII was rather fond of star stops. (U/S in ploughsoil to the north of Trench II) (U/S).

2.   Early to mid-Nuremberg, Diam. 22. Normal type (three crowns, jewelled with amulets and three *lis*/Reichsapfel` in trilobe), nonsense legends, no spandrel ornaments. This sort of jetton is common is Dissolution contexts, *c.* 1530 (331) (V).

3.   Similar to no. 2, but 23 mm diam. (348) (V). Location on fig. 34.

7.   Blank both sides, but with central piercing, diam. 23 cm. These were used with 'sterling' jettons of the early 14th century; they could hardly be earlier than 1280, when pierced English jettons began, nor after the late 14th century, when the regulation about piercing lapsed. Blanks and sterling jettons are found together. (181) (III - IV). Location on fig. 34.

7.14 Pottery (figs. 49, 56-59)

7.14a Introduction

The pottery was sorted by M.G. into type-fabrics; the distribution of these by area and context is shown on figs. MF 50-55. Their relative proportions are shown on fig. 49. Figs. 56-59 show the forms illustrated in each fabric; detail in MF.

The pottery needs studying further, in the light of excavations and publications made available since this report was written.

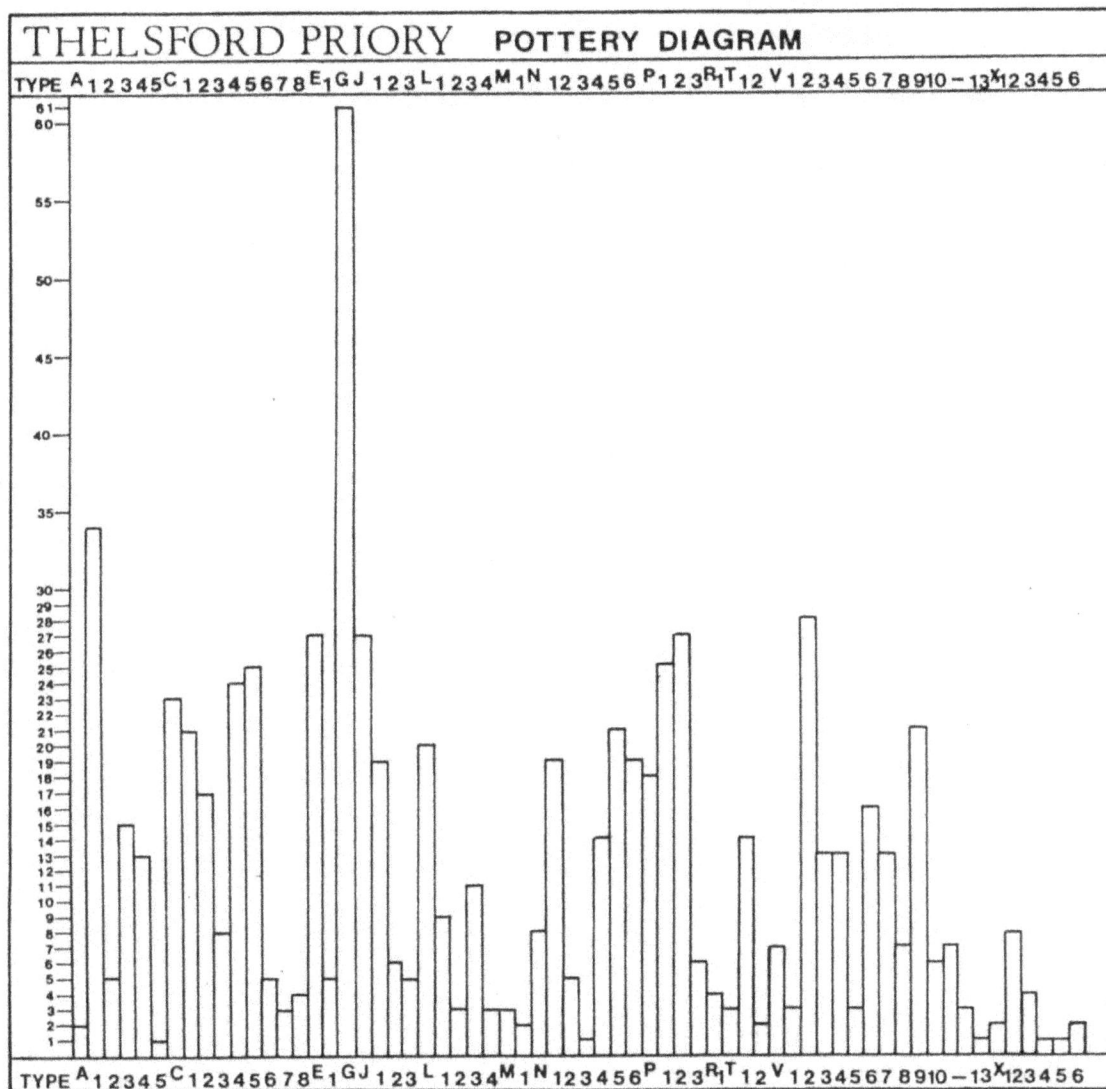

THELSFORD PRIORY POTTERY DIAGRAM

Fig: 49

7.14b The type-fabrics

A   Coarse, corky, calcareous grits, core light grey and surfaces red-brown. These were subdivided into:

        A.1   Slightly soapy, either white gritted or finely pitted.

        A.2   Similar, but more hard-fired, colour of surface more yellow-brown than red-brown.

        A.3   Less corky, with finer grits, micaceous.

        A.4   Softer fabric, shelly grits, red surfaces.

C   Hard, sandy, colour and texture variable, cooking pots, subdivided into:

        C.1   Smooth, light grey core and dark grey surface.

        C.2   Blue-grey core and surface

75

C.3	Light grey core and yellow-grey surface, micaceous
C.4	Buff-grey core and very dark grey or black surface, fine grits, giving a pimply surface, sometimes inner surface is buff-grey
C.5	Pink-grey core and surface
C.6	Grey core and grey surface, fine grits giving a pimply surface, micaceous
C.7	Like C.6, but smoother surface
C.8	Very coarse, dark grey fabric, outer surface glazed olive green

E   White, sandy, with quartz-grains, external bright green glaze (?Nuneaton)

G   Grey-white, sometimes micaceous, sandy, green-glazed, poor quality jugs (?Nuneaton)

J   Hard fired orange-buff with patchy glaze (??Nuneaton), sub-divided into:

| J | Mauve exterior surface with patchy olive-green glaze |
| J.1 | Red-brown exterior and interior surfaces, pimply texture with spotty brown, purple and green glaze |

L   Sandy, smooth surface, off-white or orange-white, sometimes with grey-core, subdivided into:

L	Fine, smooth fabric, slightly micaceous, no glaze
L.1	As L, but with green, speckled glaze
L.2	As L, but with glossy yellow or olive-green glaze
L.3	Fabric more orange, with yellow, orange or green glaze
L.4	Very sandy, orange fabric with yellow glaze

M   Smooth, buff fabric, with red inclusions, patchy yellow glaze, over painted with stripes of thick red slip (?Nuneaton) (possibly Tamworth-type jug)

N   Fine red or orange sandy (from ?Coventry or ?Warwick), subdivided into:

N.1	Red interior surface, dark red exterior
N.2	Sometimes grey core, buff interior, glossy olive-green glaze, rouletted strips
N.3	As N.2, with rouletted pads
N.4	As N.2, with applied strips
N.5	Red core, red interior surface, mauve exterior with speckled orange and green glaze, overpainted with stripes of creamy white slip
N.6	Orange red core and interior, green glaze with stripes of white slip, some cases almost lost, giving the appearance of orange-red

P   Hard, sandy, red (?from Coventry and Warwick), subdivided into:

P	Purple skinned, with patchy dark green glaze interiors
P.1	Unglazed, orange-red
P.2	Orange-red, spots of yellow, purple and green glaze interiors
P.3	Thick, apple-green or brown glaze

R   Hard fired, purple brown, with glossy dark brown glaze, like early stoneware

| T | T.1 | Fine white fabric with glossy, thick, apple-green glaze ('Tudor-Green' type) |
| | T.2 | Tin glazed earthenware, with blue glazed exterior and clear glaze interior |

V   Stoneware

V.1	Hard, smooth, very fine, red-brown core with surfaces covered with ginger brown glaze
V.2	As V.1, but purple-brown core and surfaces glazed same colour
V.3	As V.1, but pink-brown core and surfaces covered with olive green glaze
V.4	Semi-stoneware, purple-brown core and speckled purple glaze

V.5   Semi-stoneware, light grey core, dark olive grey glaze
V.6   Light pink core, with one surface glazed glossy black
V.7   Hard, smooth very fine, with dark grey core and purple-black glaze
V.8   As V.6, but glazed both surfaces
V.9   Hard, smooth, very fine, red core with surfaces glazed dark brown
V.10   Red core with gritty orange red glaze
V.11   Hard, smooth, very fine, red core with purple-black glaze
V.12   Coarse purple-grey core, usually not glazed, sometimes specks of purple glaze
V.13   As V.11, but thicker and not uniformly glazed

X   Stonewares, and post-medieval pottery
X.1   Off-white core with pale yellow or colourless glaze, stoneware
X.2   Blue-grey core with pale brown glaze (Nottingham), stoneware
X.3   Same, but with mottled glaze (Nottingham) stoneware
X.4   Light brown core with mid-brown glaze (Nottingham) stoneware
X.5   Hard, fine yellow core with mid-brown streaky glaze
X.6   Dark brown core, purple internal skin and olive-brown glaze

7.14c The illustrated series (figs. 56-59)

(Code numbers refer to Type Fabric in 7.14b; all are unglazed unless otherwise stated)

Type A.   A.D. 1200-1400. Similar in form to examples from Lyveden 9; St. Peter's Street, Northampton (Types A and B); St. Aldate's Oxford (Type T.6, Phase 8); Wythemail (Type D); and Warwick, Barrack St. (figs 6-9).

FIG. 56

Fig. 56
1.   Large bowl. A.1 (324) (III-IV)
2.   Spout of jug. A.2 (315) (V)
3.   Rim sherd. A.1 (465) (III)
4.   Rim sherd. Traces of brown glaze. A.2 (496) (V)
5.   Cooking pot. A.3 (III) (III-IV)
6.   Thumb impressed rim. A.3 (35) (III-IV)
7.   Small bowl. A.3 (308) (IV)
8.   Rim of jug. A.3 (35) (III-IV)
9.   Rim of jug. A.3 (35) (III-IV)

Type J.   Forms middle of 13th century at Weoley Castle (Fig. 49); Kenilworth Castle (fig. 5); and Warwick, Barrack St. (fig. 7).

Fig. 56
10.   Large bowl. Internal glaze, yellow and olive green. J (460) (II)
11.   Flat base. External glaze, purple spotted. J (461) (III)
12.   Flat base. Internal glaze, orange and olive green. J.3 (152d) (III)
13.   Wall of jug with pinched decoration. External glaze patchy olive green over purple. J.3 (310) (V)
14.   Rim sherd of cookpot with rim hollow. External glaze, spotty, purple. J.1 (461) (III)
15.   Rim sherd. Exterior glaze, olive green. J.3 (310) (V)
16.   Two similar rim sherds. One has traces of exterior glaze, purple spotted. J.3 (35) (III-IV). The other is unglazed (330) (V)

Type G.   14th century poor quality jugs, at St. Aldate's Oxford (Phase 10) and Potterspury (fig. 1, no. 3).

Fig. 56
17.   Wall of jug with incised rilling. Faint traces of green glaze. G (496) (V)

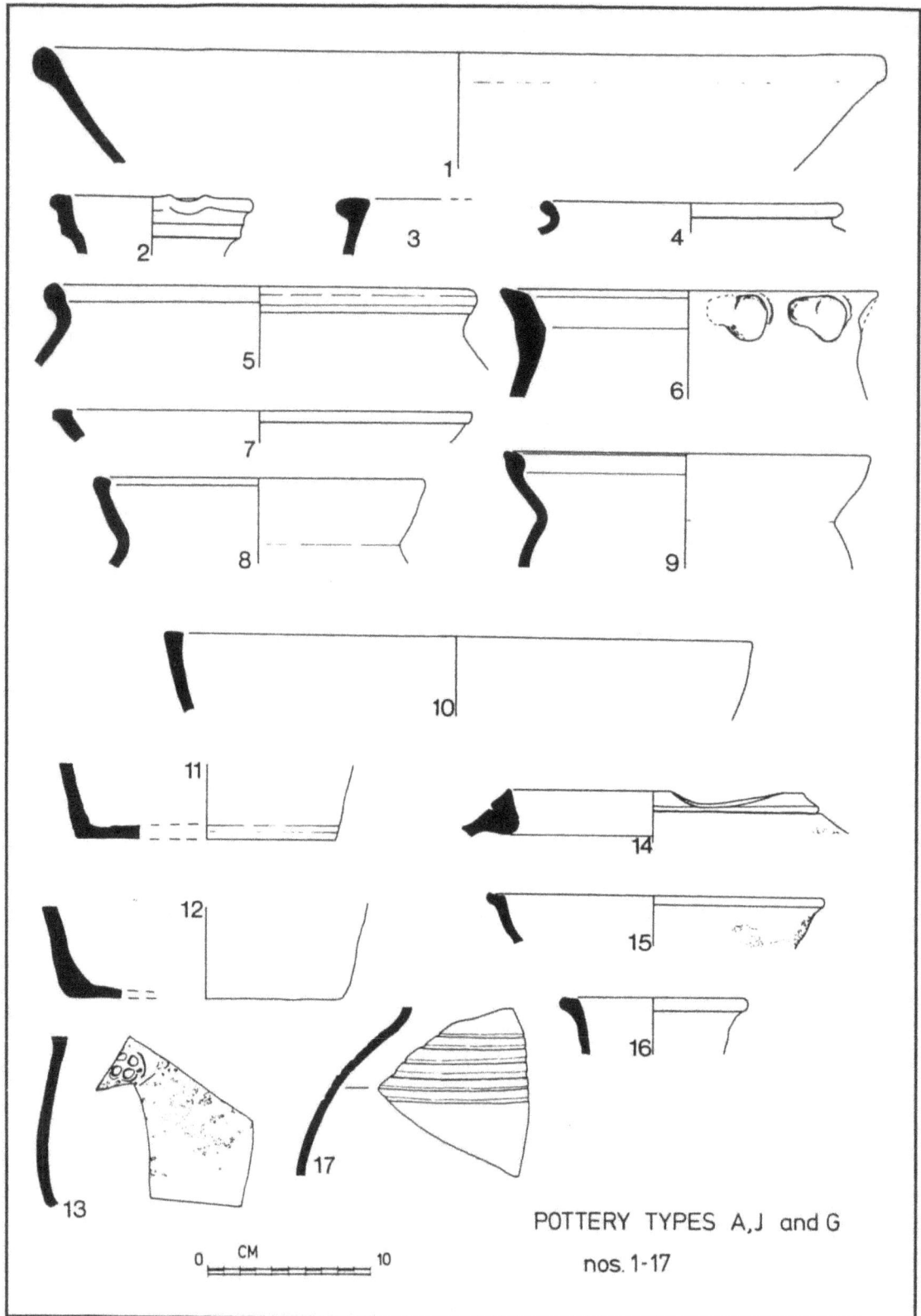

POTTERY TYPES A,J and G
nos. 1-17

Fig: 56

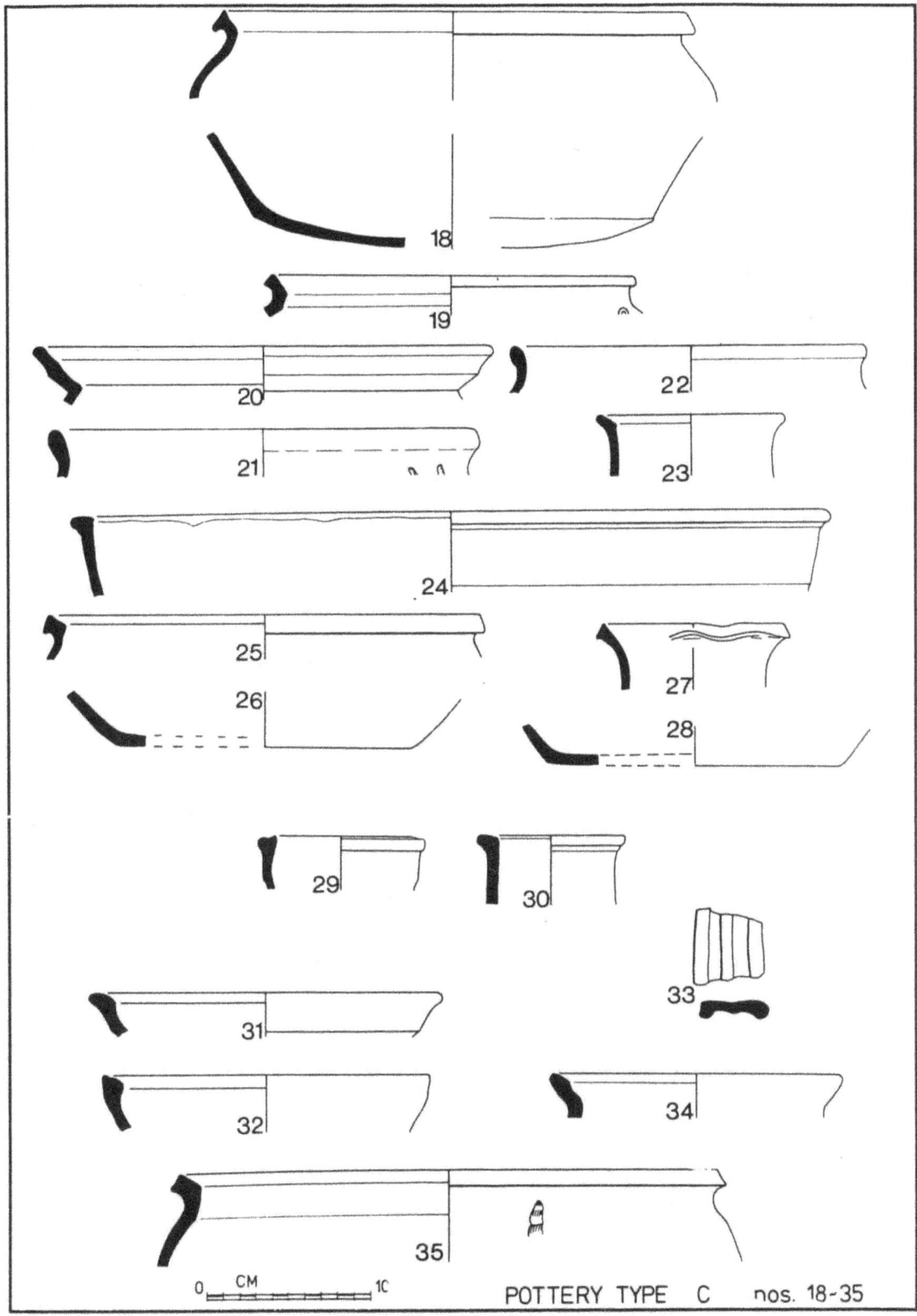

POTTERY TYPE C nos. 18-35

Fig: 57

Type C.   13th to 15th century cooking pots and jugs, as from St. Aldate's, Oxford (Phases 9 and10); St. Peter's Street, Northampton (Type V3); Lyveden (Type C); and Warwick, Barrack St. (fig. 6-9).

FIG.57

Fig. 57
18.   Rim and base of cooking pot. C.1 (308) (V)
19.   Rim sherd of cooking pot. C.2 (357) (III-IV)
20 & 21 Rim sherds of cooking pot. C.3 (152e and 304) (III and III+)
22.   Rim sherd of cooking pot. C.5 (410) (U/S)
23.   Rim sherd of jug. C.3 (35) (III-IV)
24.   Rim sherd of bowl. C.3 (334) (III)
25 & 26 Rim sherd and base of cookpots. C.4 (409a and 461) (IV and ?III)
27.   Rim of jug with 'pie crust' decoration. C.4 (483) (III)
28.   Base of cooking pot. C.4 (409a) (IV)
29 & 30 Rims from two jugs. C.5 (349 and 345) (III and V)
31 & 32 Rims from two bowls. C.6 (152e and 330) (III and V)
33.   Strap handle from jug. C.6 (349) (III)
34.   Rim of cooking pot. C.7 (351) (III+)
35.   Rim of cooking pot. C.7 (349) (III)

Type E.   13th to 14th century white fabric green glazed jugs, from the Midlands, possibly Nuneaton Type A. As from St. Peter's Street, Northampton (Type W 11).

FIG. 58

Fig. 58
36.   Thumb impressed base, apple-green glaze, exterior only (Nuneaton, fig. 105, no. 220). E (409a) (IV)
37.   Rim from bowl, apple-green glaze, exterior only. E (409a) (IV)
38.   Body sherd from jug, green exterior glaze with overlapping applied scales (See Rackham 1972, 24 and pl. 11 (368) (III-V)
39.   Rim of ?bowl or small jug, exterior green glaze covers rim also. E (309) (III-IV)
40.   Rim of ?bowl or lamp, exterior olive green glaze covers rim also. E (6) (II or III)
50.   Rim of jug, exterior olive green glaze. E (487) (IV-V)
51.   Corner from base of ?ornament, possibly statue, incised lines, yellow-brown paint on exterior and base only, splash of green glaze on interior. E (451) (V)

Type L.   13th to 14th century, possibly Midlands manufacture, similar to Potterspury ware, as found at Wythemail, Northants; St. Peter's Street, Northampton (Type W 18); and Warwick, Barrack St., (fig. 7).

Fig. 58
41.   Base of baluster jug, narrow band of brown slip on base. L (410) (U/S)
42.   Rim of jug. L (401) (III-IV)

43.   Base of bottle, heavily girth-grooved interior, traces of external light green glaze and internal spots of yellow glaze. L.1 (345) (V)
44 & 45 Rims of cooking pots. L (304) (III+) and L.3 (410) (U/S)
46.   Rim and handle of jug, light green glaze beneath handle, two knife slashes above handle. L.1 (304) (III+)
47.   Rim of jug, exterior speckled light green glaze. L.1 (304) (III+)
48.   Rim and handle of jug, exterior traces of yellow glaze and stripes of brown slip, strap handle decorated with knife slashings. L.3 (409a) (IV)
49.   Base of jug, exterior speckled green glaze, L.1 (409a) (IV)
52.   Red handle with round stab marks. L.3 (415) (IV)
53.   Base of jug, exterior yellow glaze. L.3 (330) (V)

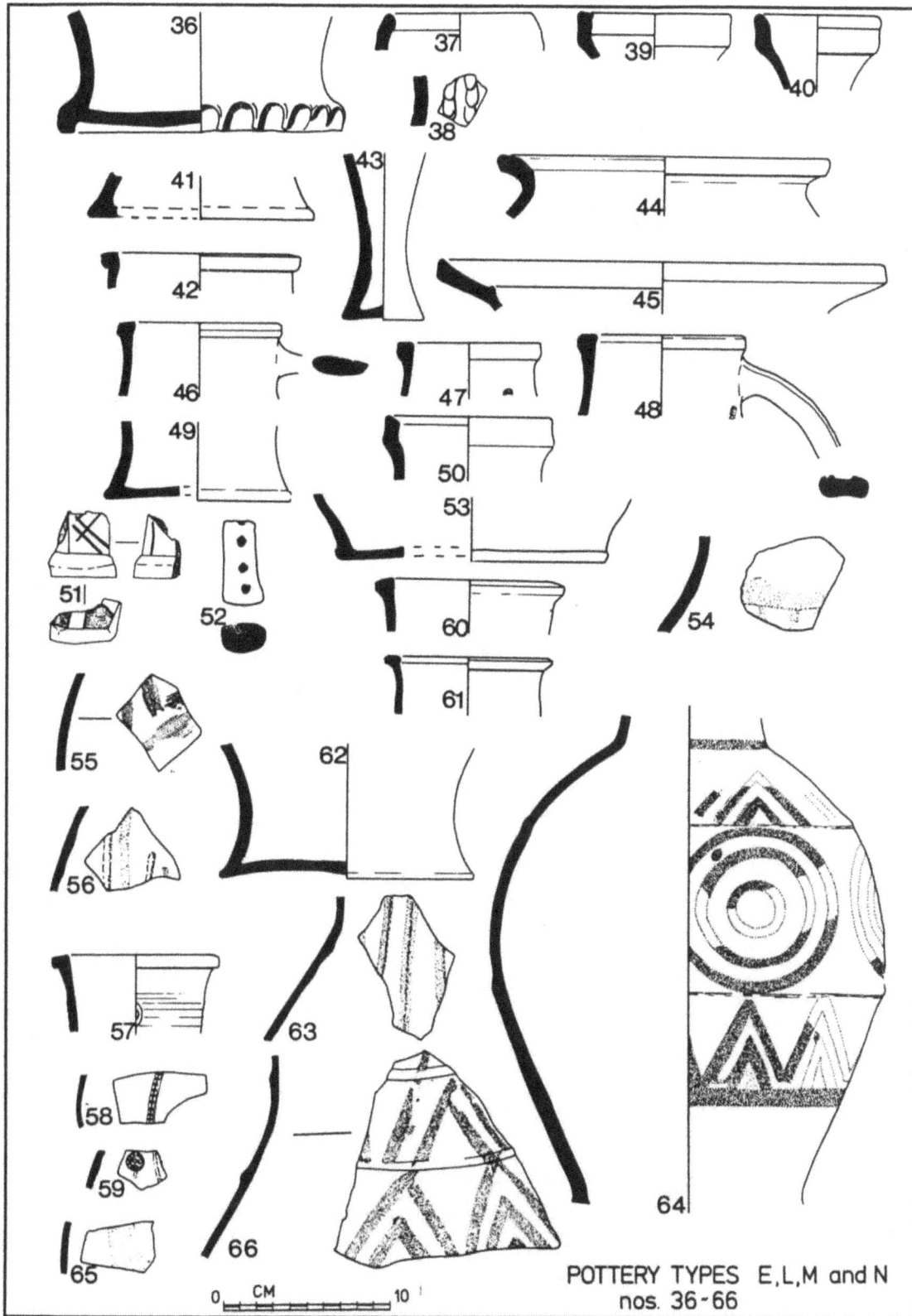

POTTERY TYPES E,L,M and N
nos. 36-66

Fig: 58

60. Rim of jug, traces of exterior speckled green glaze. L.1 (461) (III)
    61. Rim of jug, exterior apple-green glaze extends over the rim. L.3 (309) (III-IV)
    62. Base of jug, exterior speckled green glaze. L.1 (469) (III)

Type M

Fig. 58   54. Body sherd from jug, pronounced inner girth grooves, yellow glaze, overpainted with bold dark red stripes. M (*cf.* Midlands type, Tamworth etc) (410) (U/S)

Type N   Late 13th to 15th centuries, decorated jugs.

Fig. 58   55. Body sherd from jug, cream painted lines, over-glazed with speckled olive green glaze, diagonal design. Similar to St. Peter's Street, Northampton (Type W 15) with affinities in East Midlands, Essex and Cambridge. N1 (498) (II+)
    56. Body sherd, applied strips, brown slip, yellow-green glaze. Oxford late medieval ware, as from St. Aldate's, Oxford (fig. 22, no. 46) where it is dated to the second half of the 13th century to early 14th century. N.4 (494) (III)
    57. Rim sherd, horizontal rilling on exterior, pad applied over this, yellow-green glaze starts beneath the rim. Oxford late medieval ware. N.3 (368) (III-V)
    58. Body sherds from jug, speckled apple-green glaze exterior, light brown applied strips with ladder rouletting. Oxford late medieval ware. N.2 (460) (II)
    59. Body sherd from jug, light yellow-green glaze exterior, grid stamped applied pads, raised strips and lines of brown slip. St. Aldate's, Oxford. N.3 (304) (III+)
    63. Body sherd from jug, speckled apple and darker green glaze exterior, applied strips of light brown clay. St. Aldates, Oxford. N.4 (318) (IV)
    64. Body sherds from three-tiered jug, yellow brown glaze exterior; cream slip in circular and chevron designs. Possibly from Coventry or Warwick. N.5 (318) (V)
    65 & 66 Similar to 64, but less highly glazed. N.6 (494 and 409a) (III and IV)

Type P.   Late 14th to 16th century, possibly from Warwick, but similar to Lyveden (Type D); St. Peter's Street, Northampton (Type W29); and Warwick, Barrack St., (fig. 10).

Fig. 59   67,68,70 Rims of bowls. P.1 (466, 2 and 300) (III, II+ and V)
    69 & 71 Rims of bowls with spots of yellow glaze over purple red slip. P (499 and 476) (III-IV)
    72. Rim and handle of jug, thick strap handle with central thumbed groove and two thumbed points of attachment at the top, knife slashing beneath rounded inturned rim, and down handle, thick copper green external glaze, patchy over the rim and under the handle. Similar to Lyveden (fig. 30, no. 4.06). P.3 (310) (V)
    73. (See Type X below)

Type T.   *c.* 1400 to end of 16th century (*floruit* mid 15th). 'Tudor Green' type, see Moorhouse 1983, 53-61; Holling 1977, 61-66; Brears 1971, 25-6.

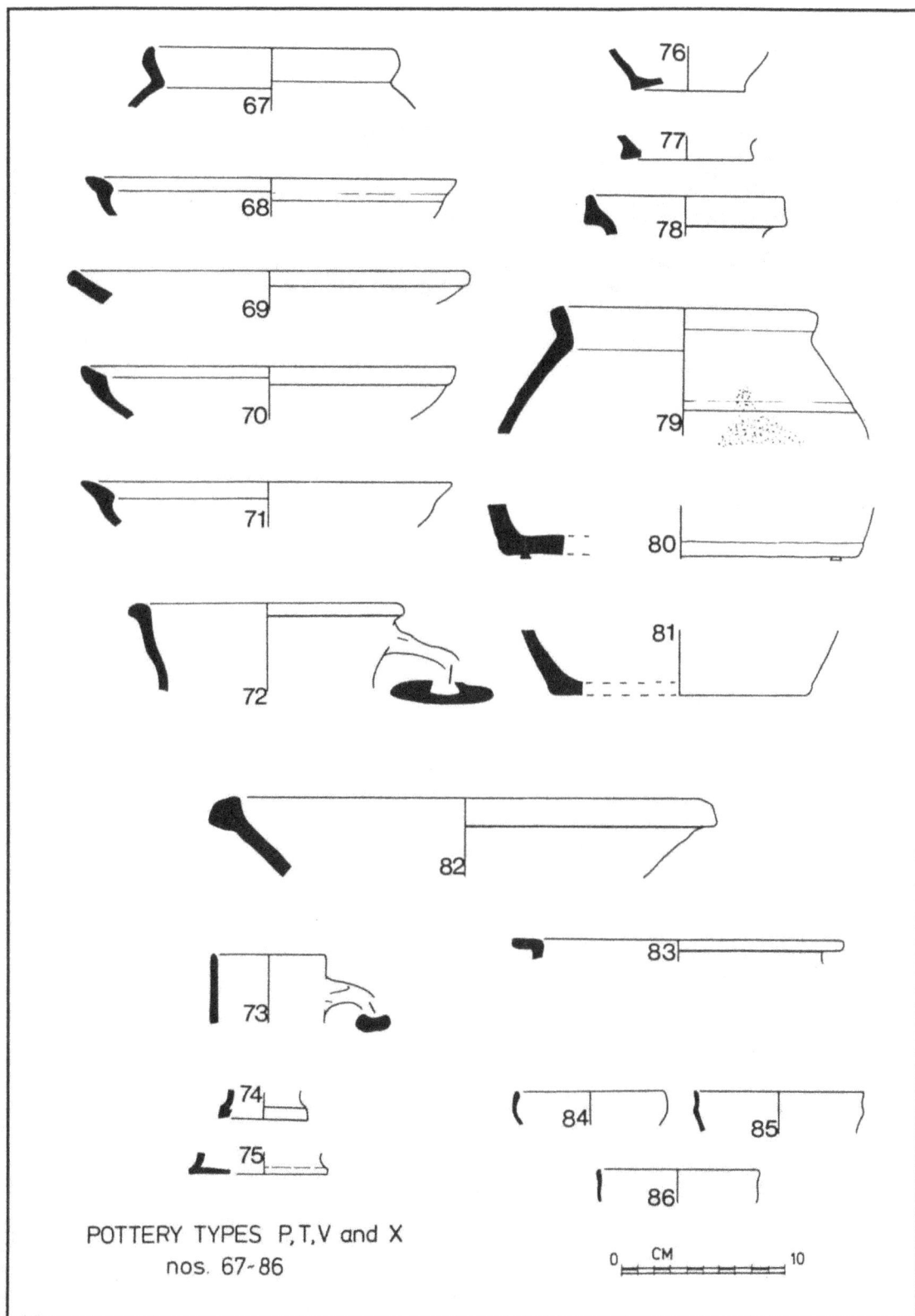

POTTERY TYPES P,T,V and X
nos. 67-86

Fig: 59

FIG. 59

Fig. 59   74.   Base of cup, lustrous green glaze interior. T.1 (438) (III + IV)

                75.   Base of wide cup, lustrous green glaze interior. T.1 (410) (U/S)

Type V. Mid 14th to mid 16th century, late medieval glazed, semi-stoneware, fine glazed ware (Cistercian); and early 17th century glazed ware (Midland Blackware), possibly from Nuneaton, (fabric D); and Midland Purple, as from St. Peter's, Northampton (Type W16), Humberstone, Leics (Type H) and Warwick, Barrack St. (fig. 10) (not illustrated):

Fig. 59   76 & 77   Bases of cups, with dark brown glaze exteriors except underneath base, and glazed interior base. V.2 (both 451) (V)

                78.   Rim of jug, unglazed. V.4 (451) (V)

                79.   Rim of cooking pot with simple curved profile and globular body. Similar to St. Peter's Street, Northampton, no. 377, p. 193. Thick purple brown glaze on body. V.4 (300) (V)

                80.   Base of straight sided jar, with applied strip under base, patches of purple brown glaze exterior and interior. V.4 (313) (V)

Midland Blackware:

Fig. 59   81 & 82   Base from jug and rim of bowl, lustrous black glaze interiors. V.6 (both 300) (V)

                83.   Rim of bowl, lustrous black glaze interior and exterior. V.8 (341) (V)

Cistercian Wares:

Fig. 59   84,85,86   Rims from cups, dark brown, lustrous glaze interiors and exteriors. V.9 (125, 345 and 372) (IV, V and V)

Type X   Stonewares, mid 16th century onwards

Fig 59.   73.   Rim and handle of ?Nottingham mug, lustrous grey glaze with ginger-brown glaze under handle, exterior only. X.1 (451) (V)

7.15, 7.16, 7.17, 7.18

Clay tobacco pipes; a block of oak from the sluice weighing 8 kgs; (513) (IV) charcoal; and fibre. The latter includes threads, now green in colour, attached to small fragment of woven fabric, probably embroidery threads; details in MF.

7.19 Human bones

No complete skeletons were recovered from graves, nor were any sent for biological examination. Remains were not disturbed unless it was essential. They were examined by M.G. in situ. Those in tombs had been robbed at the Dissolution. That in the lead shroud/coffin had been crushed by the lead. Bones were kept from two male adults, a male adolescent, two children, and part of a skull, with mark of wound; detail in MF.

7.20 Animal bone by the late Ralph Harcourt

Two samples were analysed, and taken to be typical of the extensive animal bone content of the site. In 1966 these were the only animal bones which were kept. In 1972, all animal bone was kept, and a list of species and quantities is deposited with the site record.

Sample 1 was from 152, a cesspit of period III, and produced a varied range. Apart from the usual domestic animals, there was also rat, rabbit, domestic fowl, goose, pigeon and oyster. Sheep are predominant, cattle remains consisting only of one phalanx and a few vertebral fragments. There were six complete sheep long bones, nearly a third of the total sheep remains, an unusually high proportion. From these it was possible to estimate the size of the animals, which has changed little from prehistoric to late medieval times, closely resembling the Soay, a long limbed slender breed. The pig remains were too few for special mention. There were bones from a horse of 13 hands (52 ins : 132 cms) and medium build.

Sample 2 was taken from layer 307, dumped in pond 2 at the Dissolution (period V). It could be representative of the latest period of the site. The domestic species present are cattle, sheep, pig, horse and fowl, and the only wild one is fallow deer. Cattle provided the majority of bones from this sample. There was insufficient evidence to give any idea of the age at which these cattle were killed, but there were several bones sufficiently complete for measurements to be possible, and these are compared with those of cattle from other medieval sites and of modern breeds they most closely resemble. The measurements of these, and all other bones, are deposited in the site record. Sheep bones were very few, and could have come from just two animals, one very old and one very young. The pig bones were very fragmentary, but, according to the evidence of eruption and wear of the cheek teeth, they were from animals of 2-3 years old. The fowl in question was a rooster with powerful spurs.

7.21 Bone objects (not illustrated)

Small fragment of worked bone, circular, 2 x 2 cms, incised with three lines, possibly part of a knife handle (315) (V).

Peg, 40 mm long, with notch across head and line incised near top (372) (V).

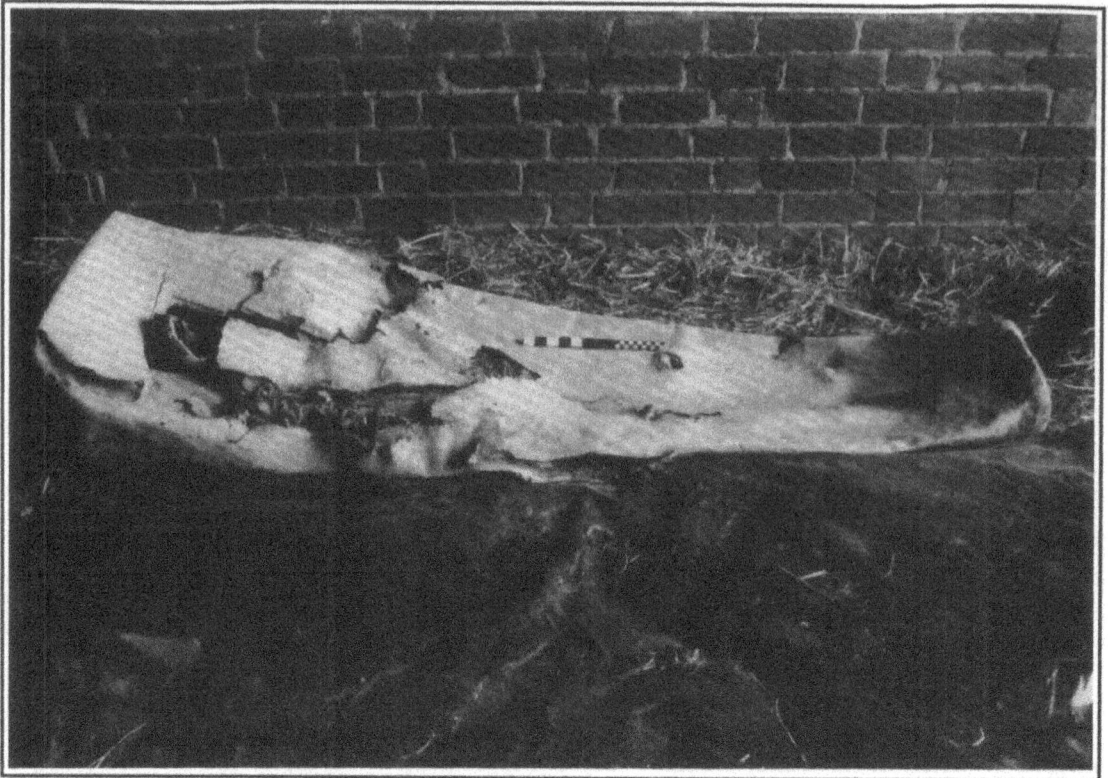

Plate V
Lead shroud, after excavation (scale in centimetres)

Plate VI
Architectural fragment from wall 206, stone 10 (scale in centimetres and decimetres)

86

Plate VII
Architectural fragment from wall 206, stone 10 (scale in centimetres and decimetres)

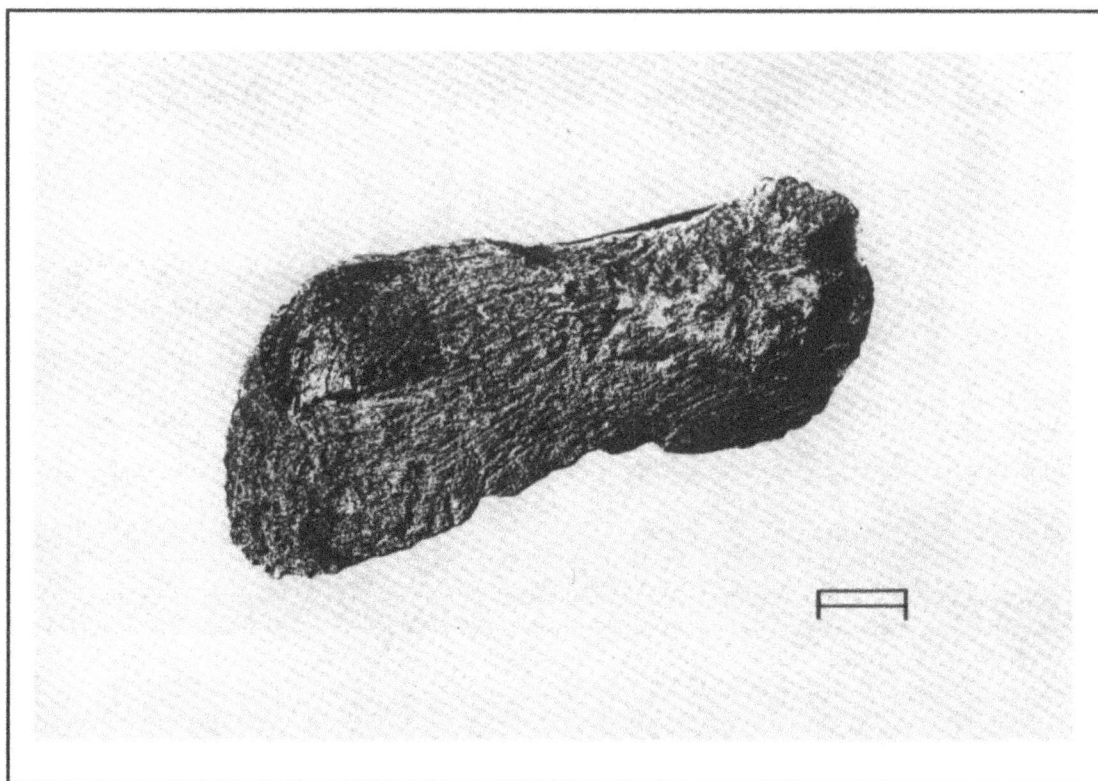

Plate VIII
Flint flake from 45, showing striations (7.1) (scale one centimetre)

Chapter 8
ARCHEOLOGICAL AND HISTORICAL SYNTHESES AND CONCLUSION

8.1 PERIOD I - pre-13th century A.D. (figs 1 and 60)

The area around Thelsford is one which is relatively dense in evidence of prehistoric and Romano-British occupation. A cursus and ring ditches lay to the south of the area later developed as fishponds (no.71 in Webster and Hobley 1965, 18); these were excavated by P. Christie in 1968 and W. Ford in 1969 (HMSO 1970). A crop-mark which may be of Iron Age date lies on the east side of the A 429, close to Thelsford Bridge (fig. 1) (no. 73 in Webster and Hobley 1965, 18). Ditched enclosures of the Roman period were excavated in 1967 by the present writer a kilometre to the south of the site near Charlecote (publication in preparation). South of Wasperton, Hooke 1985 (145 and plan, fig. 10.13a) mentions the settlement cluster of Romano-British farmsteads, some possibly of Iron Age origin, around the area of the later medieval village, and the excavated Anglo-Saxon cemetery adjacent to this complex. This excavation, which took place between 1980 and 1985 found neolithic, early Bronze Age, Iron Age, Roman and Anglo-Saxon features (Wise 1991, 256-9).

The density of features located below the priory, as shown in fig. 60, is thus perhaps no more than might be expected in any comparable area on the Avon gravels; it should however be borne in mind that only a small percentage of the area was excavated and further features may lie beneath the monastic levels which were not removed. If the whole area were to be stripped, the density of features might be higher than is apparent; and if this were so then the proximity of the Thelsford Brook might be seen as an attractive factor in favour of settlement.

Of the pre-priory features located, only one was dateable; this was 45, a Mesolithic or Early Neolithic pit, with evidence of flint knapping *in situ*. This and other features were usually in association with the buried soil(layer Q): sealed by it, within it, or cutting it. It is thus possible that several phases of occupation or frequentation are represented; the only evidence of settled use of the land is the possible negative lynchet (601), implying some cultivation of the land by the river.

No Roman, Saxon or earlier medieval finds were recovered from the area, and it seems likely that the priory settlement was initiated on land which was either in cultivation or pasture, albeit subject to flooding.

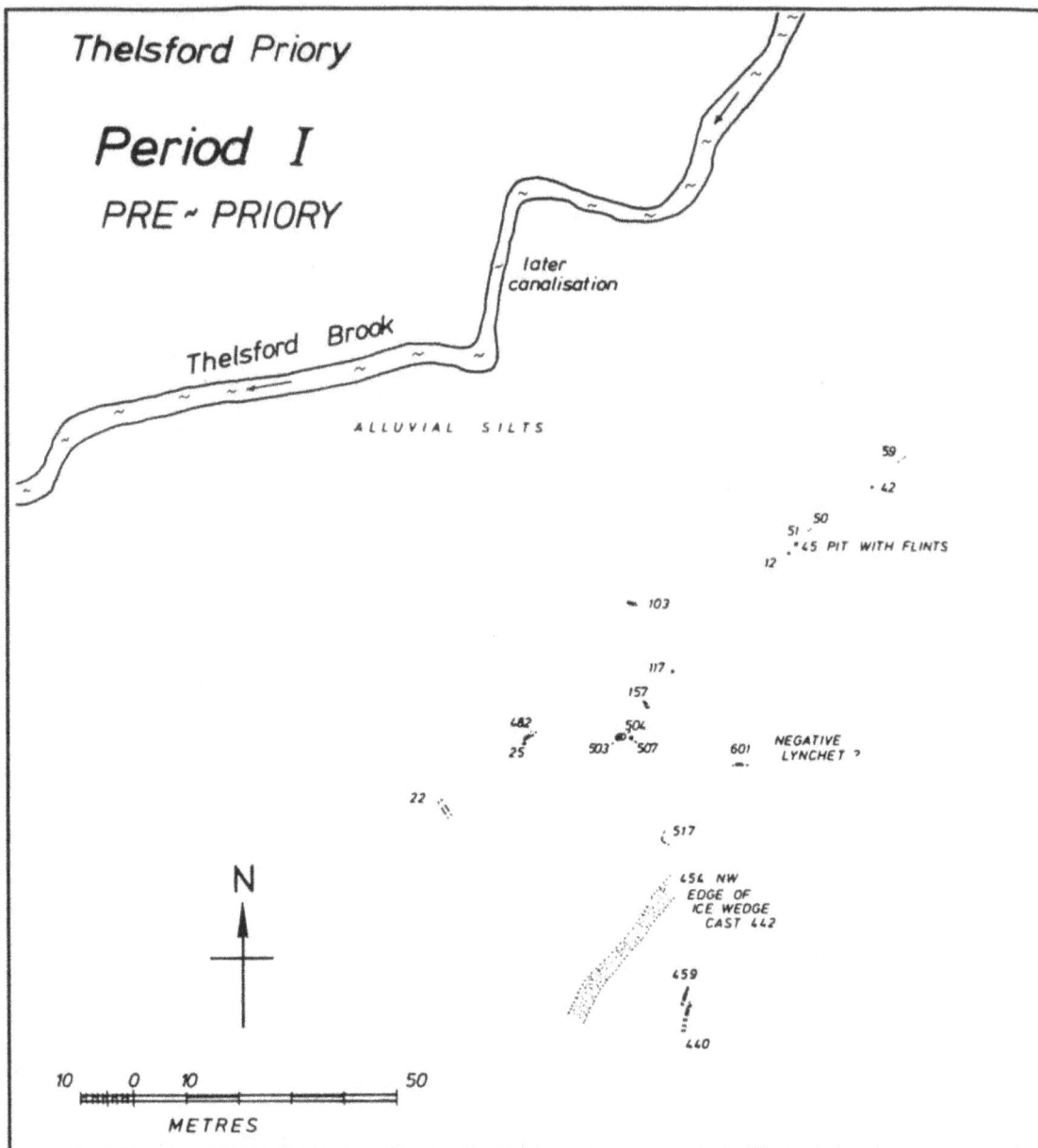

Fig 60

8.2 Period II - c. A.D. 1200 - c. 1285 A.D. (fig. 61)

The Canons of the Holy Sepulchre (4.1 and 4.3.2) were granted land which had a north facing slope and was liable to flood; it did however have the advantage of not being isolated, lying as it did close to the main road from Warwick to the Cotswolds. The apparent disadvantages of this terrain were mitigated by a monastic economy which needed a well organised water supply and easy access for the sick and for travellers to its hospital.

The first grant of land made by William Lucy in 1214 of more than five hectares (13 acres) (4.3.3) is larger than the area enclosed by the period II perimeter ditch and hedge or fence, unless the fishponds are included. This boundary defined not only the extent of the priory but should also have assisted the drainage of the site. This is a function often suggested similarly for moated sites, which are analogous in form to the Thelsford ditched enclosure.

There is no reason to believe that the Thelsford perimeter features were ever filled with water as moats, though the latter have been observed by the writer at other Trinitarian priories with associated fishponds, at Easton Royal in Wiltshire and Moatenden in Kent (9.2 and 9.6 below). The smaller element of the Thelsford perimeter, the ditch, fence or hedge, lay outside the main ditch; it may have prevented stray animals or intruders from approaching too closely to its edge.

90

Parts of the southern and eastern arms of this boundary were located in several places; the eastern arm may have been returning north-westwards at the point where it was last located, presumably extending to the nearest point on the Thelsford Brook. A possible return northwards for the west end of the southern perimeter (28) was found on the west edge of the southern arm of the fishpond

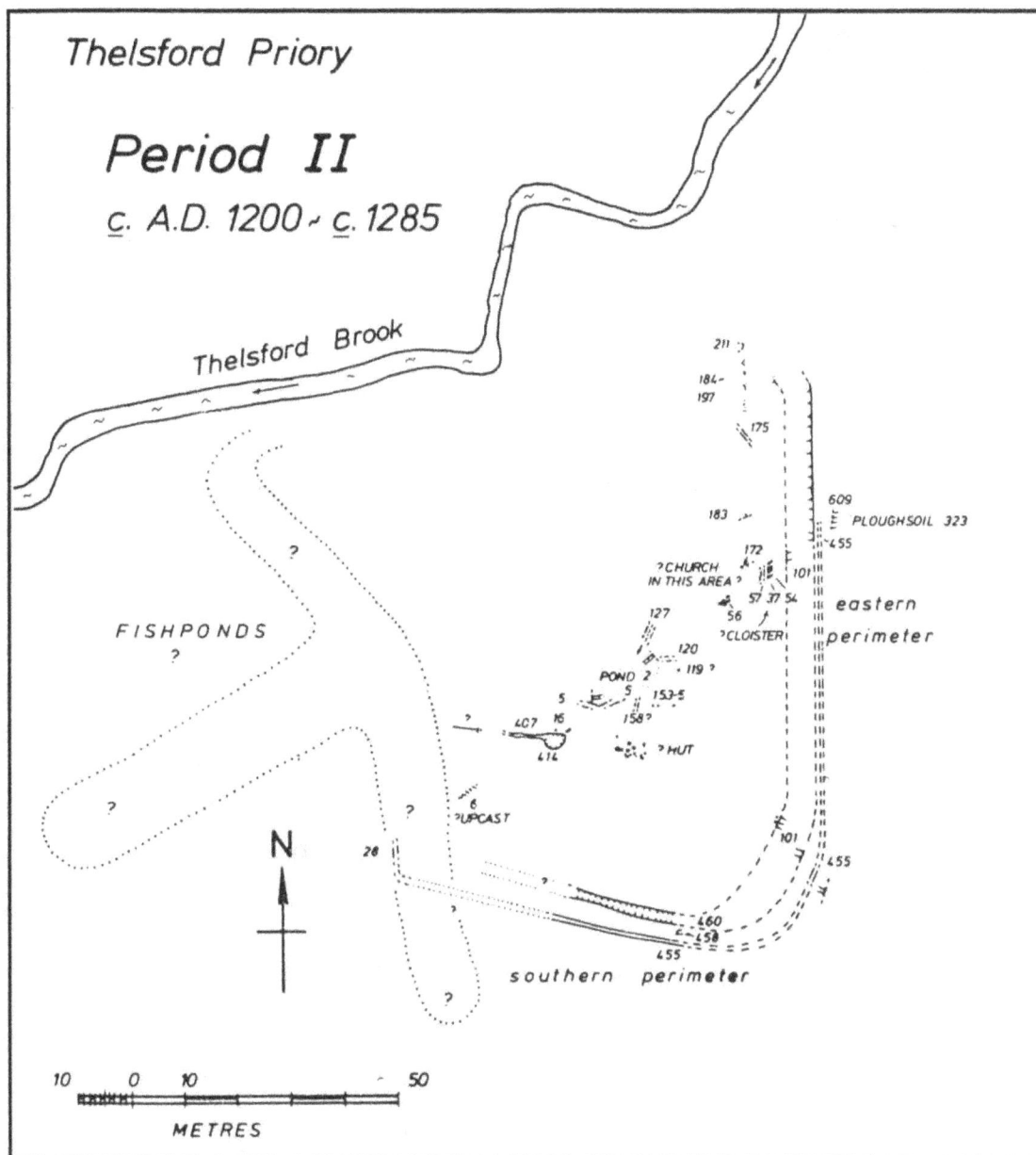

Fig 61

complex. There is however a possibility that this arm originated in period II (?upcast 6), as may also the northern arms; they are thus shown in dotted outline on this plan. The area enclosed in either case presumably encompassed the whole monastic complex of period II. The only feature located outside it, to the east, was 609, a possible lynchet filled with 323. This area was later built upon in period III.

In the NW part of the enclosed area, neither the possible mill platform nor the sluice are shown on this plan; the dating for the former is uncertain and both may have originated in period II, with an outfall to the fishpond area. If these features were however wholly initiated in period III, then the straight section of the Thelsford Brook, interpreted as canalisation for a leat in period III (fig. 62), should probably not be shown as such on this plan.

The extent of excavation did not allow of any positive location for the church or claustral complex (or hospital?) which must have existed in period II; the features of this date which were found are

91

difficult to interpret and were on diverse orientations. The possible position of these buildings is indicated on fig 61, partly confirmed by negative evidence in the area to the north and especially in the more extensively excavated area to the west. Such structures as were located appear to have been at least partly of stone and timber construction, with stone roof slates.

Other minor post- or stake-hole structures were located to the north of this area (184-197, 211). From the supposed claustral area, ditches drained south-westwards to a pond, south of which was a wooden hut; a fishpond (414) lay to the west, perhaps a predecessor of the main pond complex to the west.

No rubbish- or cess-pits were found; they may have existed outside the excavated area; or there may have been a system in the 13th century of gathering the rubbish into heaps and spreading it on the land as manure, as at Wharram Percy (Hurst 1984, 99).

It was during this period that the transfer of the priory from the Canons of the Holy Sepulchre to the Trinitarians (4.3.2) took place. Both orders had as their main concern the provision of a hospital for the poor and sick and a pilgrim' hostel; one or more of the buildings were presumably used for these functions.

Thelsford was only one of many hospitals in existence at that time. Others in the area are shown on fig. 65. There were seven other hospitals which were monastic rather than secular in the neighbourhood, including the Gilbertines at Clattercote; and most of them were under the rule of St. Augustine.

8.3 Period III - late 13th to late 14th centuries A.D. (fig. 62)

The inception of period III is equated with the dedication of the new church in 1285 (4.3.3), though work on the new layout may have preceded this by several years. The new work involved the demolition of all structures of period II and a total replanning. This included the presumed claustral buildings and other wooden structures, such as those in the NE part of the site. In the latter area gravel was extracted by shallow scoops, the spoil being used partly to backfill sections of the period II perimeter ditches.

The southern arm of the fishponds, and possibly the whole complex of ponds, may have originated in period III, though as already mentioned they could be earlier. These formed the boundary to the west, perhaps with 29 on their east side. A new southern perimeter ditch (438) extended the enclosed area in this direction; the eastern boundary may have been on the line of the present main road, perhaps (with Thelsford Bridge) dating from this time. There appears to have been an entrance in the southern perimeter; details are obscure, but there seems to have been a road here, indicated by ruts, using the hard surface of the periglacial ice-wedge cast, and heading towards the claustral complex. This may have been the road which Fulk Lucy allowed to be enclosed at this time (4.3); there was however another west-east road, on the north side of the area, located at the end of Trench VI (673); this may have led westwards to a ford over Thelsford Brook, which is still shallow in this part. There was another possible road or terrace in the SE part of the site (664). Further ditches to the west of this (469, 461) were presumably to drain the area downslope to the north.

Within the enclosed area there were several areas of structures and activity apart from the claustral complex itself. To the NW, it is suggested that a length of the Thelsford Brook was canalised and that from this a leat directed water to the north and east of a platform. The latter is very tentatively suggested to have been part of, or near to, a watermill. The eastern arm of this leat (109) led water to a complex sluice (409). Initially this was a simple ditch with a sluice-gate, the latter indicated by a sharp drop. While this sluice may have been merely to control the inlet of water to the fishponds, there is a possibility that it was (also?) the outfall from the possible watermill; or was there a mill in fact near this 'sluice' complex?

In the southern central part of the enclosed area were further drainage features, including a substantial stone-lined culvert (483) draining, with other ditches, the area to the SW of the claustral buildings. South of these were a series of structures and features which appear to have comprised the working area of the priory. There were possible industrial features here, a wooden building (burnt down), and several pits; some of these may have been for latrines or rubbish disposal.

On the west and north sides of the claustral buildings were areas of cultivated soil, suggested to have been gardens.

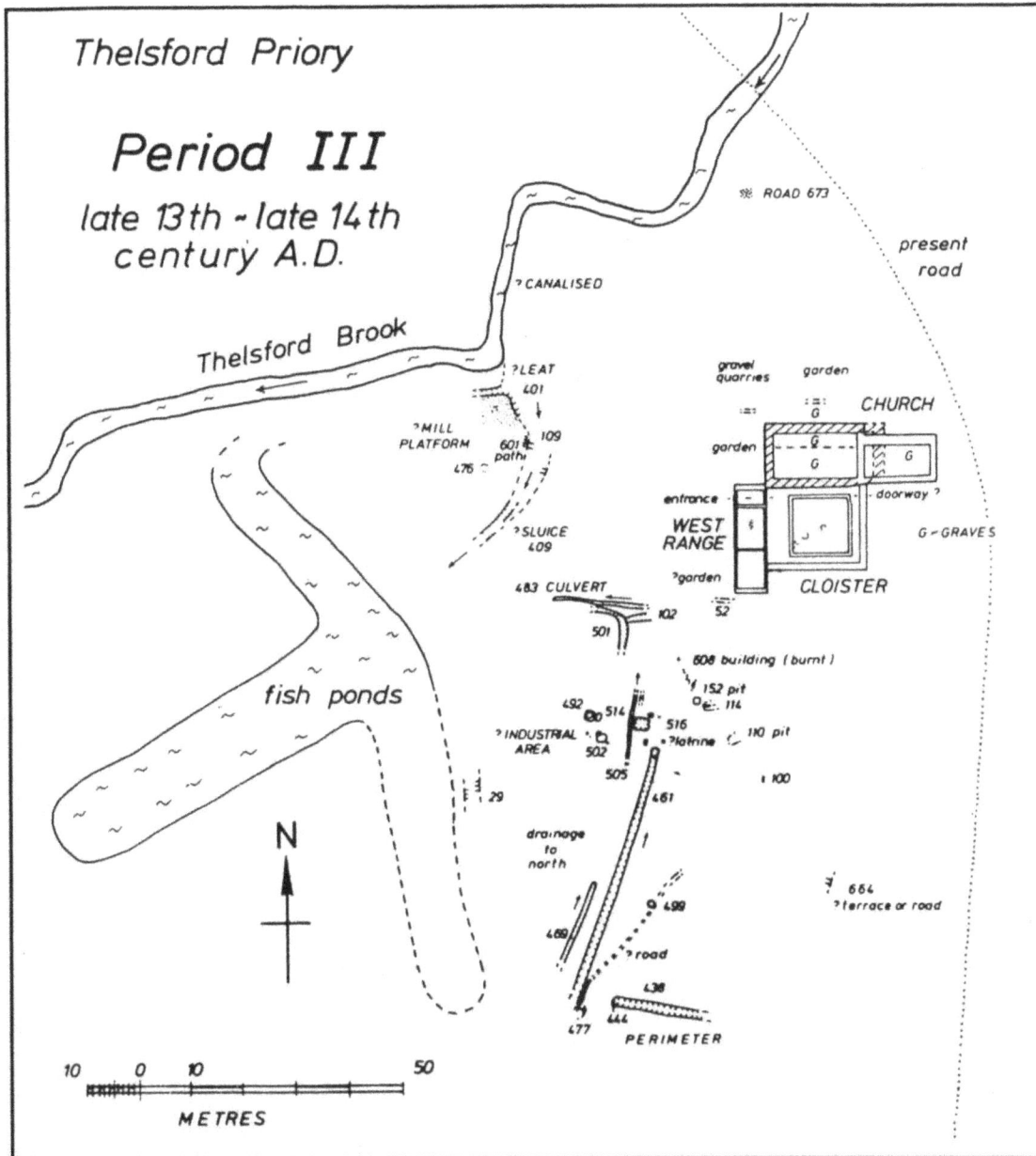

Fig: 62

Discussion of the church, cloister and west range is deferred until after the section on period IV, as the various elements of it cannot be neatly split as between periods III and IV.

The period from the late 13th century onwards was the time of maximum activity at Thelsford. By the middle of the 14th century red ceramic tile was replacing other roofing materials. A high percentage of the pottery from the site was of this period and included good quality jugs from the Midland and Oxford regions (7,14). By this time the regulation restricting riding to be only on asses had been rescinded, and there was indeed among the finds a fine 13th to early 14th century rowel spur, of unusually slender proportions and one of the earliest types to be made (7.10a, no. 56). The window glass of the 1285 church was of attractive design (7.9) and the decorated floor tiles are mostly 14th century (7.5). The architectural fragments found reused in later contexts were also of high quality (7.3a). This period of prosperity accords with the written sources, which indicate many gifts to the priory at this time.

8.4 Period IV - 15th and 16th centuries A.D. (fig 63)

It is difficult to separate many features that are solely of period IV, as a number of those of period III continued in use. Fig 63 includes only the claustral complex and fishponds as in period III and other features that seem to belong exclusively to a time after *c*. 1400, though not all lasted to the time of the Dissolution.

The possible mill platform appears to have gone out of use and may have been cultivated; the leat and sluice complex 409 however continued in use, and the latter was extensively developed with stone foundations and other associated features. If this area was in fact that of the mill, as suggested above, it was clearly altered considerably; or was a mill here wholly of period IV, replacing one further north? None of these structures lasted beyond the 15th century.

There appears to have been cultivation north of the church; and also perhaps in the southern area. A new feature here was a stony bank (415/480), which may have been associated with fields to the south, possibly acting as a boundary or flood barrier. The ditches in this area may have gone out of use, but new drainage was made in the area SW of the cloister. Also to the SW were a few features - a wall foundation, a ?path, and some pits which may have succeeded the working structures of period III.

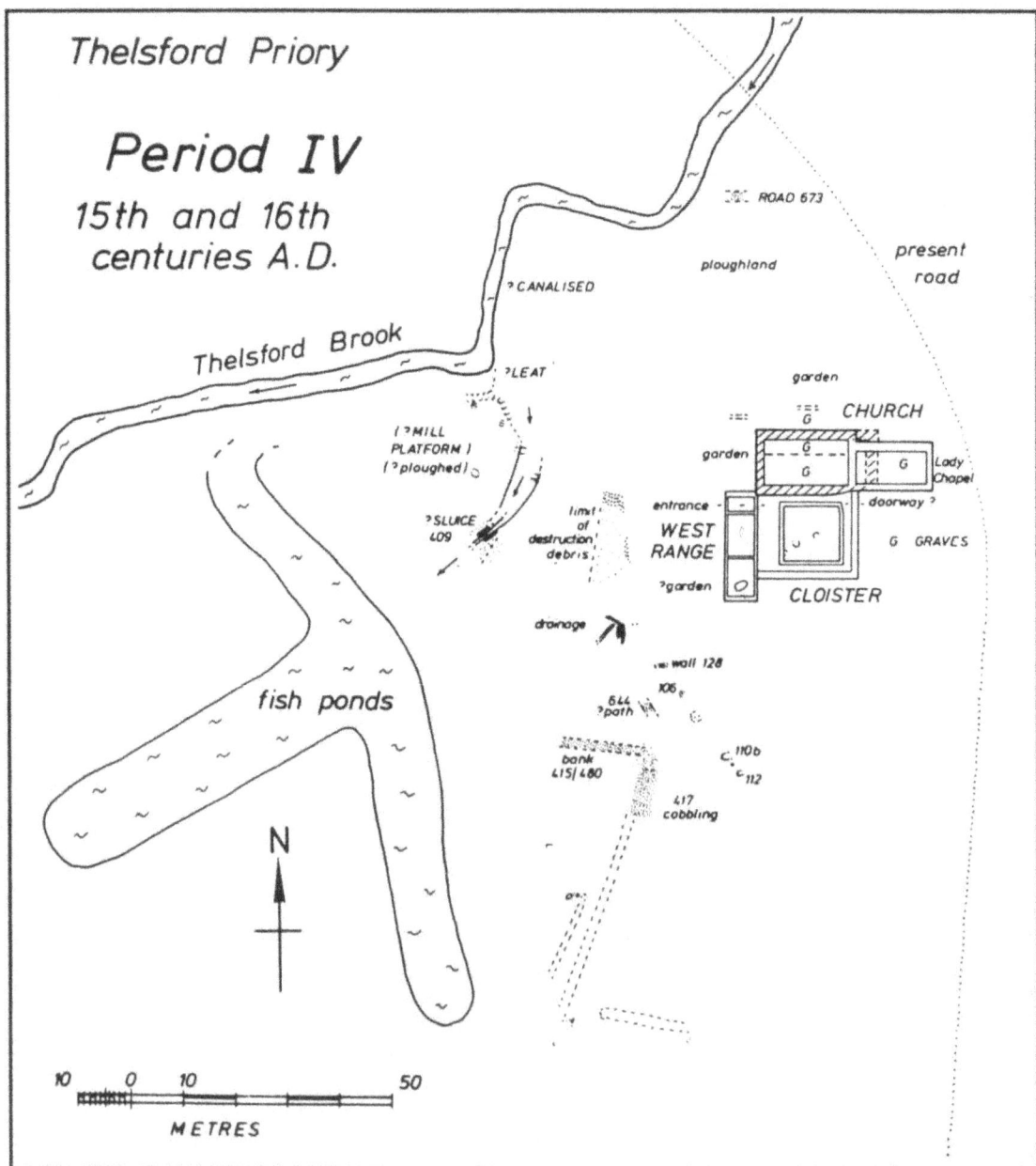

Fig 63

94

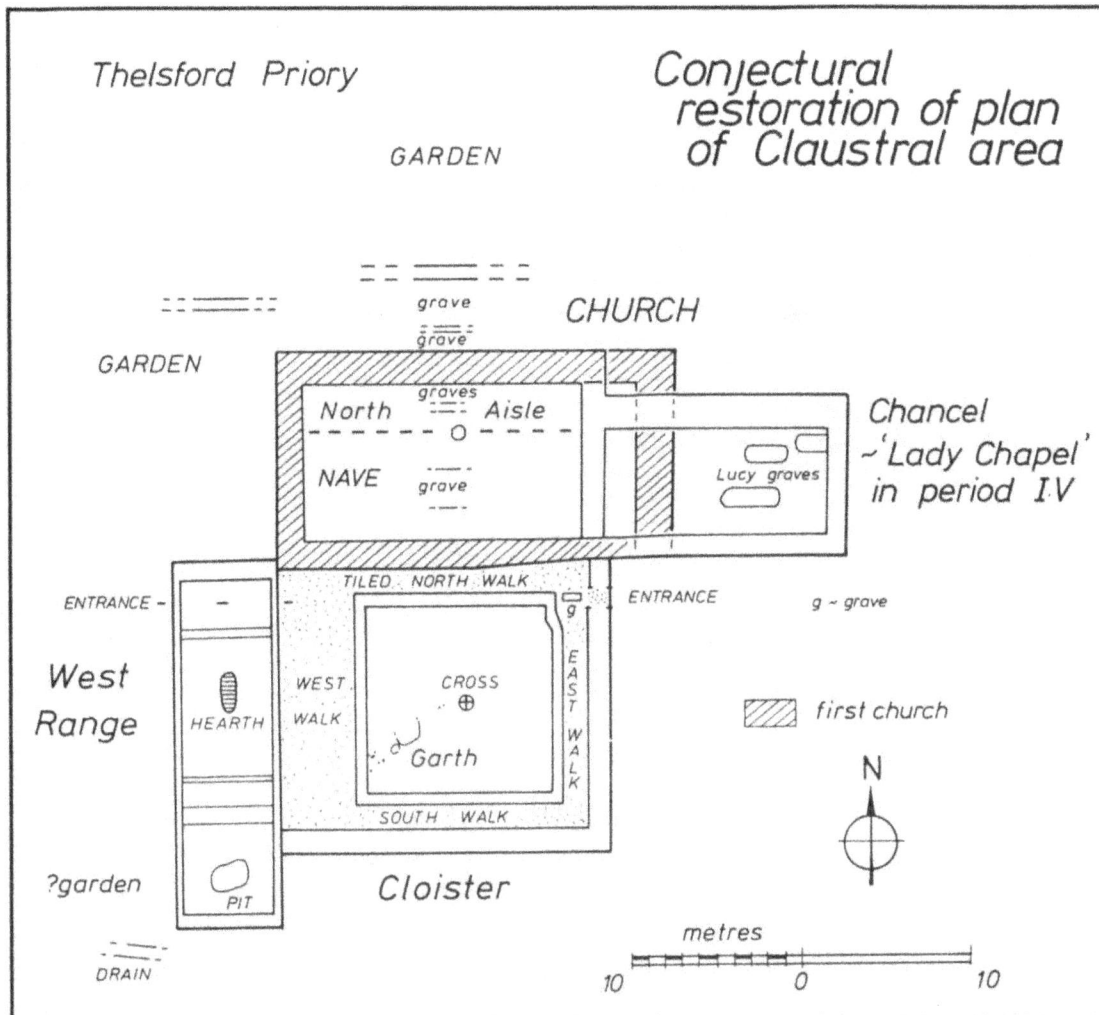

Fig 64

8.5 The claustral complex of periods III-IV (fig. 64)

Fig. 64 is an attempt at a restoration of the claustral area; this is however largely conjectural, derived as it is from a very small sample recovered principally from narrow trenches. The widths of the walls are shown as found in excavation, but in some cases these were actual foundations, in others construction-trenches or robber-trenches which may have been wider.

The new church was built partly over a length of the filled-in eastern arm of the period II perimeter ditches. Building involved extensive working of green sandstone; crushed areas of this material over the gravel scoops are interpreted as areas of builders' activity; this was also used to consolidate the ground beneath foundations and floors. The walls were principally of green sandstone with limestone infilling; the buildings were originally roofed with lias limestones slates, later replaced by ceramic tiles.

The church was initially single-celled; the restored plan shows this as c. 23 x 13 m externally, c. 19 x 9 m internally. It is suggested that the interior was divided into a 6 m wide nave and a 3 m wide north aisle, with an arcade between. This church is equated with that of 1285 referred to by Dugdale (1730, 500) and the *V.C.H. Warks.* (1908, 106-7). Dugdale also refers to a grant by Fulk de Lucy (1263-1301), which has been referred to already in relation to the extending of the enclosure and the enclosing of a road (see 4.3.3).

Secondarily, the church was extended to the east by the building of a chancel, the north wall of which was possibly directly aligned on the arcade mentioned above. In this operation, the east end of the original church was demolished and a new nave/chancel wall built further west. The chancel was c. 13 x 6 m internally and the total length of the church was now c. 33 m as drawn, possibly 100 ft.

In the time of Sir William Lucy (1301-29) there was another grant of land of two acres 'lying near to their House to join them to the Court thereof' (*V.C.H. Warks.* 1908, 106) (see 4.3.3). This could

95

have provided sufficient room for this eastern extension of the church, and the creation of an eastern cell, which could be the Lady Chapel referred to in the 15th-16th century (4.3.4). This was paved with decorated floor tiles (7.5) and contained at least four documented burials of the Lucy family, the last being in 1514 (below, 8.7).

The cloister was probably largely of timber construction; the walks were possibly originally roofed with organic material (thatch or shingles) but were later replaced with red ceramic tile. The north, east and south cloister walks were apparently all narrow, c. 1.5 m wide; the west walk was however wider (c. 4.5 m). Liddlestone Palmer (1930, 153), comments that such a wider west walk, with an entrance at its north end, was common in houses where there were a number of lay brothers. There is evidence for floor tiling only in the north walk. The cloister overall is shown as rectangular, c. 18 x 15.5 m internally (70 x 50 ft?); and the garth as c. 11 m square internally (c. 12 m externally - 40 ft?).

The position of the cloister on the south side of the church accords with that of many monastic plans. The inner walls could have supported only a penthouse roof, as at Cerfroid Priory (Plate. IX). The only other feature for which a function may be suggested is pit 41 (Trench I, fig. 29). This is almost central and could have held a stone or timber cross, again as at Cerfroid.

The west range was also presumably largely of timber construction on stone footings, also with organic roofs later replaced by ceramic in the mid 14th century. The plan as shown may be of more than one phase. There was a major central hearth in the largest room, and a pit (?of period IV) in the southern room. The floors were probably stone paved over a mortar base. This west range may originally have been for the lay brothers, but Liddlesdale Palmer (1930, 153) suggests that in the later periods, with the disappearance of the lay brothers, such buildings were converted for the use of the prior and guests; hence perhaps the large and substantial hearth. This was presumably central to avoid a location against the west cloister wall.

8.6 Period V - post-medieval

The plan of the priory probably survived in this form until its dissolution in 1538. In the robbing-trenches of the church there was no pottery later than the end of the 16th century, though some post-medieval pottery was found elsewhere. The ponds and low lying areas of the site were backfilled with roof tiles and other debris, and there was destruction debris over all the top layers of the buildings. Many of the stones may have been used at Wasperton Manor and Thelsford Farm; this was perhaps originally the 'Court' mentioned in documents.

The fields to the south probably remained in cultivation. Intensified ploughing (Butzer 1982, 129) or over-grazing of these slopes may have led to soil erosion. The lower levels of the site were however probably flooded and were only useful for grazing. It is only since the 1939-45 war that the site has been ploughed. There has also been considerable backfilling of hollows and degrading of high features, causing damage to such walls as had not been robbed out and had remained as earthworks.

8.7 Mortuary procedures, by Philip Rahtz

Although the circumstances of the excavation did not allow a full examination of the areas in which burials were encountered nor of the human remains which were seen, some general conclusions may be drawn. They contribute to the corpus of high medieval mortuary procedure, a study of increasing anthropological and archaeological importance.

Research in a relatively well-documented period allows conjectural correlation between written and archaeological evidence. Archaeology provides merely the residues of the material aspects of mortuary procedure, altered and decreased by centuries of burial. These residues comprise firstly the graves themselves, whose precise location and orientation in or around the priory church must have been a matter of meaningful deliberation, either by the deceased (as expressed orally or in a will); by the relatives; or by the canons themselves, if the decision was left to them. Secondly, there are the containers for the dead: coffins, etc. Thirdly, inside the container there are the body residues; and grave-goods or fittings, of which particularly fine examples were recovered at Thelsford. Fourthly, there is the filling of the graves; in some cases this derives from the time of burial, in others only from when the sealing of the tomb was broken at a later date. In either case the filling was probably not very significant in content or mode of deposition, even though potentially informative on absolute date or relationship to phases of destruction or deposition. Fifthly, among the material residues are the sealing materials of the grave, often in form and location affording a potentially permanent marker or memorial, visible to contemporary observers and later generations. Sixthly and finally, although not strictly classifiable as mortuary procedure except in what is revealed about attitudes to the earlier dead, there is the archaeological evidence of destruction of the graves and the robbing of their contents.

Detailed examples of written sources related to Thelsford (4.3.4) include the provision by William Lucy (d. 1492) of the sum of 40s to the canons for 'observation of his exequies'. His son Edmund (will proved 1498) wished to be buried on the north side of his mother Margaret; he made elaborate provision for his funeral in the Lady Chapel at Thelsford, including the gift of a cross of silver gilt to the chapel, and of a marble slab 7 x 4 ft (2.1 x 1.2 m) over the grave. On the day of his burial 40 marks were to be spent there by priests, clerks and poor people, while on the anniversary of his death twelve of these poor men should hold torches round his grave, each of them receiving a black gown and hood and 4d in money. Money was also left for the keeping of his anniversary for twenty years after his death. Edmund's second wife, Joan Hungerford, asked in her will (dated 1514) to be buried at the side of her husband. Hers was the last known burial at Thelsford (*V.C.H. Warks.* 1908, 107).

It is always tempting to relate such details to graves and their contents discovered in excavation. Unfortunately since only a small part of the Lady Chapel was dug, this can only be conjectural. In the trench excavated (fig. 32) there were three graves with the remains of four individuals, which *could* be (in order of death) Edmund's mother Margaret, his first wife Jane, Edmund himself, and his second wife Joan. In terms of spatial distribution, the most southerly grave 24 could be Margaret, to allow one of the graves to the north to be Edmund; but the skeleton in 24 was tentatively identified at the time of excavation as that of a large male! Of the other two graves, the middle one (43) was the later; this contained a coffin, lead shroud and silver belt fittings to be discussed below; the third, to the north and east of 43 (21) contained two bodies. Neither of these could be sexed at the time of excavation, but were adult.

A further source of evidence for identification comes from the silver fittings in 43 (fig. 47 and 7.12c), from a leather belt, perhaps securing a fabric shroud? The skeleton could be that of Edmund; although lions rampant are quite common (inf. Susan Wright). Michael Farr (Warwick County Record Office) suggests however that the three lions 'passant gardant' on the chape could be the arms of Richard Ludlow, the father of Joan, Edmund's second wife (*cf.* the hall windows at Charlecote where these arms are displayed); the lozenges, he suggests, would be right for a woman in place of a shield. The lions could therefore be of the Ludlow family, and the fleur-de-lys ('flower de luce') on the other side for the Lucys. If this is indeed, following this argument, the grave of Joan, then either grave 24 to the south or 21 to the north and east could be Edmund, for her grave to be 'by the side of'. If 21, then the other skeleton in 21 might be Edmund's first wife Jane. The skeleton in 24 was marked with a stone floriated slab; but not the 'marble slab' referred to in the will. The identifications of the four historical figures with the four people found in a limited cut through the Lady Chapel must remain a matter of conjecture, although it is likely that one or more are of the Lucy family.

To return to the spatial aspects of burial; three graves were also found in the nave of the church, three to the north and one in the east cloister walk to the south (fig. 36). All were orientated west-east, with the church, as were those in the Lady Chapel.

Most graves were unlined pits cut to varying depths through floors, other layers or into the subsoil. Some were however lined on sides and base with bricks, held by hard white mortar; these should perhaps be called vaults rather than brick-lined graves.

The use of brick in the building of tombs for more prosperous families is referred to by Wight (1972, 158-60), who comments that most of the tombs cited were encountered during the excavation of monastic sites. Those in Kent were dated to the late 14th century, and those at the London Charterhouse were of similar date. Also in London (with a date of 1480 scratched on the leaden shroud) was the brick-built tomb of Anne Mowbray, child-bride of the elder son of Edward IV, one of the 'Princes in the Tower'.

Some of the graves or vaults contained wooden coffins. These were represented by coffin nails (7.10b, type B), by wood 'stains', or, in the case of 43, by angle irons (fig. 41, no. 34, 7.10a). Other coffins may have been of wood only, without nails.

Inner containers, apart from fabric shrouds, are represented only by the lead shroud in 43 (fig. 46, 7.12b). These were, as in antiquity, used to protect and preserve the corpse, sometimes very successfully. Their use is well-documented by the 15th century and the example found in the chancel at Thelsford is probably of this date. There is an example from Hailes Abbey of a lead shroud within a wooden coffin from an early 16th century tomb of an Abbot or benefactor. This tomb was within the screen wall on the south side of the chancel and is now on display in the museum of the Abbey. There are also undated examples from Farleigh Hungerford Castle Chapel of six adults and two infants, four with faces moulded or cast onto them.

The body residues at Thelsford were poorly preserved and very disturbed; they include both adults and children,but no biological data are available. It seems likely that all are of the lay population, rather than of ecclesiastics; and probably of the local gentry, who would have provided resources in return for burial and subsequent rites. The Lucys are the only family so documented.

The graves or vaults were covered in some cases by sandstone or limestone blocks (in one case with traces of painted plaster), in one case concave on the underside; and/or as well as by grave slabs, one of which bore a floriate cross design (24) (6.5a; not illustrated). The 'marble' slab given by Edmund Lucy was not found.

All graves located had been badly disturbed either at the Dissolution or later. The skeletons themselves were disarranged, notably in the area of arms or thorax, perhaps in the search for rings or other valuables. Covers were broken, for use elsewhere. Only in one case (43) did the inner container and skeleton survive these depredations, but in this case the lead itself had sagged and severely crushed the skeleton.

Much data on mortuary procedures remain buried at Thelsford, deep enough not to be ploughed; these could be recovered by future archaeologists.

The bones that were preserved (7.19) are in Warwick Museum and could be examined further.

8.8 Materials and resources

The constitutions of the Trinitarians stipulated that only one third of their income should be spent on their own maintenance and fitting frugality is reflected in the material remains of Thelsford Priory.

The only building to be constructed entirely of stone was the church. This building was the only one to be completely robbed out after the dissolution of the priory, suggesting that the other walls of the claustral complex contained little stone. The walls of the church were of dressed green sandstone blocks with a filling of broken limestones, both of which materials could have been quarried fairly locally. Either through scarcity of suitable stone or in accordance with local vernacular architectural traditions, the majority of the buildings were probably timber framed on stone footings. It is possible that green sandstone was dressed on the site as there was an area of chippings and crushed green sandstone to the north of the period III church (6.15b above). These chippings were not wasted but were used as the foundation for tiled floors and walls and to make up soft or uneven ground. Lias limestone roof slates were found both in the area of the church and by the ?mill platform. There was evidence throughout the site that red ceramic roof tiles were replacing earlier stone tiles or thatch by the middle of the 14th century. The ancillary buildings were constructed of timber, probably with thatched roofs, with the exception of the possible mill which may have had flagged floors and a lias limestone roof.

Interior decoration of the church is represented by traces of white rendering of the stone mouldings and the presence of tile impressions on a mortar bedding. There were also broken decorated and plain floor tiles which had been discarded by the 16th century stone robbers. Enough window glass survived to show that some of the church windows had been painted: there was also some plain window glass.

There were two finely carved architectural fragments (7.3a, stone nos. 10 and 11, pls. VI and VII) built into the inner wall of the period IV cloister (6.12c). These may have come from a structure dismantled when the 1285 church was extended and its east wall demolished. These stones could both have formed part of canopied tombs recessed in the wall of the 1285 church. Intermural interments were, according to Braun (1970, 170), quite normal where there was no room for an elaborate free-standing tomb in a church as small as that at Thelsford. Usually the north wall was chosen near the east end, especially if it was the founder's tomb. This was also the position of the Easter sepulchre, which often incorporated the founder's tomb, in which case it would be as close to the altar as space would allow. The sepulchre was designed to provide accomodation for the sacred elements from Maundy Thursday until Easter Sunday. Cox (1923, 267-73) explains that the rites connected with this ceremony were observed in every church until the Reformation. He comments that at the end of the 13th century it became customary to place a structural stone sepulchre to the immediate north of the altar, its usual form being a recess in the wall covered by a decorated arch and figure sculpture, sometimes in niches. Evans (1949, 170) says that the earliest permanent stone niches used for this purpose date from the 13th century and that they became more elaborate in the 14th century, and were a characteristically English form of monument.

Stone 10 could possibly have come from such a structure built close to the east end of the north wall, although it is strange that, in this case, it was not re-erected in the new Lady Chapel when this wall was demolished.

Throughout the whole life of the priory considerable attention was paid to drainage and water management. Perimeter ditches were constructed, the stream canalised, the fishponds excavated, and the stone sluice and stone culverts created. Good drainage and plentiful clean water would have been essential for the daily needs of a priory whose function was the reception of travellers and the care of the sick.

The Trinitarian constitutions proscribed the eating of both meat and fish except at certain festivals; the prohibition on the purchase of these items meant that they had to provide them from their own resources, as it was decreed that the inmates of the hospital should be allowed them. A large quantity of fish could have been supplied both from their own fishponds and from their fishing rights in the Avon, which would have been more than ample for their own needs. No doubt the surplus could be sold locally to augment their revenues (c.f. Aston ed., 1988).

Meat would also have been readily available, from both wild and domestic sources. The rights granted for grazing on common land and other meadows and on the outlying estates would have allowed ample opportunities for breeding their own stock. In the cesspit sample of period III, sheep were predominant, but there were also a few pig and cattle bones and also rabbit, domestic fowl, goose and pigeon; oyster shells in this pit and elsewhere were presumably imported from a more distant source. In another sample from the latest levels of the site (307) cattle were however predominant, and fallow deer was also represented.

For a mainly vegetarian diet, however, there were the ample gardens and arable areas available, the former in close proximity to the claustral area, the latter on the southern slopes.

When the sluice and ?mill with their associated water courses went out of use in the 15th century, and a flood barrier or boundary bank was built across earlier industrial features, there may have been a change in emphasis from fish to a more pastoral and arable type of farming. There is also some evidence that the southern slopes of the priory were terraced at this time and some of the drainage channels which had run down this slope were filled in.

The Trinitarians were not allowed to ride horses or other animals until the middle of the 13th century and no stabling was therefore needed in the earlier life of the priory. Horse bones were however found in both the samples (of later date); and there are several examples of horseshoes, spurs, and bridle fittings among the finds; stables are mentioned at the time of the Dissolution (4.3.3). Domesticated animals (apart from the fowl) are represented only by a cat footprint on a tile; rat bones were found in cesspit 152.

With the exception of objects connected with their patrons, the Lucy family, (such as the seal matrix and possibly the silver buckle and chape and ?family monuments), the finds were not exotic and were mostly connected with the daily life of the priory. Four of the glass fragments may be from distilling apparatus (7.9b), two being found in the area of the cloister and two in the destruction debris. It is quite common for distilling apparatus to be found on monastic sites, although not always recognised as such. From the 14th century onwards, distilled alcohol was prescribed for medical reasons and therefore a monastic site with a hospital, such as Thelsford Priory, would find use for its own products. The apparatus could also be used for alchemical experiments connected with religious studies (Moorhouse 1972, 86-7).

The iron objects were mainly from knives, keys, latches, horseshoes and spurs, including an unusual rowel spur of the earliest type (7.10a, no. 56) and a substantial socketted hook, originally hafted on a wooden handle, which came from the bottom of a small pond and may have been used for the retrieval of nets (7.10a, no. 44). The copper alloy objects included a hinged strap end or book clasp, a thimble and pins, buckles, rings and part of a candlestick. The seal matrix (7.11c) belonged to the Lucy family; Harvey Bloom (1906, 163) says that it was common practice in the 12th and 13th centuries for a knighted family to assume a device which was allusive and specifically mentions the Lucy family using the 'luce'. Dugdale (1730, 503) says that William Lucy, who was knighted c. 1309, bore for his arms 'Gules seme of crosslets, with three Lucies hauriant d'Argent, as by his seal appears'.

This means that there was a red shield 'sown' in little crosses, with three pikes with heads 'palewise'; that is standing on their tails with heads above water. On our seal the luce was however a 'fleur-de-luce' rather than a pike and was probably an earlier personal seal of the Lucy family. This must be a personal seal rather than the seal of the priory (7.11c). The priory seal is illustrated in *V.C.H. Warks.*, pl. I, and shows three figures, one of which was St. Radegund, within an oval setting (*c.f.* 4.3.5).

Even allowing for the limitations of the excavation, the quality of 'currency' found was very small: three silver coins and five jettons (7.13).

The majority of the pottery was from cooking pots, of standard Midlands type, which could have been obtained locally. Hurst (1964, 147) comments that coarse pottery such as cooking pots, bowls and jugs were rarely traded more than twenty miles. The glazed jugs were also from places no further apart than Nuneaton and Oxford and were of the types in general use at this period in this area.

It would seem therefore that most of the portable finds were obtained fairly locally. The influx of visitors and the extensive recruitment and money-raising journeys of the canons are not reflected in the type of objects which were recovered from the excavations. Moorhouse (1983, 66) has suggested that itinerant monks were often responsible for the movement of pottery, causing non-local wares to be found on sites especially when there was also a guest house or hospital here. The fact that this has not so far occurred at Thelsford may be one more indication of the simplicity and frugality of the domestic arrangements.

8.9 Conclusion (Fig. 65)

The various stages of the physical development of the priory reflect the demands made upon the canons. In period II the hospital and the reception of travellers was their main concern, but by period IV the fulfillment of obligations to their founders in the Lucy family for intercessory prayers and for burial in the priory made the church and the Lady Chapel the focus of their attention, at a time when the chantry movement had been established as one of the foremost manifestations of religious life (Cook 1968, 8).

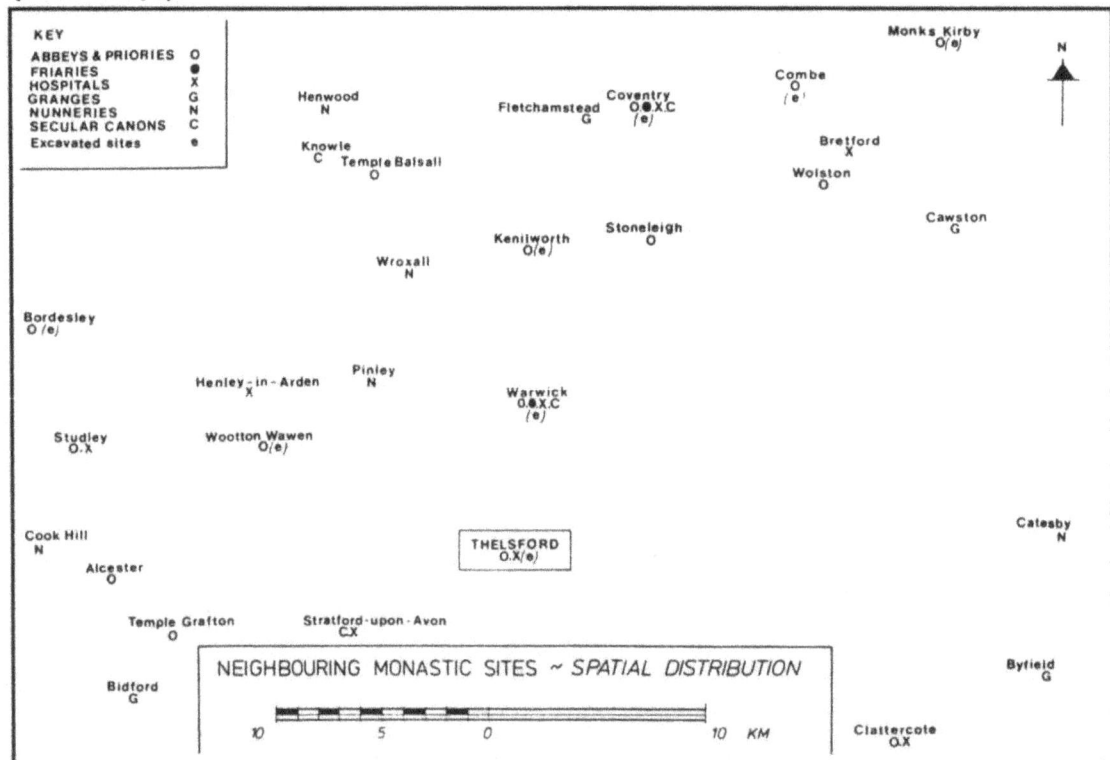

Fig 65

Comparison with other monastic sites is difficult and with other Trinitarian sites almost impossible, although a gazetteer of these is appended (chapter 9 below). The map of neighbouring monastic sites (fig. 65) shows a blank space to the east of Thelsford, possibly because there are no major rivers in an area which is also crossed by the Fosse Way and the 'Welsh Road'. In the region

100

there have been no excavations at hospitals, but seven of the abbeys and priories (including Thelsford) have been excavated in recent years. The large Cistercian abbeys of Bordesley (Rahtz and Hirst 1976 and Hirst *et al* 1983) and of Combe (Wilson Hurst 1967, 182), and the Benedictine St. Mary's, Coventry (Hobley 1971), far outstrip Thelsford in scale. The excavation at the Benedictine alien priories at Wootton Wawen (James 1982, 37-48) and Monks Kirby (Webster and Cherry 1980, 242) were not on a large enough scale to produce comparative data. Of the two Augustinian sites, that of St. Sepulchre's at Warwick has already been mentioned (4.1). There were two excavations at Kenilworth, in 1980 and previously in 1922-3; the latter are described with a plan in a note in *Trans Birmingham Warwickshire Archaeol. Soc.* (1930), 212, which once again show buildings of a larger scale than those at Thelsford. Norton Priory, Cheshire, which is also a house of Augustinian canons, exhibits some similarities in the plan of the claustral buildings, although they are double the size of those at Thelsford (Greene 1972, 1974 and 1980; and Runcorn Development Corporation 1972 and 1973). The Norton church was extended, as at Thelsford, because of the demand for the burial in it of the local laity, and there were also timber buildings, in this case in the 12th century.

The only standing Trinitarian church in England is that of Ingham, Norfolk, which is not really representative. Having originally been the parish church, it became collegiate, with a monastic chancel and a parochial nave, with the cloisters (now destroyed) to the north. There is a standing church at Adare (Co. Limerick), which seems from its plan (Dunraven 1865, plan 13 and drawing 14) to have been originally a small aisleless church of 7 metres width internally but with the chancel subsequently extended to make a length of 33 metres for the building; there was a massive tower, and the cloister was on the north side (plan. fig. 77). At Peebles (Scotland), Gordon describes the church as being 102 feet (31 metres) in length and 32 feet (9.75 metres) wide, the 'side walls' being 24 feet (7.30 metres) in height and 3 feet (0.90 metres) thick (Gordon 1868, 299). The cloisters, which were to the north, were 32 feet (9.75 metres) in width and the buildings 'on the other sides' were 14 feet (4.26 metres) in height, 16 feet (4.87 metres) in width and vaulted. The engraving of the first Trinitarian priory to be founded in France at Cerfroid (pl. IX) shows buildings which approximate to those which could have been at Thelsford, although only the latest buildings, erected in 1540, are shown. The church is long and aisleless, with a cloister and conventual buildings to the south side. The cloister walk has a penthouse roof, and there is an entrance to the cloister between the west range and the west end of the church. Within the precinct there are well-tended gardens, with arable fields and orchards to the north. There is a hospital and graveyard to the SE and what may be fishponds to the south. The only conventual building which has a chimney is that of the west range.

There have been few excavations at the sites of the minor orders in England, as the chart in Clarke (1984, 87) shows; and none of them has concentrated on the ancillary buildings within the precincts. Little is known therefore, as Clarke (1984, 88) points out, about the architecture and development of these smaller houses and the light this could throw on their sociological, religious and economic life. If future work were ever possible at Thelsford, it should be concentrated on the excavation of the timber buildings to the north of the church and the discovery of the period II church; also of the hospital which may lie to the SE of the claustral buildings. A interdisciplinary study of the estates of Thelsford Priory, as suggested by James (1982, 40) in conjunction with those of Wootton Wawen, would reveal a good deal of evidence about the agriculture and economy of both institutions.

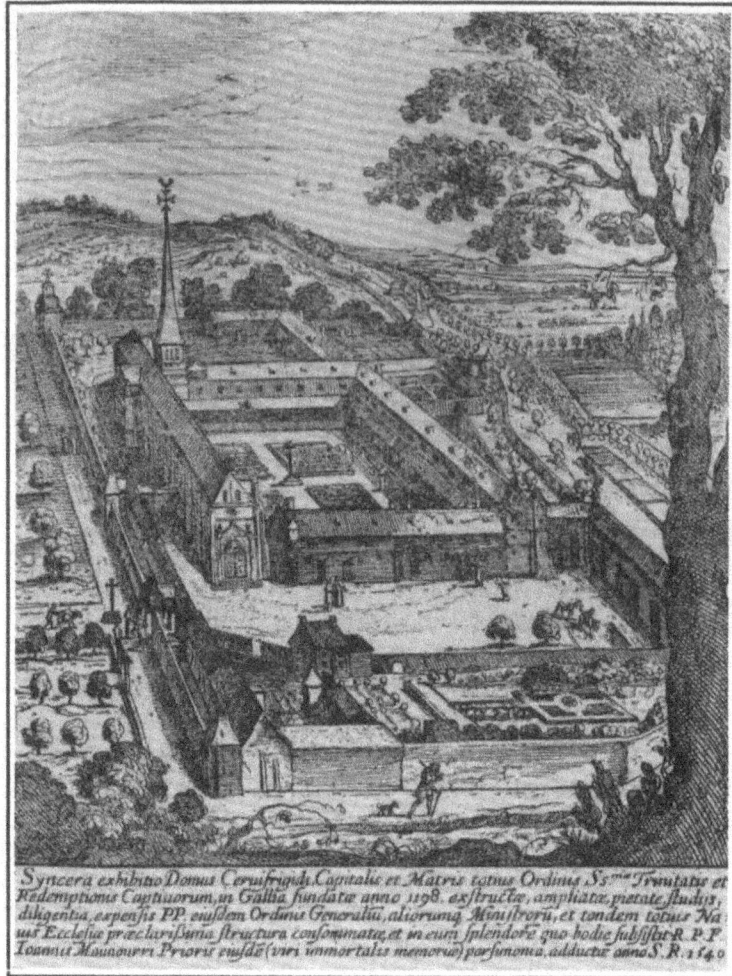

Plate IX

Monastery of Cerfroid (Aisne) in 1633 from Antonin 'Les Origenes de l'Ordre de la Tres Sainte Trinite'

Chapter 9
GAZETTEER OF TRINITARIAN SITES

9.1 Introduction

I am grateful for a grant from the Colt Fund, administered by the Society for Medieval Archaeology. With the help of this all the Trinitarian sites in England, Fail, Ayr in Scotland and the only one in Ireland (Adare, Co. Limerick) were visited by the writer. A photographic record was made, air photographs obtained and, where possible, sites were surveyed. This gazetteer is only a summary of the results obtained; it restricts itself to topographical features and the present state of the sites. The history of each site is only referred to where it is of importance to this. General histories may be found in the following documentary sources:- Tanner 1787; Dugdale, *Mon. Angl.* 1830; Knowles and Hadcock 1971, 205-7; Midmer 1979; and those specified under each site.

The map of the Trinitarian houses in England (fig. 66) shows that they are widely distributed. This distribution probably reflects a particular preference by each of their patrons for the Trinitarian Order, as much as a preferred topographical position. Four of them are now rural sites and six are urban, though Hounslow was merely a village in the 13th century. The sites at Hertford and Knaresborough are outside the town, but those at Newcastle-upon-Tyne, Oxford and Totnes were by entrances to the towns. All of them, except Ingham, were adjacent to a major medieval road. Three of the sites, Newcastle-upon-Tyne, Hertford and Thelsford, took over premises which had become derelict from other orders, all being hospitals. Hounslow, Ingham and Totnes had also belonged to other orders, but may not have been derelict. Eight of the houses were founded in the 13th century and two in the 14th. Those dedicated to the Holy Trinity are Easton Royal, Hounslow, Moatenden and Oxford, denoting that, according to their constitutions (see 4.2), they were taking on a site which did not have a previously-dedicated church. Those houses whose dedications linked another saint with that of the Holy Trinity were Hertford (with St. Thomas the Martyr), Knaresborough (with St. Robert of Knaresborough, whose tomb they maintained as a pilgrimage site), Ingham (with All Saints) and Totnes (with the Holy Spirit and St. Katherine).

Dedications without the Holy Trinity were at Newcastle-upon-Tyne (St. Michael, although also known as Trinity House) and Thelsford (St. John the Baptist and St. Radegund). Totnes and Knaresborough were situated near the banks of the Rivers Dart and Nidd, Hertford close to the River Lea and Oxford near the Cherwell. Easton Royal was near a tributary of the Bristol Avon, Thelsford of the Warwickshire Avon, Hounslow of the Thames and Moatenden of the Beult. Ingham, a collegiate church was also the parish church and atypical. Six out of the ten houses were either hospitals or priories with a hospital on the site. The three sites without a hospital were Moatenden, Oxford and Ingham, all of which were founded for specific functions unrelated to hospitals. Only two of the houses remain intact underground in an open area: those of Easton Royal and Knaresborough. The sites of Moatenden, Ingham and Thelsford are partially destroyed, those at Totnes, Oxford and Hounslow are built over, and those at Hertford and Newcastle-upon-Tyne are completely destroyed.

ENGLISH TRINITARIAN HOUSES

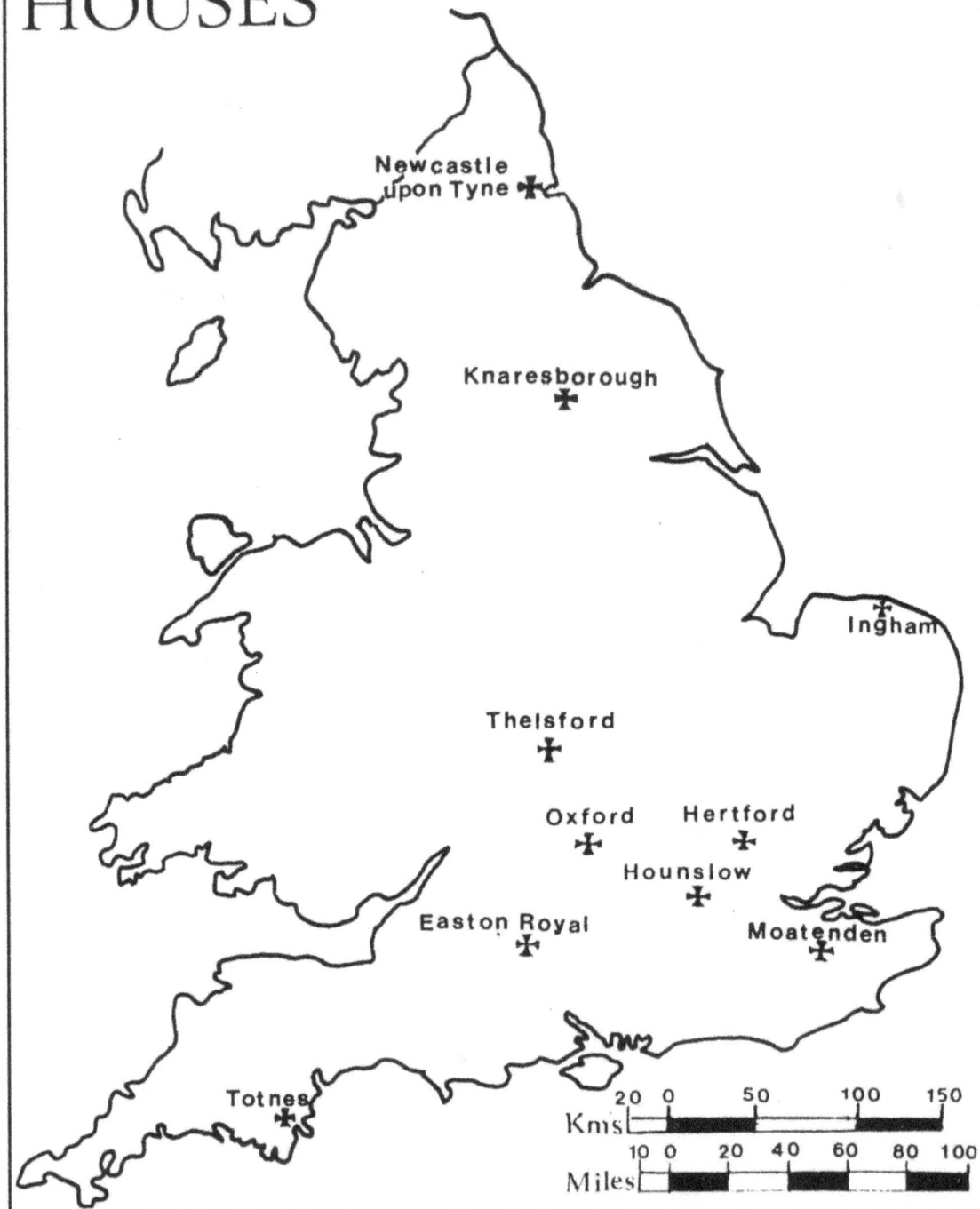

Newcastle
upon Tyne ✚

Knaresborough ✚

Ingham ✚

Thelsford ✚

Oxford ✚   Hertford ✚

Hounslow ✚

Easton Royal ✚

Moatenden ✚

Totnes ✚

Kms   20 0   50   100   150

Miles 10 0   20   40   60   80 100

Fig 66

Net incomes at the Dissolution were, in order of wealth, Hounslow £72, Ingham £61, Moatenden £58, Easton £42, Knaresborough £35, Thelsford £24, Newcastle-upon-Tyne £6; and Hertford, Oxford and Totnes had ceased to exist.

The material discussed in the foregoing is summarised in Table B appended.

TABLE B
Attributes of the Trinitarian houses of England

GEOGRAPHICAL

Rural sites	Urban sites	Adjacent to medieval road	Adjacent to river
Easton Royal	Hertford	All except Ingham	All except Ingham and Newcastle-upon-Tyne
Ingham	Hounslow		
Moatenden	Knaresborough		
Thelsford	Newcastle-upon-Tyne		
	Oxford		
	Totnes		

FOUNDATION DATES AND DEDICATIONS

Founded in 13th century	Founded in 14th century	Holy Trinity	Holy Trinity with another saint	Without Holy Trinity
Easton Royal	Ingham	Easton Royal	Hertford	Newcastle-upon-Tyne
Hertford	Newcastle-upon-Tyne	Hounslow	Knaresborough	Thelsford
Hounslow		Moatenden	Ingham	
Knaresborough		Oxford	Totnes	
Moatenden				
Oxford				
Thelsford				
Totnes				

FUNCTIONS

Hospitals	Recruitment or pilgrimage centre	Academic	Collegiate	Occupying houses of other orders
Easton Royal	Knaresborough	Oxford	Ingham	Hertford
Hertford	Hounslow			Hounslow
?Hounslow	Moatenden			Ingham
Newcastle-upon-Tyne				Newcastle-upon-Tyne
Thelsford				Thelsford
Totnes				?Totnes

PRESENT ARCHAEOLOGICAL STATE

Intact in open	Partially destroyed	Built over	Destroyed
Easton Royal	Ingham	Hounslow	Hertford
Knaresborough	Moatenden	Oxford	Newcastle-upon-Tyne
	Thelsford	Totnes	

9.2 Easton Royal (Wilts.) SU 210 604.
8.85km (51/2 miles) SSE of Marlborough.
(plan, fig. 67)

Sources: Chettle 1947, 365-377
          Bashford 1955, 66-7
          V.C.H. Wilts. 1956, 234-7
          Bashford 1977
          Air photographs, O.G.S. Crawford Collection 9512. 11.5.34

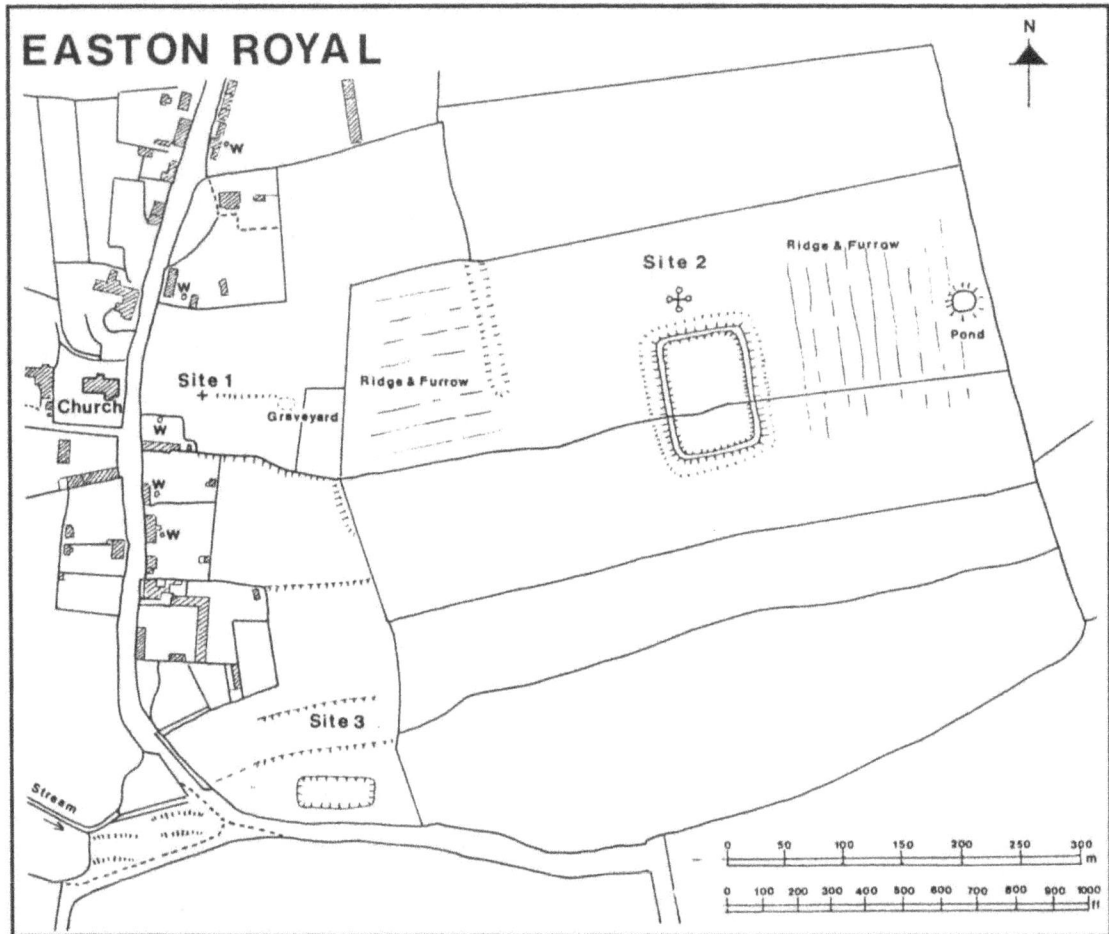

Fig 67

Founded as a hostel for poor pilgrims in 1245, it became Trinitarian in 1251. It lay on a road, possibly Roman and now non-existent, between Winchester and Cirencester and under the northern scarp of Salisbury plain. The village, now a *cul-de-sac*, is subject to flooding at the lower, southern end, under Easton Hill where the old road used to cross the stream. Chettle (1947, 377) suggests that there was considerable traffic on this road by both rich and poor, and possibly some misuse of the canons' hospitality. In 1392 they pleaded that they could not maintain their establishment of one minister and six priests, which they needed to fulfill their obligations, and also could not find the money to pay for their hospitality and the upkeep of their buildings. There was always a close relationship between the parish church and the priory. In 1325 Robert Drueys built a chapel on the north side of the parish church dedicated to St. John Baptist, to be served by a priest from the hospital. In 1368 the parishioners, reduced in numbers, asked that this church should be demolished, and the materials be used to enlarge the priory church, where they would maintain and use the nave, chancel and cemetery. In 1371 there is mention, in a grant from the patron Sir Henry Esturmey, of a

106

mill, together with other gifts of land in the vicinity of the priory. The priory, including the church vestments and ornaments was destroyed by fire in 1493, and although some money was raised for rebuilding, *V.C.H. Wilts.* (1956, 326) describes the church and 'mansion' as ruinous in 1535 and the outhouses in decay. The close relationship between church and priory has led to some controversy about the position of the conventual church. The present parish church, built in 1591 and restored in 1852-3, was thought to lie over the priory church. Bashford (1955) sites the priory church sixty yards (54.86 m) to the west of the parish church (see fig. 67) and the conventual buildings close to it. Bashford (1977, 14) mentions that in 1953 a waterpipe laid through 'Cemetery Field' uncovered late 14th-early 15th century floor tiles and masonry, which could not have come from an earlier church pulled down in 1369, and must be from the priory church sited with the 'mansion' (Seymour's Court in Court Meadow) in this area. The Seymour family are thought to have lived somewhere on the site until at least 1735. The church at Easton Priory had become the burial place of this family, who were hereditary wardens of Savernake Forest. The monument to the last of these pre-reformation wardens, Sir John Seymour, was left abandoned in the ruins until his son rescued it, and re-erected it at Great Bedwyn parish church.

The priory church was pulled down in 1590 after the body of Sir John Seymour had been removed. In 1591 the Seymours then rebuilt the parish church, probably on its original site, and dedicated it to the Holy Trinity. The fact that the priority dedication was only to the Holy Trinity and no other saint, is indicative of the fact that the conventual church was on a new site (see constitutions of the Trinitarians, 4.2).

Bashford (1977) mentions that two ponds to the south of the priory were filled in during 1955. There are surface indications of one of these ponds, shown in the plan (fig. 67) as Site 3. Above the pond there are signs of terracing of the slope.

Bashford is probably right in placing the conventual buildings between the present graveyard and the church. In this area (Site 1) there were many mole-heaps, which contained fragments of roof tile, building stone and medieval nails, although the only surface indication is a mound near the present graveyard and a mound to the south of it. To the west of this, surface indications have been obliterated by post-medieval ridge and furrow; a long depression to the east of them may be part of a hollow-way. Further west, in Beech Meadow, there is a rectangular area (Site 2) defined by a bank and ditch, where the O.S. places its antiquities mark for the priory. However, within this enclosure there are no surface indications and the mole-heaps show no building debris. Bashford (1977, 16-17) having studied the Ailesbury Estate Maps of 1814, states that there were at that date strips of arable subdividing the larger fields, five of them being on Manor Farm, and also twenty small enclosures bearing the name of 'several'. This rectangular enclosure may be one of these 'severals'.

The plan (fig. 67) is based on O.S. sheet for 1900, and the site was surveyed by the writer and Deirdre MacLaverty in March 1985. I am grateful to Dr. B.N. Eagles for information about this site.

9.3 Hertford TL 320 120. (plan, fig. 68)

Sources: Andrews (undated)
             Andrews 1912
             V.C.H. Herts. 1914, 452-3

As it was originally a leper hospital, the site was outside the town. It occupied a position c. 800 metres from the south bank of the River Lea, with 'Trinity Hill' rising SE of it. It was adjacent to the junction of the road from Hertford to Ware with the main road to London, and close to Ermine Street. This was originally the St. Mary Magdalene Hospital founded by the Valosgnes for lepers; there were a master and brethren there in 1199. After many claims being made against it, the Trinitarians took it over in 1261, when it ceased to house lepers and changed its name to 'the hospital for the poor of the Trinity and St. Thomas the Martyr'. Until 1448 it was under the direction of Easton, and after that it is mentioned with Moatenden. In 1359 King John of France, who was in captivity in Hertford Castle, visited the 'dwelling of the brethren of the Trinity' to hear mass; there must therefore have been a church or chapel at the hospital. It was last heard of in 1504 and probably did not survive until the Dissolution, when it was described as being a messuage belonging to Moatenden called 'le Trinitie'. When the Denny family, to whom it was granted, sold it to John Spurling it was called 'Trinity Close' on which 'Trinity House' stood together with 'Friars Grove'; an indenture of 1767 refers to it as

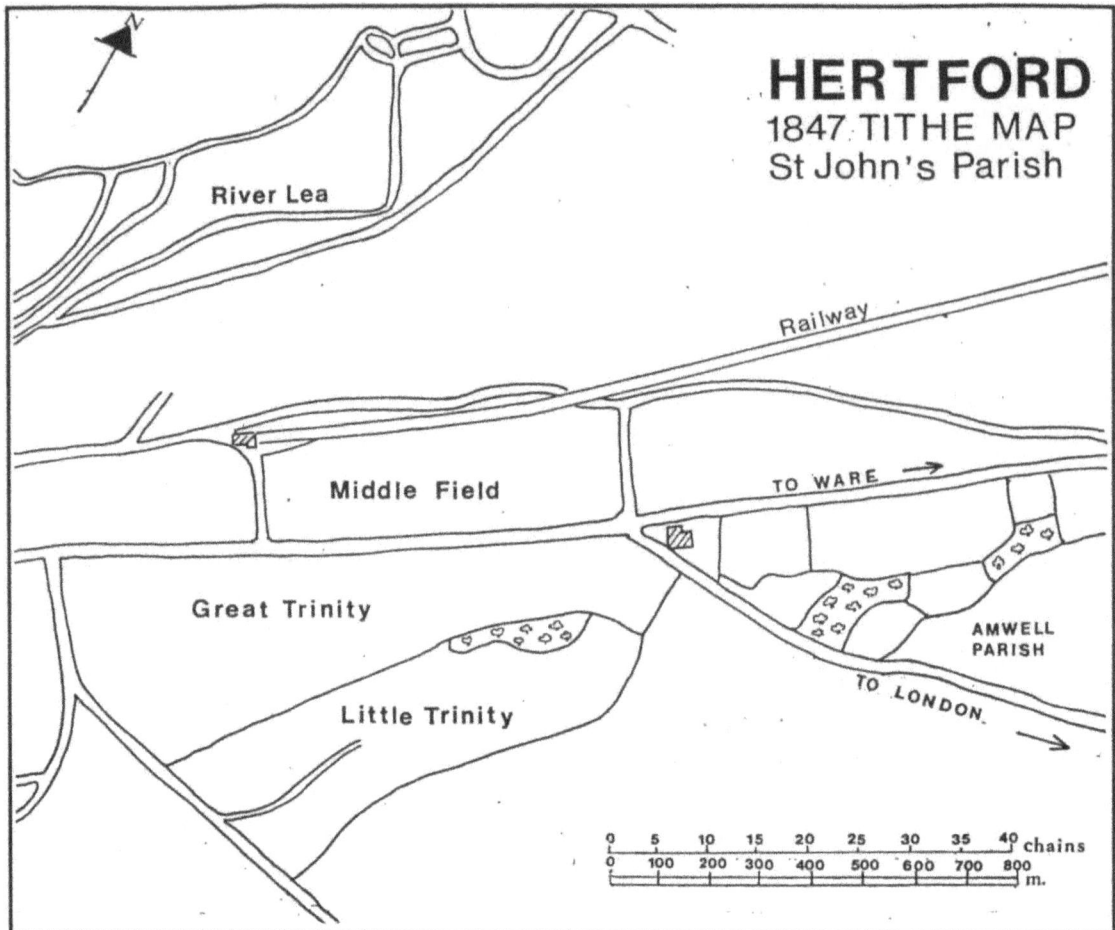

Fig 68

'Trinity or Spittle Field'. The plan (fig. 68) shows a road which led into an empty field in 1847, the field being called 'Little Trinity', with a copse adjoining. It was not possible to check any of the features shown on this 1849 Tithe Award map as the whole area is now covered with factories, which have destroyed the site without record.

9.4 Hounslow (Middlesex) SU 123 769.
9.65 km (6 miles) NE of Staines (plate X)

Sources: Newcourt 1708, 1, 655-6
             Lysons 1795, 3, 414-7
             Aungier 1841, 482-94
             Bate 1924
             V.C.H. Middlesex 1962, 107
             V.C.H. Middlesex 1969, 191-3

The site of the priory, on the north side of what is now Hounslow High Street, was originally on open land west of the town. It was on Hounslow Heath and adjoining a main highway, previously Roman, from London to Windsor and the West.

The first mention of a hospital at Hounslow was in 1200, but there is no indication of the order to which it belonged. It is unlikely to be Trinitarian at this early date; the first reference to the Trinitarians is in 1252, when Henry II presented the minister and 'friars' with a silver chalice and thurible. The main benefactor in the middle of the 13th century was Richard of Cornwall, brother of Henry III, who also founded Knaresborough in 1257 and who died in 1272. As the dedication was to the Holy Trinity it may have been a church built by the Trinitarians on new land. Richard of Cornwall also gave them 80 acres (32.37 ha.) by the River Crane and part of Hounslow Heath. The manor of

108

Hounslow was in their possession by 1296 when they were granted a weekly market and annual fair. In the 14th century they received many gifts of land, including a mill and two fisheries at Kingston-on-Thames. As they were on the road from Westminster to Windsor they frequently received royal patronage, and in 1376 Edward III erected a grange at Hatton on their land, for which they provided a chaplain to celebrate mass there. They supplied a warden for the St. Lawrence Hospital at Crediton and a chaplain for Totnes. Nearly 200 oz of plate were collected from Hounslow by the royal commissioners, and an attempted lease of their land in 1537 mentions 'all the barnes, stables, garners, orchards, dove house, gardens and all other houses and edyfycyons, whyche they have in or aboute the seyd monastery ... the churche, and the only mancyon place, with chambers wher the seyd mynastre and convent do lye, the kechyn, breuhouse and bakehouse within the seyd monastery and house' (Aungier 1841, 489). Two seals are known from this priory and illustrated in Aungier (1841, 493) one being of the provincial minister and the other from Hounslow; both are at the British Library. Another seal matrix from Hounslow was found 'about a mile from Carlisle' in the River Peteril and is illustrated in the *Gentleman's Magazine* for Dec. 1784. Four letters of confraternity were issued from Hounslow, including the one mentioned in 4.2 above to Henry, Prince of Wales (later Henry VIII). Clark-Maxwell (1926, 56) gives the reference numbers for these at the British Library and P.R.O. The *Valor Ecclesiasticus* (Aungier 1841, 490) gives their holding of land as 73 acres (29.54 ha) of arable and pasture and 33 (13.35 ha) of meadow, at Hounslow as well as properties elsewhere. It was always an important Trinitarian house and often the residence of the provincial minister. After the Dissolution the manor and site of the priory were annexed by Henry VIII to Hampton Court, and after this they passed through many hands, as described in Lysons (1795, 3, 415-7), Bate 1924 (28-51), and *V.C.H. Middlesex* (1962, 197). An engraving (pl. X) appears in Lysons (1795, 3, opp. 38) and he describes the church as having some 13th century features in the south wall of the chancel (three stone seats and a double piscina) and 'some ancient painted glass', including a window showing St. Catherine. He mentions a nave, chancel and south aisle (the latter, as the drawing pl. X shows, should be *north* aisle), which appears to-be 14th century. It was expected after the Reformation that it would become the Hounslow parish church but this did not happen until 1858. Until that time it was a 'chapel of ease' and, like the manor house which stood by it, was private property, although used continuously for public worship. In 1557 the estate comprised 117 acres (47.34 ha), the fair, the market and court-leet, and there is a reference to the right of holding courts in 'the great hall of the manor house' (Bate 1924, 29). This manor house was built on the priory ruins at the end of the 16th century and was described in 1711 as an 'ancient brick structure' when Bulstrode rebuilt the north and east wings and repaired the church after a fire (Bate 1924, 32).

In 1828 both buildings were demolished and a large parish church erected on the site (Bate 1924, 36). This Victorian church was destroyed by fire in 1943 and the present modern church was dedicated to the Holy Trinity on 18th May, 1963, by the Lord Bishop of London (Order and Form of Dedication of the Rebuilt Parish Church of Holy Trinity, Hounslow).

9.5 Ingham (Norfolk) TG 389 258. 2 km. (11/2 miles) NE of Stalham (plans, figs. 69 and 70).

Sources: Gough 1786-96, 119-120
Blomefield 1808, 9, 326-7
Stothard 1817
Cotman 1819, 23-26, 29-31
Neale 1824-5
Lee-Warner 1879, 194-209
Gairdner 1888
V.C.H. Norfolk 1906, 410-2
Maxwell Lyle 1911
Cooke 1920, 141-181
Pevsner 1962, 176-8
Knowles and Hadcock 1971, 205
Harvey 1978, 95
Wilson 1980, 248-50

Cattermole and Cotton 1983, 235-79
Platt 1984, 208
Park 1988, 130, 132-6
Martindale 1989, 142, 66-74
Pestell 1991
Church Guide to Holy Trinity Church, Ingham, undated
Air Photograph J.K. St. Joseph OH 58

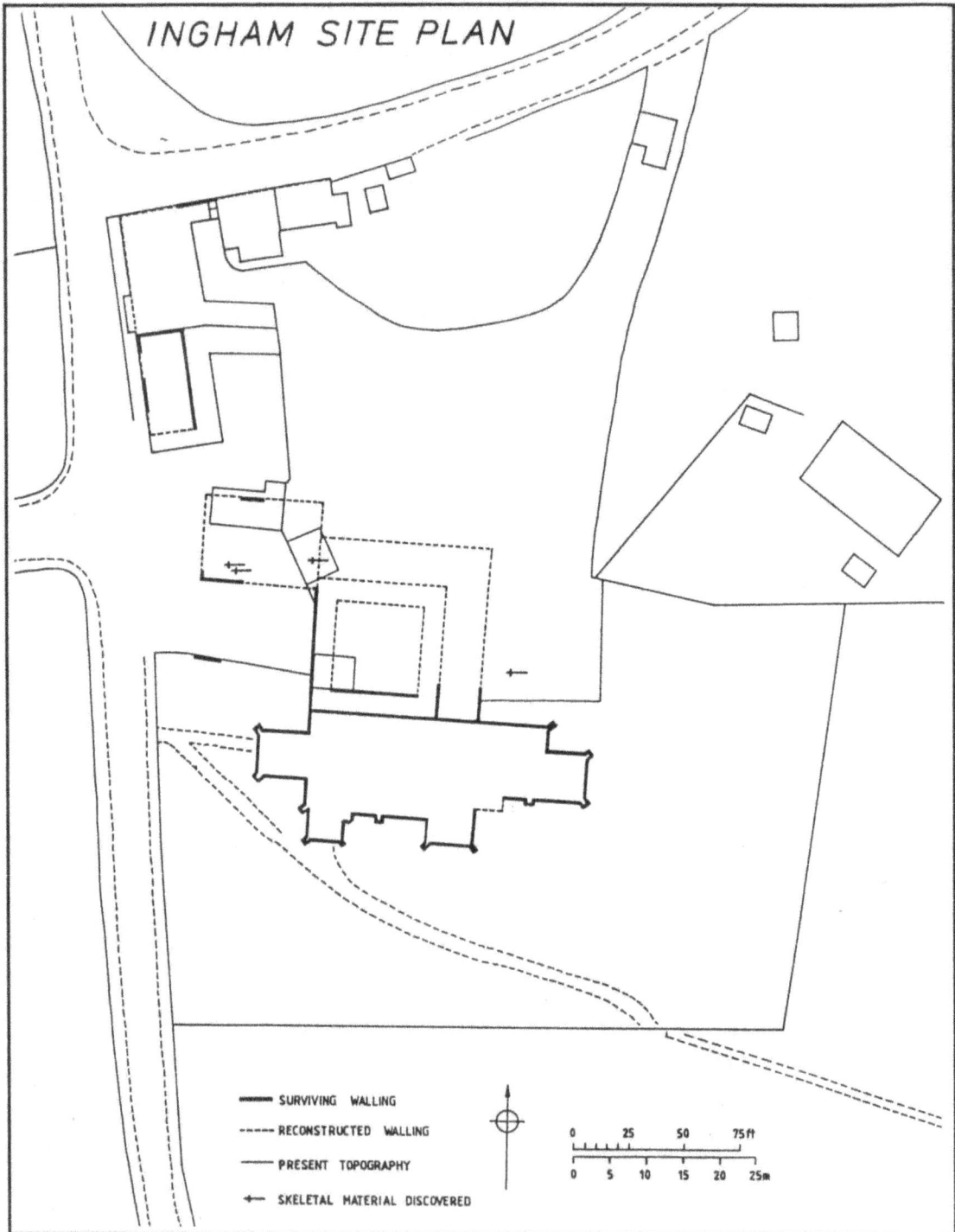

Fig 69

110

HOLY TRINITY INGHAM

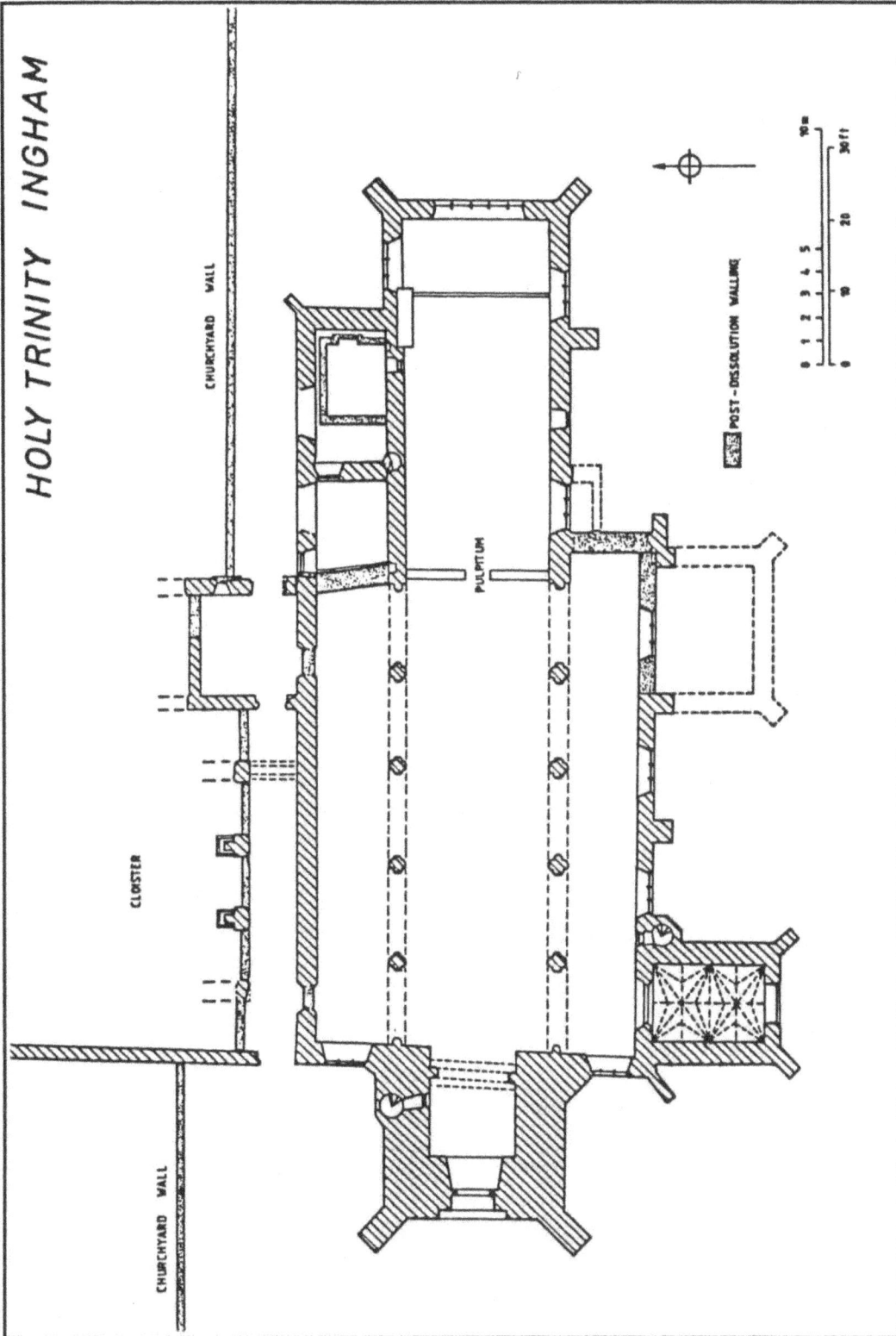

CHURCHYARD WALL

CLOISTER

CHURCHYARD WALL

PULPITUM

POST-DISSOLUTION WALLING

0 1 2 3 4 5   10   20   30ft
0   10m

Fig 70

The church of the Holy Trinity and the site of the priory are on a slight rise, 3 km. from the Norfolk coast. The original church, thought to be Norman because of a remaining 12th century font, was rebuilt by Miles Stapleton who obtained licence in 1355 for it to become collegiate, i.e. served by secular canons. However in 1360 it became Trinitarian, an order more like the regular canons. The choice of the Trinitarians for his new foundation by Sir Miles Stapleton may have been dictated by his knowledge of the Trinitarian house at Knaresborough, through his family ownership of lands at Bedale and also at Knaresborough, where a Miles de Stapleton is recorded in 1307 as being 'Constable of the Castle of Knaresburgh and Keeper of the Forest' (Wheater 1907, 95). This was the grandfather of the founder of Ingham, whose interests in Norfolk had been established by marriage with Joan de Ingham in 1350. The bishop's ordinance of foundation names the superior as 'prior, minister seu custos', a title especially framed to meet the Constitutions of the Trinitarians, and yet including the word 'custos', the head of a college rather than a priory. There was also a sacrist for the parishioners, and two more canons. By the 16th century there were six canons in addition to the minister and sacrist. Platt draws attention to the fact that the minister and his canons, anticipating the suppression of their community, had sold in 1534 their entire estate to a near neighbour, William Woodhouse, without the consent of the patron Sir Francis Calthorpe. The county commissioners for the Norfolk suppression accordingly found, on their arrival, no religious person there in 1536. Woodhouse appeared before the commissioners and alleged that Ingham was a house of Crossed Friars and not of monks or canons, and therefore outside the statute. The commissioners surprisingly agreed and granted it to Woodhouse.

All of the conventual buildings have been destroyed by a gravel pit, but the cloister probably lay to the north of the present nave; its suggested plan is shown on fig. 69. This position is based on the fact that the north cloister walk still survives, with blocked arches of the inner cloister walk wall incorporated into the present churchyard wall. The base of the west and east walls of the east range, and the east wall of the west range are still visible in its footings. On the north wall of the nave and along the extent of the north cloister walk, the flints are knapped to the height of the joist holes which supported the pent-house roof which covered this walk. Above this line the flints of the nave wall are not dressed. There are blocked doors leading from the nave into this north cloister walk, the most easterly of the doors having an arch to the west of it into the north walk. Waste ground on the north side of the present churchyard wall, in the area of the west range, has not been destroyed by the gravel pit, and excavation there would prove the existence of conventual buildings. To the north of this lies the 'Swan Inn' which is shown on the plan (fig. 69), and lies on the same orientation as the priory buildings; it is reputed to have been part of the monastic complex. The area covered by the priory may have been quite large, for, in 1362, another acre (0.404 ha) was conveyed to the prior for the enlargement of his house, together with permission to enclose a road.

Two letters of confraternity exist in the possession of P.R.O. and British Library, their reference numbers are given in Clark-Maxwell (1926, 57).

The site was surveyed and the plan of the church drawn by the writer and Nicholas Clayton in April 1985. In 1990-1 Tim Pestell carried out an extensive survey of the Priory buildings, its precincts and documentary history for his BA dissertation (Pestell 1991). I am grateful for the architectural history which he has contributed to this gazetteer, and for his two plans (figs. 69 and 70).

Architectural History by T.J. Pestell

Ingham Priory was one of the last two Trinitarian houses established in Britain, both being founded in 1360. Ingham seems to have developed from a chantry foundation established in 1355, making it differ from the other Trinitarian houses. The priory was therefore based on an existing parish church of which only the thirteenth century Purbeck marble font survives, supplemented by a few architectural fragments reused in the nave north wall.

The church of the Holy Trinity was completely rebuilt for the priory although the process may have begun in the 1340s judging by the tomb to Sir Oliver de Ingham (d. 1344) and the design of the fine east window. The chancel was possibly completed by Sir Miles Stapleton, founder of the priory, who went on to incorporate it into his own building scheme. This new programme can be followed through the *Calendar of Patent Rolls* and other contemporary sources which demonstrate that the priory was originally conceived of as a chantry college. In 1355 Innocent VI issued a mandate to the Bishop of Norwich to grant licence to rebuild and enlarge the church and 'elect therein a College, in honour of the Holy Trinity and All Saints ... making it a conventual church with due statutes and ordinances' (*VCH Norfolk* 2, 410).

Four years later in February 1359 licence was granted for the alienation in mortmain and appropriation of the church by the chaplains (*CPR* Pat 33 Edw III pt.i m30). The granting of subsequent licences in 1360, 1362 and 1365 chronicle the establishment and expansion of the priory, including 'Licence ... (for) the prior and Trinitarian Friars of Ingham ... to enclose a way in Ingham leading from Pallyng to Staleham beneath their manse ... provided that they make on their soil there another way ... equally convenient for those passing by' (*CPR* Pat 39 Edw III pt.ii m29). This redirected road survives today and preserves the northwestern boundary of the priory (fig. 69).

These sources show that the foundation was clearly envisaged as a chantry college, yet apparently also a monastic house. In the Bishop of Norwich's 1360 Ordinance of Foundation, the head is referred to as "prior, minister seu custos' (Lee Warner 1879, 194-5) a title not only describing the head of a religious house, but a specifically Trinitarian house, and finally the 'custos' or head of a college of secular canons. The establishment of the priory therefore seems to have taken place in 1360, being the final element in moves which started five years earlier.

These documentary sources are also important for enabling an unusually tight dating of the construction of the conventual church. They have been accepted by Harvey who explains the 'London' appearance of the early Perpendicular features as being attributable to the involvement of Robert de Wodehirst (Harvey 1978, 95). Wodehirst worked in London at Westminster before rising to become Master of the work at Norwich Cathedral cloister by 1385. His known appearance in Norfolk by 1362 provides the perfect context for such work as the sedilia and original nave window tracery at Ingham which, although now replaced, is depicted in the engraving of the church by Neale (1824-5).

The conventual church is the best preserved Trinitarian building in England due to its reversion to fully parochial status at the Dissolution. The church has been altered over the years, notably in the thorough Victorian restoration of 1875-6, but it remains essentially unchanged. Fortunately, the many excellent monuments in the church attracted the attention of various antiquaries whose descriptions and illustrations allow the extent of the changes and various losses to be assessed. The church consists of a large western tower with a clerestoried nave and aisles, a Lady Chapel in a south transept, a three-storeyed south porch and a chancel. The priory buildings, now very fragmentary, lay to the north of the church.

The chancel was monastic and nave parochial, a stone pulpitum dividing the two. Little survives of this; that which does suggests that the original was once very elaborate. The rood screen that would have been placed in front of the pulpitum has not survived. The chancel contains the choir stalls, well repaired in the 1875-6 restoration although now lacking their misericords which remained until at least 1865. William Cooke, a local antiquary, records that in the restoration of these stalls "they had to be removed from the side walls on which were the red and blue crosses of St. Victor" (Cooke MS, 154). Ingham was notable for the collection of monumental brasses it once contained, memorials to subsequent generations of the Stapleton family. Most were robbed in 1799/1800 but we are fortunate in having illustrations by Gough (1786-96), Stothard (1817) and Cotman (1819) of those now lost and they make it clear that the brasses were amongst the best in the county. The chancel also houses the monument of Sir Oliver de Ingham, Sir Miles Stapleton's father-in-law, in a tomb built into the chancel north wall. Although much damaged, this tomb is still clearly of the highest quality and is one of only three in Britain with the effigy of a knight resting on a bed of cobbles (reviewed by Martindale, 1989). The form of this tomb has occasioned much debate and has been seen by Wilson as the work of royal master mason William Ramsey (Wilson 1980, 248-50). Another fine monument now in the nave but probably originally in the chancel is to Sir Roger de Bois and his wife Lady Margaret de Gimmingham. Both were named a co-founders in the priory foundation charter. This altar tomb is also of high quality and retains many traces of its original polychromy.

The porch is unusual in having three stages. The ground floor has a two-bay tierceron-ribbed vault emphasising its pretensions, with the two upper floors, now made into one, reached by a newel staircase. Each floor had its own windows, the first floor had a niche looking into the nave and although much scarred, both appear to have had fireplaces, now totally removed and heavily patched. These support the tradition that the rooms were used as living quarters for the sacristan. The tower was added to the nave, as seen by the two eastern buttresses impinging slightly on the nave aisle west windows. The fine western doorway has the arms of Stapleton above the centre, and within the north spandrel; the Trinitarians cross appears in the south spandrel. From the evidence of wills, the tower appears to have been finished in about 1533 (Cattermole and Cotton 1983, 252-3) and the parapet

113

eastern face bears the arms of Calthorpe (which family married into the failing Stapleton line) and again the Trinitarians cross.

The church contains the remains of several other features now lost. The south transept, demolished in 1799 and traceable in grass parchmarks, was probably served by a small sacristry which stood in the angle between nave and chancel. The only trace of this today is a blocked doorway and the scar marks of a thin removed wall. To the north of the church are the remains of the priory, although most of the conventual buildings have been destroyed by a large gravel pit. The cloister south walk survives, running along the nave north wall. The cloister arcade of three arches, and blocked entrances to the east and west walks survive in a stretch of walling which now marks the limit of the churchyard. Assuming the garth to have been square, the cloister would have been very small at some 210.25 sq. m., including the walkways.

The nave has two north doors leading into the cloister south walk, consistent with a fully monastic conventual church, and a blocked upper door, representing the night stairs entrance. Two further rooms, originally one, are abutted to the chancel north wall, and were open extensions of the nave north aisle. A later wall divided this into two rooms and joist holes demonstrate that both originally had upper floors. Tradition, recorded by local antiquarian William Cooke (1920) calls these the Jesus Chapel (east) and the Sacristry (west). If these ascriptions are correct, the eastern room would be a more suitable candidate for a sacristry as it communicates with both the room to its west and with the monastic chancel. In addition, the connecting doorway's facing of dressed stone with a brick relieving arch behind demonstrate that it was normally viewed from the west. The upper floor above the western room has a large opening of uncertain function and to its east a Tudor niche of moulded brick with recesses indicating former shelves. This is clearly a later insertion into the wall. A Victorian vestry now stands within the easternmost room.

Recent work has assessed the damage to the priory site and collated information on the other remains of the priory. The gravel quarry has clearly destroyed most of the site and has undermined parts of the cloister arcading along the south walk. However, outside the quarry area the digging of foundations and drainage trenches has revealed wall footings, most probably part of other conventual buildings. The west walk of the cloister had no attached conventual buildings, the exterior (west) face being a blank wall, but at its northernmost extent, the stub of a return wall heading west survives. This wall has been traced to the north, and together they almost certainly indicate a former structure (see fig. 69). The apparent great width of this building suggests that it was originally aisled. Another building traditionally ascribed to the priory is the Swan Inn next door to the church. Certainly this is within the assumed precinct boundary but the building as it stands dates from much later. Close internal examination suggests that the bases of some walls are possibly of pre-Dissolution date, the walls above being much altered with patchings, blockings and rebuilds. Finally, parts of the properties built along the precinct roadline are of pure cobble construction and suggest that they are the much damaged remains of the original precinct wall. Further investigation is clearly required.

A blocked opening in the churchyard north wall with medieval brick jambs seems to be a stretch of the original churchyard walling dividing off the priory precinct. Skeletal material found to the north of this area, that is, within the suggested precinct, has been seen as associated with a gibbet which apparently stood here in later medieval times. However, with the redirection of the road for the expansion of the precinct it is more likely that these burials represent interments made within the original parochial churchyard before this part was enclosed as part of the priory.

A few items from the priory survive including a manuscript written within its walls, a 'Meditation on the Passion', now in the Bodleian Library (Bod. MS.758). A colophon records that it was written in 1405 by a Ralph de Medylton on the commission of Sir Miles Stapleton, son of the founder. There is a cast of an imperfect impression of a 14th century seal from the priory in the British Library, portraying the Trinity within a triple arched niche above a shield portraying a lion rampant, the arms of Stapleton. A different seal attributed to Ingham was illustrated in the *Gentleman's Magazine* of 1775 216, again depicting the Trinity within a triple-arched niche but with different arms and inscription. Three painted wooden panels discovered patching a seat in the church in 1782 have now disappeared. Fortunately, they were copied as half-size watercolours on the commission of the antiquary Sir John Fenn and are now preserved in the National Monuments Record archive. The panels originally formed an altarpiece dated by Park (1988, 132-6) to the late fourteenth century. They depicted six scenes from the life of St. Nicholas and were known to be in existence until as recently as 1883. Given the Stapleton family's particular devotion to this saint, the altar piece almost

114

certainly represents another instance of the family's patronage of Ingham. With the funeral monuments, which themselves form a coherent group, all these items provide an eloquent testimony to the wealth and status of the Stapleton family and their importance in the establishment and life of the priory. This very personal involvement is again reflected in the decision to establish the priory adjacent to the family's seat, the manor house and farm at Ingham.

Assessing the number of canons based at Ingham is difficult. When founded, provision was made for 13 religious including the Minister and a sacrist, but Blomefield records that in 1360 there were "but a custos and two chaplains or brethren" Blomefield (1808, 9, 326-7). These numbers doubtlessly fluctuated until in the sixteenth century there were six canons as well as the minister and the Sacrist. However, some measure of the priory's standing within the English Trinitarian movement is seen by this foundation having a value of £61 by 1535. Whilst small in comparison to many religious houses, this was the second richest English Trinitarian house despite being one of the last two founded. By contrast, Newcastle, also founded in 1360, had a value of only £6 in 1535 (Knowles and Hadcock 1971, 205). Ingham's value seems to be the origin of the mistaken notion in some antiquarian sources that this was the head house in England and that the Trinitarians were sometimes called 'The Order of Ingham'.

Ingham Priory was not officially dissolved. Anticipating the supression of the house, the canons had sold their entire estate to local landowner William Woodhouse in 1534 without the consent of their patron Sir Francis Calthorpe. Woodhouse was therefore brought before the Crown commissioners at Coxford and alleged that Ingham was exempt from their attentions, being a house of Crossed Friars and not of monks or canons. Surprisingly, after a perusal of the Statute, the commissioners agreed (*L & P Hen VIII* xi, 261), no doubt to the relief of both Woodhouse and several, richer, ex-canons.

The plan of the church is based on one first made by M. Gray and N. Clayton in April 1985. Other details are taken from fieldwork conducted in December 1990 and July 1991. I would like to express my gratitude to Mr. N. Kent, churchwarden, Mr. K. Fiddy, ex-proprietor of the Swan Inn, Mr. and Mrs. Scott and Mr. B. Foreman, for their time and help during my fieldwork. Research into the history and archaeology of the priory is continuing.

9.6. Knaresborough (Yorkshire) SE 360 652 (plans, figs. 71 and 72)

Sources: Hargrove 1809, 69
Wheater 1907, 298-319
V.C.H. Yorks. 1913, 296-300
Cummins 1924, 80-8
Bazire 1968, 17-2
Jennings 1970, 95-108
Air Photograph, Acrofilms (unnumbered and undated), and J.K. St. Joseph BFW 93.95

The priory of the Holy Trinity and St. Robert occupied a classic monastic site adjacent to the River Nidd and bounded on its north side by limestone crags, which contain caves. It is now in Abbey Road which runs SE along the Nidd from Knaresborough.

The success of this priory rested on its association with Robert of Knaresborough, known as Saint Robert, although he was never officially canonised. This connection became so well known that the whole Trinitarian Order in England became known, for a time, as the 'Robertines'.

The life of Robert, the foundation of the Trinitarians and the history of Knaresborough Priory are all related in his Metrical Life (Bazire 1968). After Robert's death in 1218, the small chapel of the Holy Cross, built on the site of the original St. Giles' chapel, where the saint had lived in a cave, became the scene of miraculous cures, with medicinal oil flowing from his tomb. There is a possibility that this was sulphur water from a spring adjacent to the chapel. When the Trinitarians were granted the hermitage and forty acres of land near to it, they took full advantage of these events to attract pilgrims. It was not until thirty four years after the death of Robert however that there is official recognition that the Trinitarians had colonised the site, when in 1252 Pope Innocent IV

115

granted an indulgence to those who had helped to build the priory. During the intervening period, immediately after Robert's death in 1218, the hermitage was granted to the rector of Knaresborough. It was given nine years later to Brother Ives, who had been Robert's companion; it was during his life that the miracles of healing started to occur. Ives was also granted the adjacent forty acres, which King John had given to Robert after a visit to him in 1215. It must have been on this land that the first Trinitarian buildings were erected, although it is not known precisely when the first of the canons arrived there. The Metrical Life (Bazire 1968, 73) says that Ives gave the site to Coverham Abbey, but that it was desolate for some time before the Trinitarians colonised it. This would indeed accord with the arrival of the Trinitarians at other sites, as they tended to take over places abandoned by other orders. By 1252, when the papal indulgence was granted, there must have been buildings on the site, but it is only in 1255, when Henry III gave three oaks for the fabric of the church, that the Trinitarians are expressly mentioned by name.

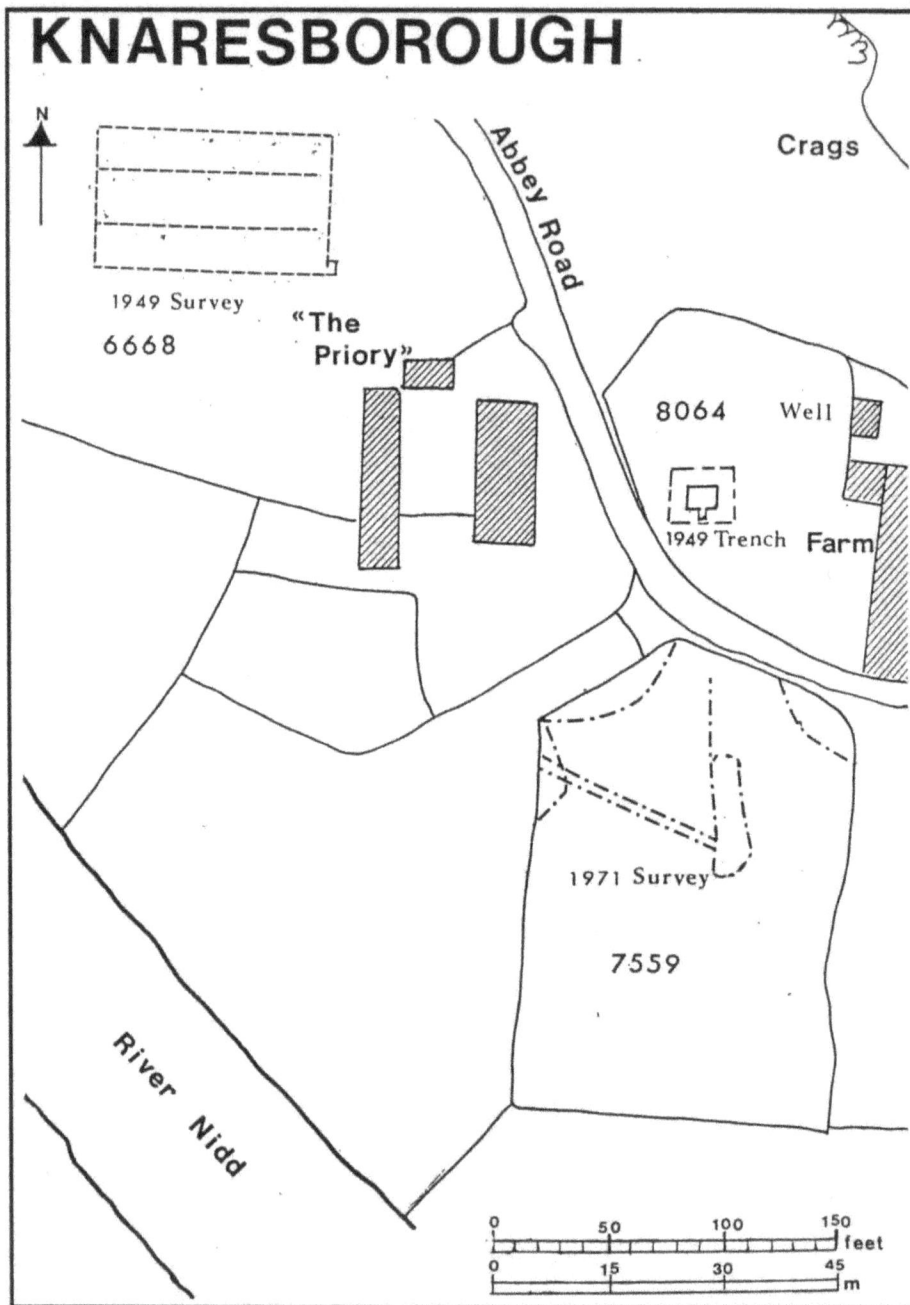

Fig 71

The first patron was Richard, Earl of Cornwall (who also founded Hounslow), whose charter is dated 1257. He gave, amongst other gifts, the chapel of St. Robert. Its position is not certain but it was probably 400m away on the north bank of the Nidd near Grimald Bridge on the Knaresborough-Wetherby road. In this place still exists a cave where Robert is reputed to have lived and the site of the Chapel of the Holy Cross (plan, fig. 72). This is a complex site, cut into the limestone bedrock adjacent to the river. Three steps lead down into the cave, whose height is between 1.8m and 1.9m, with ledges and recesses in two of the corners. Outside this cave is the remains of the Chapel of the Holy Cross with a raised altar platform. In front of this is a cavity, which may be the grave which Robert is reputed to have dug for himself, and which attracted pilgrims because of the healing oils which are said to have flowed from it. This cavity may have been adapted in the 18th century for cold bathing from the spring as mentioned in Hargrove (1809, 69). A deep drain runs from the mouth of the cave to the river on the south side. The lowest courses of the south and east walls of the chapel survive, the northern wall being the side of the limestone cliff. To the west of the chapel, immediately outside the entrance to the cave, is a living area with a bench carved out of the rock around its perimeter. A flight of steps leads down the cliff face to the site of the cave and chapel.

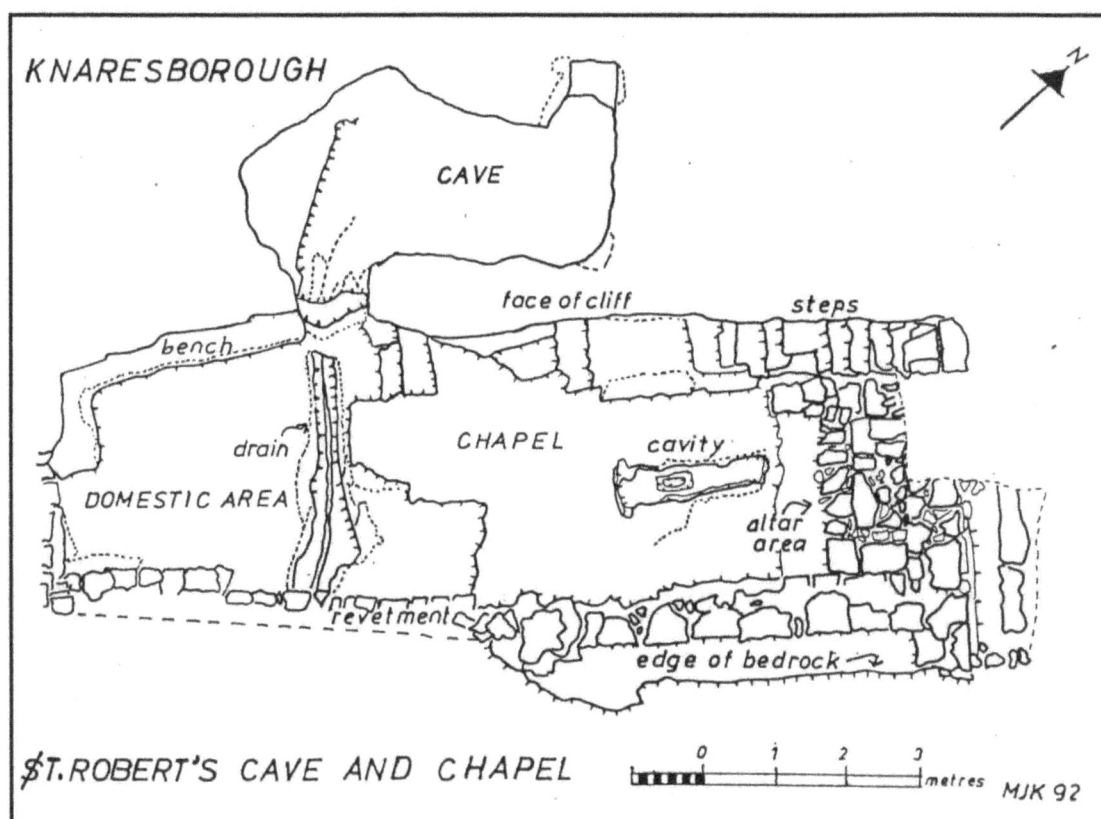

Fig 72

It is not known how long Robert's bones rested in the tomb which he prepared for himself. There was dispute with Fountains who wished to own such prestigious relics (Jennings 1970, 97). The Trinitarians may have moved the bones into their newly built church, as in 1252 Pope Innocent IV granted an indulgence to 'those that help in completeing the monastery of St. Robert of Knaresborough where that saint' body is buried' (V.C.H Yorks. 1913, 297).

The original charter allowed the canons to build a mill on the river, and they were also given grazing land. In 1300 the buildings were still under construction as the archbishop of York granted forty days indulgence to those who gave alms for the building of the church. These buildings were partly destroyed by the Scots in 1318, but in 1350 more indulgences were granted to finance building and repair work. A large number of pilgrims were still being attracted there in the 15th century, as the pope authorised the minister and six other priests to hear the confessions of the crowds coming to the church at the feast of Holy Trinity.

At its suppression in December 1538, the account for the sale of goods mentions the King's Chamber and the Knight's Chamber, as well as two other chambers, a hall, and ancillary buildings, including a kitchen and brewhouse (Jennings 1970, 107-8). A belfry is mentioned with five bells weighing 9 tonnes altogether. Also mentioned are one mill, three granaries, one barn, one dovecote and apple orchards. One of the fields called 'Esper' was, according to Hargrove (1809, 69), the site of the fishponds, which he describes as well constructed, one pond measuring 52ft by 35ft (15.85 by 10.66m) and the other of the same breadth, but 26ft (7.92m) longer. He also mentions a 'large drain capable of receiving the water of both' which was 6ft (1.82m) deeper than either of the ponds, 206ft (62.78m) long and 20ft (6.07m) wide. These ponds are still in existence in the fields opposite the Abbey Farm and show on the air photographs. The gatehouse of the abbey (erected 1435-50) and nearby smithy still existed in 1629 and must have been pulled down when the present 'Abbey House' was built in 1657. In 1700 Celia Fiennes mentions in her diary visiting the 'ruines of an Abbey where there has been many bones taken up and some preserved as relics' (Fiennes 1982, 92). A map in P.R.O. of 1587 (44/411) shows the remains of a criciform church with two adjacent buildings, which have been sketched on to a tithe map (Jennings 1970, 108). Two seals exist, 13th century for the priory and 15th century for the minister, both showing St. Robert reading a book under a tree. These are illustrated by Clay (1928 pl. V, nos. 9 and 10); the priory seal (BM. Cat., No. 3378) and the minister's seal (cast cxxxvii 70) are in the British Library. Nine letters of confraternity exist; one in 1465 was to Henry Rychmond (afterwards Henry VII), and their reference number is given in Clark-Maxwell (1929, 212-3).

Two excavations and two surveys have taken place. In 1862 trenching exposed the north transept of a cruciform church with towers or turrets at the angles and a stone coffin with three skeletons. This is reports by Gomme (1902, 272). A second excavation was carried out by S.C. Barber, assisted by V.Brown, in 1949, and the plan of their cuttings is shown (fig. 71). In field 6668 the SE buttress of the church was exposed, after a plan of the church had been delineated by Colonel Merrylees, official dowser to the army. He also reported graves to the north of the church, but they were not excavated. In field 8064 a small cutting exposed a limestone flagged floor, with a masonry drain which had a semi-circular base of millstone grit. The excavators considered it may have been a malthouse. To the east of this was a well, c. 2m in diameter and c. 2m deep, which was fed by a spring. The photographs, plans and elevations of this excavation are deposited with the writer of this report.

In 1971 members of a Harrogate extramural class under the direction of C.V. Bellamy surveyed field 7559 and the results of work with a probe, a resistivity meter, a proton gradiometer and a fluxgate meter are shown on the plan (fig. 71). There is a large circular mound in this field which may be a dovecote. The results of this work and a summary of the 1949 excavations have been prepared by B. Thompson, and a copy is deposited with the present writer.

Part of the south perimeter wall still exists in the garden of 'Abbey House', and some 14th century architectural fragments are incorporated into the garage wall of the 'Priory'. The latter is on north-south orientation and its lower courses show evidence of being on earlier foundations. Many of the field walls contain dressed stone.

St. Robert's cave was rediscovered in the mid nineteenth century, when it was cleared to make the site accessible to the public and an iron rail installed on the cliff top. It was cleared once again in the 1920's in advance of a visit by Queen Mary. In 1989 the Harrogate Museums Service, under the direction of Mary Kershaw, undertook a clearance and recording project, removing only 20th century debris (previous archaeological deposits having been removed in the earlier clearances). The site was extensively photographed and all features drawn to scale. The site will soon be made accessible to the public once again, Ampleforth College having made over its rights of access. I am grateful to Mary Kershaw for her information about St. Robert's cave, and for supplying the plan (fig. 72).

9.7 Moatenden or Moddenden (Kent) TQ 818 464. 21/3 km (13/4 miles) NW of Headcorn (plans, figs. 73 and 74)

Sources: Hasted 1782, 2, 391-3
Lambarde 1826, 299-302
Furley 1878, 10, 26-8
V.C.H. Kent 1926, 205-8
Atkins 1957
Pevsner 1980, 321
Payne 1979
Aldridge 1991
Air Photograph, taken by R. Seward, Institute of Archaeology, London.
Air Photographs, taken by J.K. St. Joseph, Cambridge University Collection, (ADJ 19, 20)

The site is near the main road A 274 from Maidstone to Tenterden and on a small tributary of the river Beult. It was originally one of the four manors of Headcorn and was probably a moated farmstead before the arrival of the Trinitarians, owned in the early part of the 13th century by Robert de Rokesley, seneschal to the Archbishop of Canterbury (As such it is listed in *Kent Manorial and Moated Sites 1979, 46).* Part of the moated site is the remains of this earlier manor. Aldridge 1991 says that Robert accompanied Henry III on his campaign into Gascony. This is an interesting connection with the benefactor of both Hounslow and Knaresborough, Richard, Earl of Cornwall, who was the brother of Henry III. This influence may have assisted in the choice of the Trinitarians rather than any other order for the new foundation at Moddenden. Tradition states that Robert de Rokesley founded a Trinitarian house on land which he already owned, possibly in 1224, which would make it probably the first foundation of the order in England. However *V.C.H. Kent* 1926 (205) gives the earliest reference as 1235-6 when 'the prior' and Robert de Rokesley were named in a royal writ. The first time that the house was expressly named as Trinitarian was in 1253, when they were granted a right to hold a fair at the feast of Trinity and six days after. There is no record of a hospital, and, being near continent, it may have been a recruitment and administrative centre; it provided several provincial ministers for the order and, like Knaresborough, it was interested in the affairs of the house at Oxford (*V.C.H. Kent* 1926, 207). Five letters of confraternity from this house are still extant; one in 1477 admits as brother and sister two people who had aided in an expedition against the Turks (Clark-Maxwell 1929, 213). In 1538 Cromwell had personal possession of the estate, but after his attainder the property was leased to Sir Anthony Aucher, who held the lease from 1540 to 1544 when he purchased the site of the priory and its lands for £806 12s 3^{1}/2d. He was probably the builder of the present house on the site which dates from 1545, although the crown post of this roof could be earlier and part of the west range of the priory (Aldridge 1991). A seal of the priory is illustrated in Hasted (1782, 2, 392). Aldridge 1991 mentions that a lead papal seal of Innocent IV (1243-54) was found close to the front door of the present house about twenty years ago and that several finds have been made in the garden, including parts of stone coffins, two sections of a carving of an angel's wing, decorated floor tiles, and sherds of pottery. Both Furley (1878) and Atkins (1957) mention stone coffins and part of the sculptured frieze of an angel. Furley says that in his time there were no standing remains. Atkins mentions, and Aldridge confirms, that in the Archaeological Society's room at Maidstone Museum there are two carved roof spandrels from Sutton Valence Church which show the rebus of Richard de Sutton, the last minister of Mottenden and vicar of Sutton, which include the Trinitarian cross.

The site survives as a large moated enclosure with a house of Tudor origins in its confines. The 1841 Tithe Map shows that at that time there was still water in some of the moats, and that the ditch originally went round all four sides of the enclosures, although the western side was partly dry. Pevsner (1980, 321) mentions the house as Tudor, with bricks on the ground floor and stone quoins, as well as four windows and a round headed doorway. Field Officers of the Ordnance Survey visited the site on 29/11/61 and recorded the house as a timber framed structure faced with 18th century and modern brick, incorporating stone windows and four centre arched doorways, probably re-used

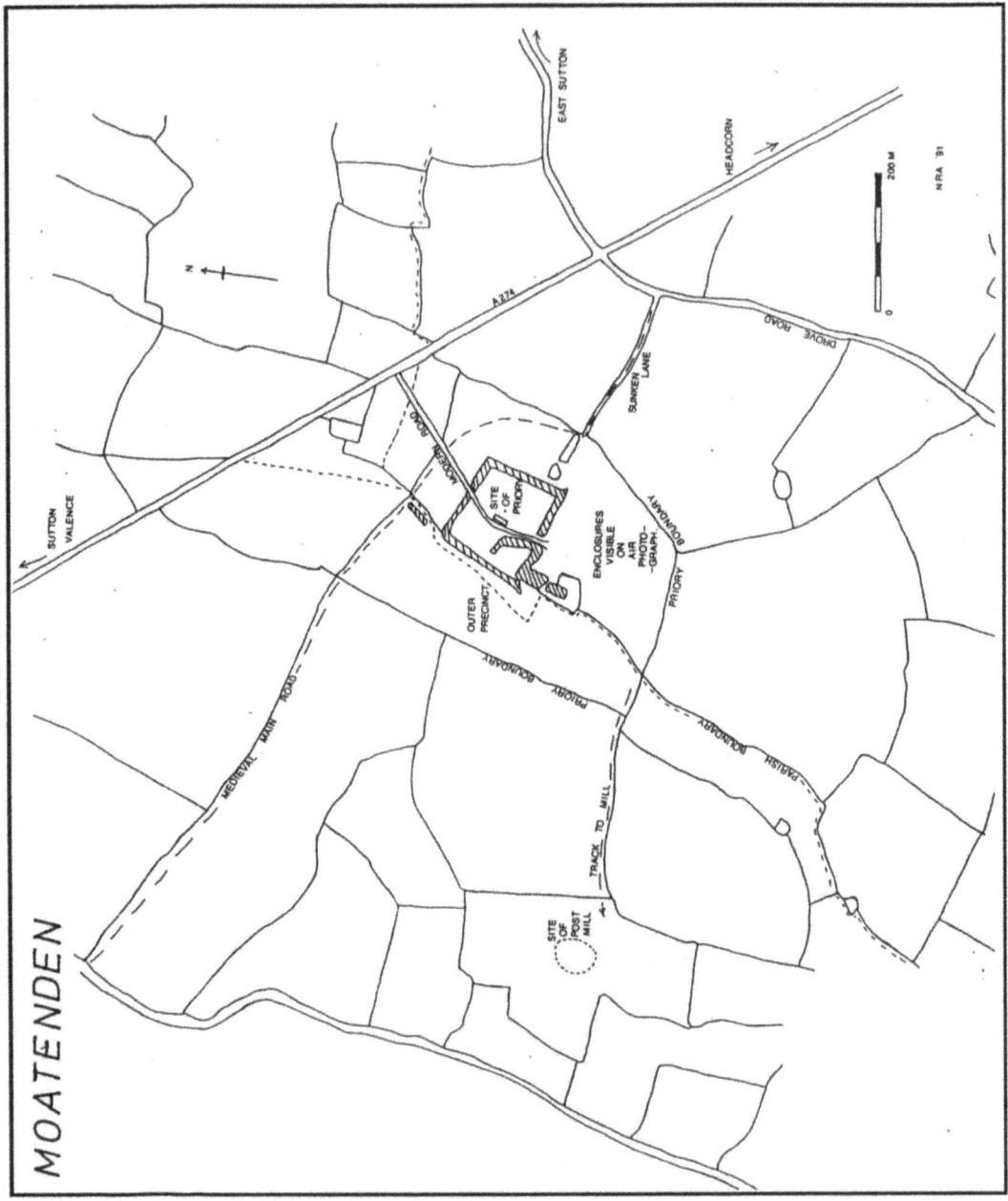

MOATENDEN

Fig 73

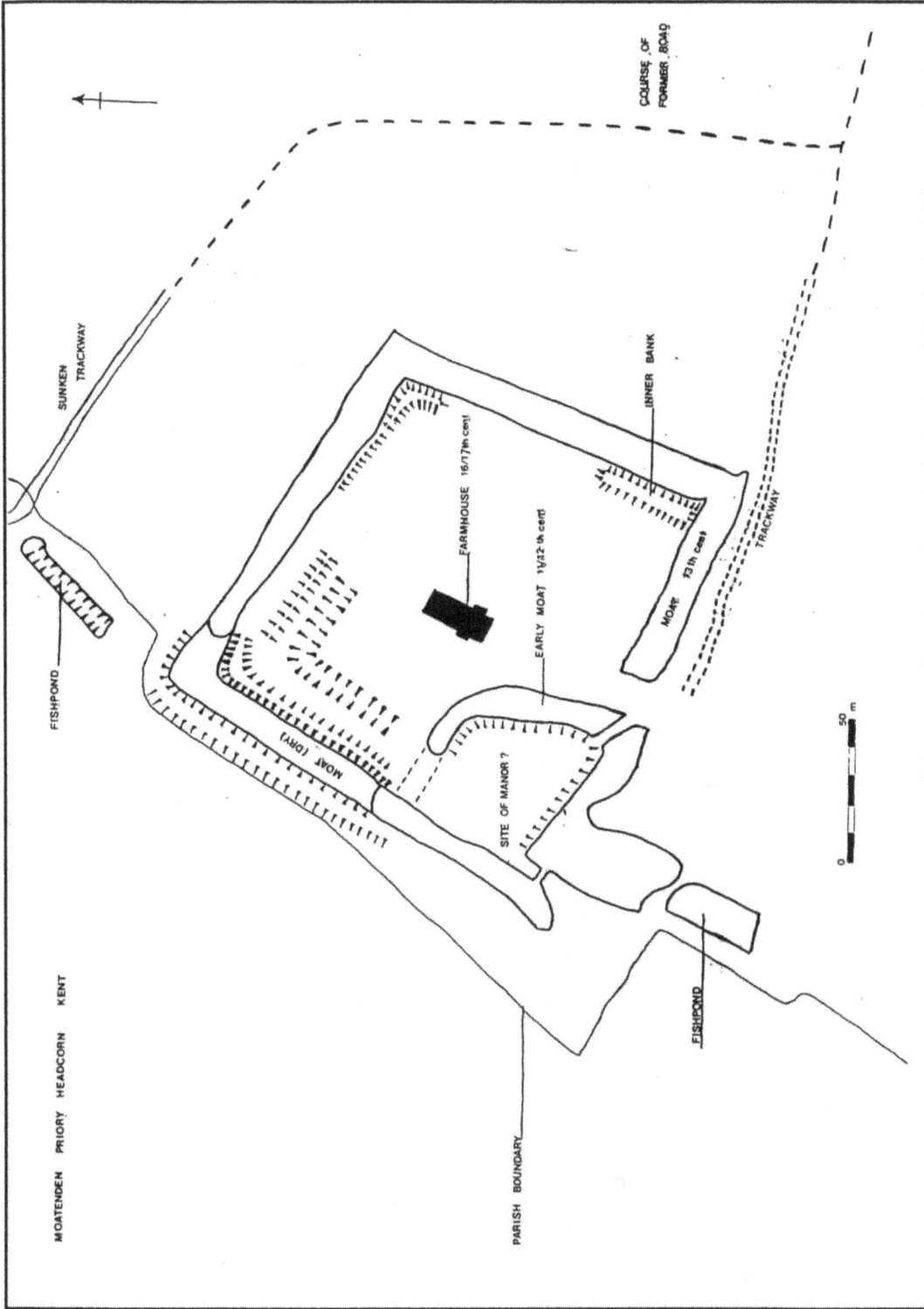

MOATENDEN PRIORY HEADCORN KENT

SUNKEN TRACKWAY

FISHPOND

COURSE OF FORMER ROAD

INNER BANK

FARMHOUSE 16/17th cent

EARLY MOAT 11/12 th cent

MOAT 13 th cent

TRACKWAY

MOAT (DRY)

SITE OF MANOR ?

PARISH BOUNDARY

FISHPOND

0   50 m

Fig 74

121

material from the priory. An architectural Survey of the house was made by Neil Aldridge and K.W.E. Gravett on 13/11/91. I am grateful to them for permission to use a summary of this information in this record. They found three distinct periods of construction from evidence both inside and outside the house. The earliest part of the present house is the crown post, dated between 1480 and 1550; there was possibly originally a gable facing north at the crown post end of the house. In the time of Anthony Aucher, about 1545, there was considerable work including a 'chequered' pattern wall painting, which could be 1550-1600, along the southern side of the partition wall under the crown post. This early timber framed house seems to have been partly rebuilt soon after 1600 with three gables added to the eastern side of the house and a central chimney. The centre and southern end of the house were encased in brick in the middle of the nineteenth century. This house is a Grade II listed building, the northern end being perhaps around 1540, the middle seventeenth century and the southern part late seventeenth to early eighteenth century. It is likely that this house lies over the site of the Trinitarian priory building (Resistivity Survey Jan/Feb. 1992).

In 1991 Neil Aldridge carried out an extensive survey not only of the house mentioned above but also of the surrounding earthworks. His plans are reproduced in figs. 71 and 72, and the results of his work summarised. He has identified the pre-priory moated farmstead, which belonged to Robert de Rokesley, in the south west corner of the site (see plan fig. 71), this being one of the four original manors of the parish of Headcorn (Payne 1979). He suggests that the main moats were dug at the time of the establishment of the Trinitarian priory, and enclose an area of about 1.82 ha ($4^{1}/2$ acres). It can be assumed that the ditch originally went round all sides of this rectangular area, although the western side is now partly dry. The average width of the ditch is 12-14 metres; a small watercourse feeds the west moat. To the south of the early homestead moated area is a square ended pond, probably an earlier fishpond. Another smaller pond is sited to the north west of the priory moat and this one is now dry. Aldridge has traced the priory precinct on Air Photographs by hedge lines, and this is shown on plan fig. 71. Also visible on the air photographs are a series of ditched field enclosures within the precincts of the priory, and a sunken lane which approaches the priory from the east. The lane continued across the modern access road along another sunken track and headed north west towards Sutton Valence, following a bank which could have been the rabbit warren referred to in Hasted 1782 (393).

No excavation has taken part on the site except by Stuart Rigold, but it has not been possible to trace the unpublished report of this work.

I am grateful to Rebecca Payne for her permission to use information from her unpublished thesis, and also to Neil Aldridge for allowing me access to his extensive study of this site.

* 3x drawings

9.8 Newcastle upon Tyne (Tyne and Wear) N2 25 64 (plan, fig. 75)

Sources: Brand 1789, 1, 400-10
             Oliver 1831, 113

This house was always a hospital; it was known variously as St. Michael's from the fact that it stood upon a hill, Holy Trinity from the order and Acton's Hospital from its founder. It occupied a site a Wall-Knoll which, according to Brand, was a street leading uphill from Fisher Gate and thus named from the Roman wall at the top of it (Brand 1789, 400). The Carmelites left the property vacant in 1307 but the Trinitarians are not heard of there until the date of their foundation charter in 1360. Their founder was William de Acton, burgess of Newcastle. The first warden, William Wakefield came from Berwick (Northumberland), when the house there was destroyed by the Bishop of Durham. The establishment consisted of three canons (one of which was the warden), three poor and infirm persons and three clerks to teach in the school, and instruct in the chapel of the house. The foundation charter also stipulated that three beds were to be kept prepared for 'accidental guests'. The minister of St. Robert's at Knaresborough was to visit them annually about Trinity

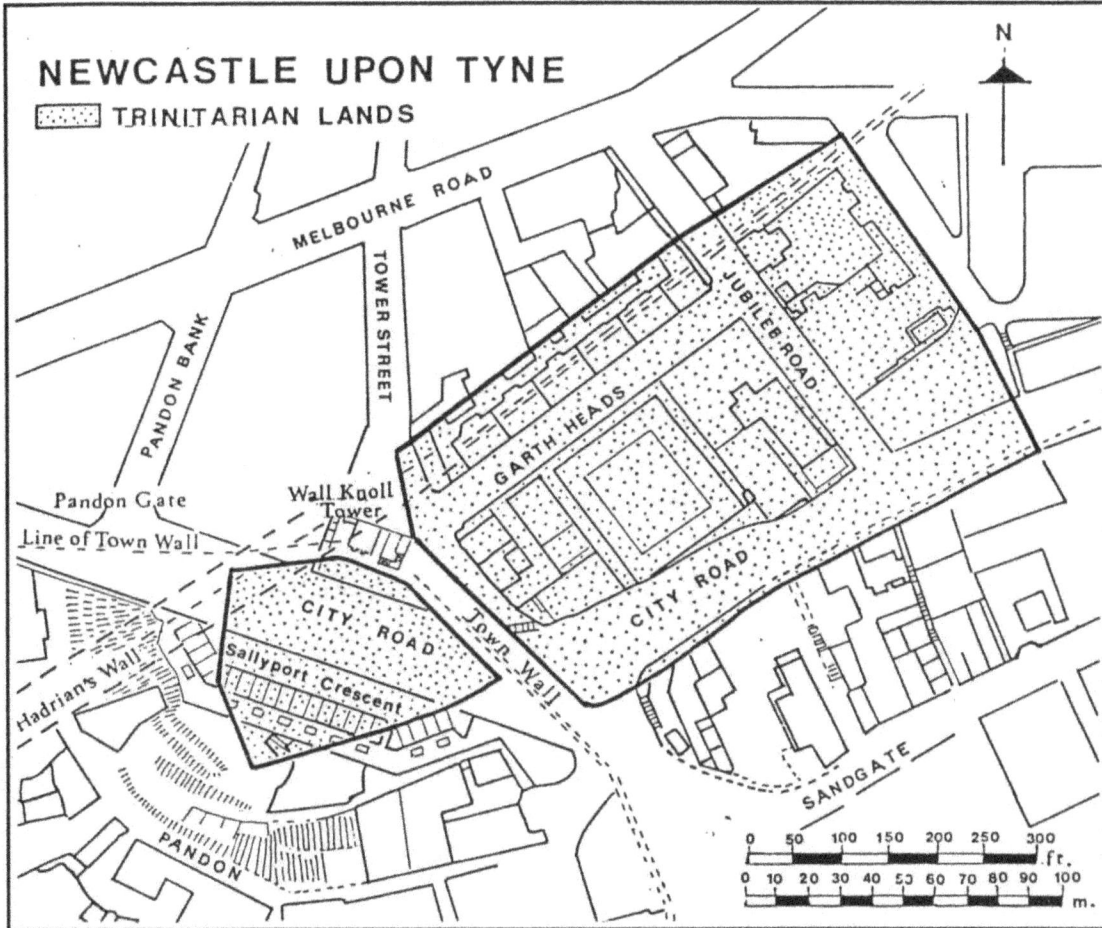

Fig 75

Sunday, on which occasion he was to be presented with 'a horse-load of fish'.

In 1370 Edward III granted a licence of mortmain to William Wakefield in aid of support of a chaplain to perform divine office for the souls of the Thorald family and all faithful departed in St. Nicholas' church. They received several grants of land, notably in 1378, 1394 and 1397. In 1496 there is a record of the ordination of two priests from this hospital (Brand 1789, 406). When the house, after its dissolution, was conveyed from William Dent in 1548 it was described as 'the priory of St. Michael de Wall-Knoll' with a garden and orchard of about an acre (0.40 ha) of ground as well as a close near the town wall of four acres (1.61 ha), 34 'messuages', three gardens and a close, also a close called Coleriggs and four ridges in Shield Field (Brand 1789, 410). It was conveyed to William Jennison, the mayor, and alderman Richard Hodshon, in trust for the corporation. It would seem that it stayed in the hands of the mayor and burgesses, as they leased it out in 1602 to Ambrose Dudley as 'waste ground on which was one capitall house latelie knowne and called by the name of Walknoll' together with all garths and gardens belonging to it for 99 years (Tyne and Wear Archives Department 544/71, 15). The building is marked on Speed's Plan of Newcastle (Brand 1789, 410) and Brand also says that in his time 'some vestiges of old buildings, doorways, etc., still remain' (Brand 1789, 410). It would seem that there were still remains of the priory there in 1831, although by now in a bad state, as Oliver (1831, 113) describes it in these words:- 'On entering Pandon from Pandon Bank, on the lefthand rises Cobourg Stairs, leading to the Alleys, where a manufacture for weaving sail-cloth is situated, immediately opposite to which a doorway, window and other vestiges of St. Michael's Priory still remain, amidst a cluster of houses and stables, the area of the convent is now used for a dunghill and stable-yard, and a smith's shop occupies the site of the burying-ground'.

The site of the priory buildings is on the north side of Sallyport (plan, fig. 74) and south of Wallknoll Tower, marked on the 1951 OS map with an antiquities mark as 'site of chapel'. The Wallknoll Tower is the only part of the town wall to survive in that area. It was an advantageous position for the Trinitarians as their hospital was close to Pandon Gate, a main thoroughfare through the walls into the city. In this respect it was similar to both Oxford and Totnes. The final remains of

123

the buildings were probably destroyed by 19th century workshops and housing. It now lies under City Road, which was constructed in 1880; Sallyport Crescent became pre-war council flats.

I am grateful to Barbara Harbottle for her help in this section of the Gazetteer.

9.9 Oxford (Oxon) SP 51 06 (plan, fig 76)

Sources: Loggan 1675, Maps SE V and NE V
              Clark ed. 1890, 478-88
              Clark ed. 1899, 326-7
              Hurst 1899, 146-7
              V.C.H. Oxon. 1907, 150-2
              Oxeniensia 1943-4, 203-5
              Pantin ed. 1960, Salter Maps SE IV and V, NE IV and V and 197
              V.C.H. Oxon. 1979, 368, 406, 465
              Hassall 1978, 261

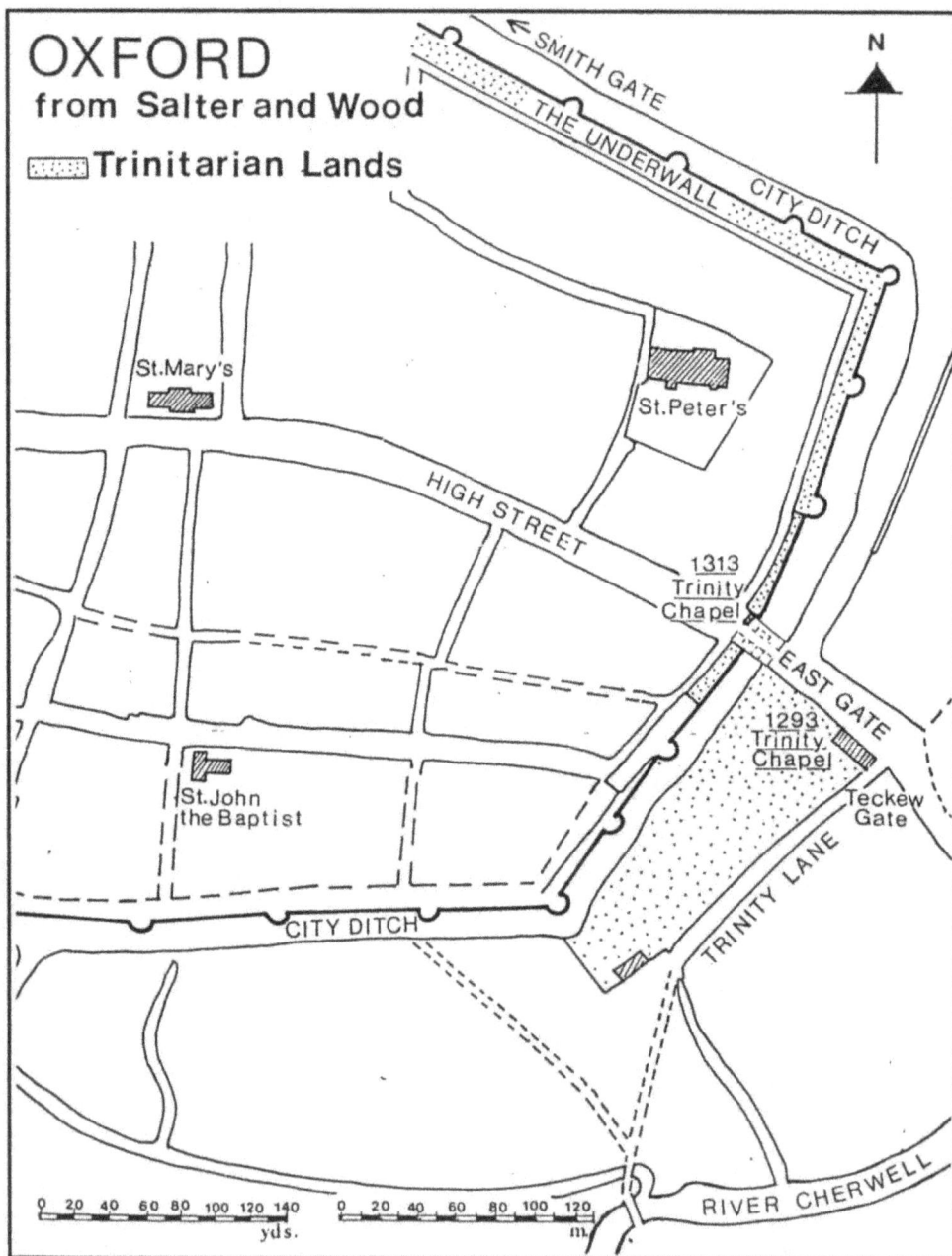

Fig 76

124

There is confusion in Clark 1889 about the existence of two Trinity Chapels but *V.C.H. Oxon.* 1907, (151 footnote 3) says that Wood is correct and his editor Clark is wrong in the latter's assumption of there only being one chapel.

Before 1286 there were Trinitarian students at the university, as at that date Oxford was mentioned in connection with the house of St. Robert at Knaresborough, whose benefactions assisted their maintenance there (Wheater 1907, 311). The Trinitarian presence at Oxford University is possibly explained by the need for these canons to have theological training before taking up pastoral work in their dependent churches as well as within their own priories. The opportunity to study seems to have embraced all within the order who wished to study, unlike the Benedictines students whom Foster 1990, 107, sees as candidates for monastic administration. That there was an increase in academic interest by the mendicant orders in theological education at the Universities is mentioned by Foster 1990, 100. It was Edmund, Earl of Cornwall, son of the founder of Hounslow and Knaresborough, who in 1292 obtained land from the Hospital of St. John outside the East Gate (plan, fig. 76). The exact measurements of the land between the East Gate and Teckew Gate and its dimensions to the south are given in Salter 1, 197 (Pantin ed. 1960). It was adjacent to the City Wall and eleven tenements were converted into a house and a chapel, from which the city claimed a rent. The inmates comprised a minister and five brethren, who were to take charge of novices of the Order who wished to receive academic training. It was known as 'domus Trinitatis' and 'aula Trinitatis'.

In *c*.1310 the Trinitarians obtained the use of a chapel owned by St. Frideswide's and already dedicated to the Holy Trinity, which stood within the East Gate, on the north side. With this was included a shop and two plots of vacant land each side of the gate within the walls. In 1311 the city granted the land known as 'Underwall' from the Smithgate in the north as far as the East Gate. In 1313 the Trinitarians had licence to move from their house outside the wall to their new site within, on condition that the Trinity chapel within the gate was to be a chantry for founders and benefactors, the chaplains to be maintained from their former house. It would seem therefore that both chapels were served concurrently, until a reduction of their numbers to only one brother at the Black Death, when the chapel outside the walls was served in 1351 by a brother from Hounslow. In 1379 the Underwall was sold to the founder of New College, and from 1351 until 1391 their land outside the east wall was held by the King as an escheat. The chapel within the East Gate was abandoned, and they only retained their original chapel these chapels having no parochial functions. In 1391 Richard II allowed the city to seize the land as a distraint for non-payment of rents. In 1447 the minister from Hounslow leased out all the Trinitarian lands which remained to the city, and in 1471 they conferred the chapel and all its lands to a hermit on condition that he should maintain a chaplain there. However, owing to the intervention in 1486 of Robert Gaguin, the head minister of the order, the site was surrendered by the city to the provincial minister of the order at Mottenden, in whose possession it remained until the Dissolution. The site became known as 'Trinity Hall', with a warden appointed by the minister of Mottenden, with secular students amongst its inmates; at the time of its dissolution it was occupied by a priest, an anchorite and other students who lived by begging alms from the colleges. Robert Perrot of Magdalen College converted this hall into a barn and stables and several tenements for the relief of four poor bedesmen called 'Trinity Men'. In 1563 the city appointed them as beadles of beggars in the four wards (*V.C.H. Oxon.* 1979, 465). Trinity Lane is now called Rose Lane, and the area outside the former East Gate is covered by 19th century houses, which adjoin the Botanic Gardens. Hassall (1978, 261) notes that the original East Gate 'consisted of a single square tower with a round-headed archway. The room above was the Holy Trinity chapel. The gate was rebuilt in the 17th century as two square towers flanking a single wall. That gate was in turn demolished *c*.1771' There is an illustration and notes about the East Gate in *Oxeniensia* 1943-4, 203-5. Excavations on the site of the infirmary hall and adjoining chapel of St. John's Hospital were carried out by Brian Durham in 1986 and 1987 for the Oxford Archaeological Unit (Youngs, Clark and Barry, 1987, 154-5 and Youngs, Clark, Gaimster and Barry 1988, 270-1). This hospital was refounded by Henry III in 1231, and it was his nephew, Edmund, Earl of Cornwall who gave the St. John's Hospital lands to the Trinitarians in 1292.

I am grateful to Tom Hassall for checking the information in this section.

9.10 Totnes (Devon) SX 80 60 (plan, fig. 77)

Sources: Windeatt 1880, 166-7
             Beresford and St. Joseph 1979, 198-9
             Air photograph, Beresford and St. Joseph 1979, 198-9

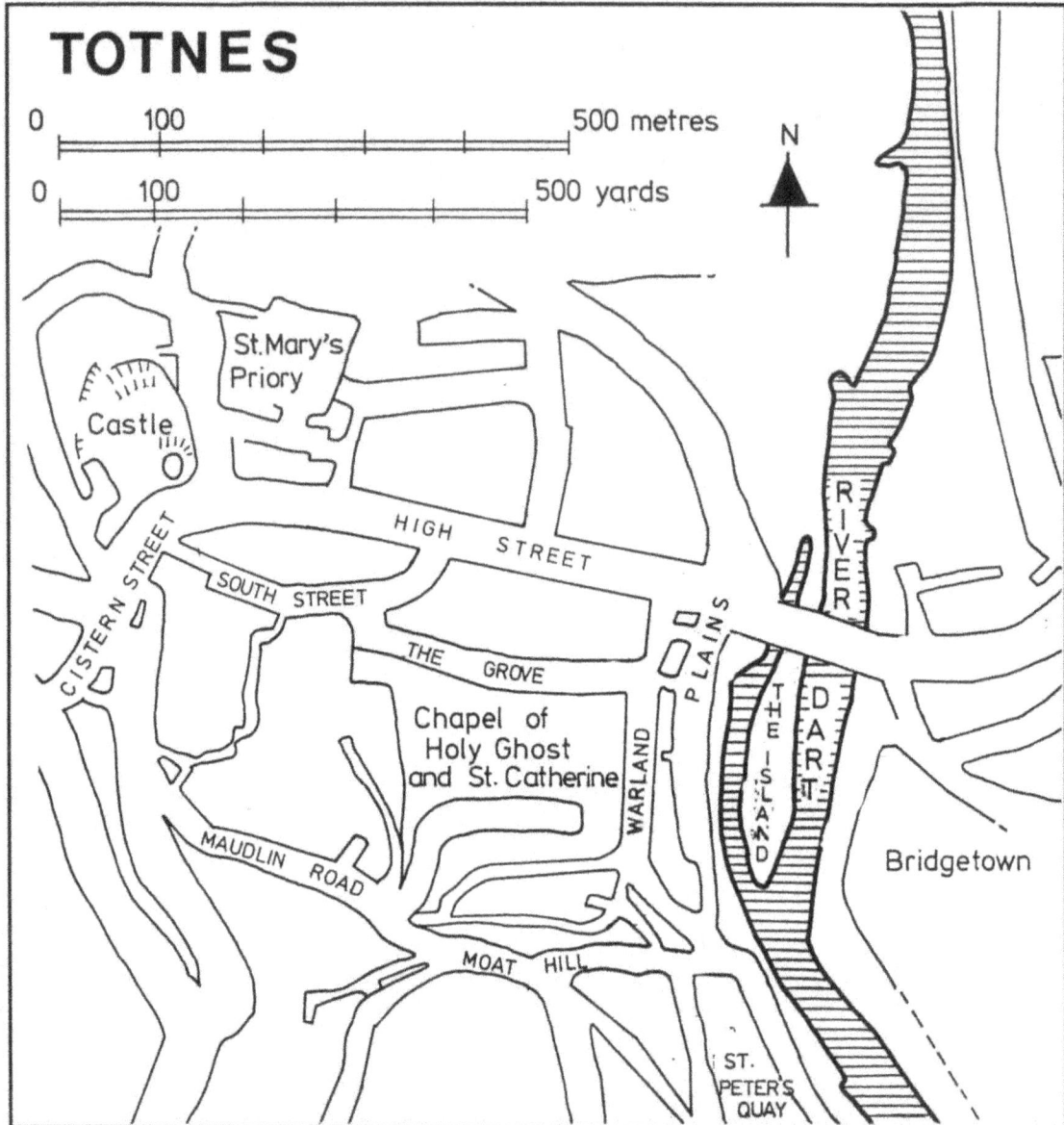

Fig 77

This site was also known as Little Totnes or Warland. Both Dugdale (*Mon. Angl.* 1830, 6, 1562) and Tanner (1787) make these separate houses, but it is clear that there was only one house at Totnes and that Warland/Werland is part of the town of Totnes (plan, fig. 77). Little is known of the history of this hospital, but the Trinitarians are thought to have been given a site here in 1270 by Walter le Bonard and his wife Agatha, together with considerable lands in the area. The dedication was to the Holy Ghost and St. Katherine; as there is no dedication to the Holy Trinity, a chapel may therefore have existed already. It is at its suppression in 1508 referred to as a hospital. Aungier (1841, 492) says that the place of *custos* or warden at the hospital at Crediton was generally given to a brother at Hounslow, and also that a Hounslow brother served the chapel at Warland, whose collation was absolutely vested in the bishop of Exeter. From 1427-37 it is known that a brother from Easton Royal served this chapel (Chettle 1947, 373). Bishop Oldham suppressed it in 1508 and gave its lands to the vicars of Exeter cathedral. The site was near the west bank of the River Dart, opposite an island. It

126

was outside the walls of the medieval town but near the town bridge. Beresford and St. Joseph (1979, 199) note that in the 15th century there was extensive extramural development to the east of the town walls, and a new borough was planted across the river, but close to Warland, in 1293. The suffix 'land' is an Anglicised form of 'lon', implying attachment to a monastic house or church.

There was 19th century building over the site after the land was sold in 1801, under the Land Exemption Tax, when it ceased to belong to Exeter cathedral. Little remains to show the exact position of the hospital except for a stone cottage with traces of earlier foundations in a street still called Warland. The name however survives in 'Warland House' in this same street, and in a modern development named 'St. Katharine's Mews'.

The plan (fig. 77) is taken from the Street Guide to Totnes published by *'Geographia'*, which is based on the OS map of the town.

9.11 Scotland and Ireland

Sources: Gordon 1868, 1, 286-311
Gwynn and Hadcock 1970, 217
Cowan and Eason 1976, 107-112

Individual houses in Scotland and Ireland are not listed in this gazetteer as, with the exception of Fail (Ayr) and Adare (Limerick) they were not visited and surveyed, therefore their present position was not ascertained.

Useful comparison between the Scottish and English houses has been made by Tim Pestell (Pestell 1991, 107-112) and his table showing all the Trinitarian houses in the British Isles is appended. Although he sees a similarity in function between the Scottish and English houses, he notes that in Scotland their tighter geographic distribution was advantageous. He believes that the closely clustered group of sites with hospitals on the east coast could have been connected with the pilgrimage route to St. Andrews'. He calculates average values between the English houses and those over the border, as £29.8 for England and £155.1 for Scotland, at the time of their dissolution, three of the Scottish houses exceeding any English values at this time. However this comparative wealth may not reflect the success of an order instituted for charitable purposes, as they may have kept more of their 'tertia pars' (the third part of their income reserved for the relief of captives) for their own use. Coulton sees the Scottish houses failing in this duty (Coulton 1933, 227) whereas Fuller (Fuller 1811, 2, 43) sees the English houses still fulfilling these obligations (see 4.2). Pestell attributes their wealth to their tight distribution, but the three wealthiest houses were away from the east coast group.

As Cowan and Eason (1976, 107) point out, the number of Trinitarian houses in Scotland has frequently been exaggerated through confusion with other orders and through uncritical repetition of erroneous statements of earlier authors. For example, Gordon (1868, 1, 286-311) lists thirteen houses when the total authenticated by Cowan and Eason (1976, 107-112) is only eight.

The head house of the order is usually seen as St. Mary's at Fail, as the minister at Fail was provincial of the order in Scotland. Not only was he in direct consultation with the minister-general in Paris, but also guardian of all the Trinitarian possessions in Scotland, his consent being necessary for all transfers of property (Dillon 1958, 73, 82, 84). The minimum income of Fail in 1561 was the largest of any house in the British Isles (Table C).

127

TABLE C
TRINITARIAN FOUNDATIONS IN THE BRITISH ISLES

House	County/Country		Foundation	First Ref.	Dissolved	Value
Aberdeen	Aberdeen	(S)	*-1274*		1561	£54
Adare	Limerick	(I)	*-1226*	1272	1559?	
Berwick	East Lothian	(S)	-1240-8		1488	
Dirleton	East Lothian	(S)	*1444*	1507	1588	
Dunbar	East Lothian	(S)	*1218*	1240-8	1529	
Easton	Wiltshire	(E)	*1245*	1251	1536	£42
Fail	Ayr	(S)	*c.1252*	1335	1561	£580
Hertford	Hertfordshire	(E)	*-1199*	c.1261	c.1535?	
Hounslow	Middlesex	(E)	*-1200-1*	1224-52	1538	£72
Houston	East Lothian	(S)	c.1270		1531	
Ingham	Norfolk	(E)	1360		1536	£61
Knaresborough	Yorkshire	(E)	*1235*	c.1252	1538	£35
Mottenden	Kent	(E)	c.1224	1235	1538	£58
Newcastle	Northumberland	(E)	1360		1539	£6
Oxford I	Oxfordshire	(E)	*-1286*	1293	c.1313	
II			c.1313		1538	
Peebles I	Peebles	(S)	c.1448		1463	
II			c.1474		1560-1	£327
Scotlandswell	Kinross	(S)	c.1250-1		1591-2	£280
Thelesford	Warwickshire	(E)	*-1200-14*	1224-40	1538	£24
Little Totness	Devonshire	(E)	*1271*		1509-19	

Italics are for uncertain dates.

First Reference, where given, is for dates where foundation is unclear.

It should be clear that there is difficulty in assembling all the necessary data, for example values of houses. In England the assessment is *c.*1535, in Scotland *c.*1561.

Fail (Ayr) NS 421 288 2km (11/2 miles NW of Tarbolton)

Sources: Cooper 1880, 143-150
             Groome 1895-1900, 36.
             Dillon 1958, 68-132

St. Mary's priory at Fail is not lacking in documentary material though there is little on the ground to verify this information and no archaeological work appears to have been undertaken.

The most useful topographic information is in Groome (1895-1900, 36) who places the site on the right bank of the rivulet Water of Fail at Failford. Dillon 1958 (68) says that ruins once stood on 'a little used back road between Ayr and Galston, a paradox in stone - everybody knew of it, nobody knew anything about it'. This observation is still true today, as it is difficult to make much sense of the monastic plan from the existing evidence.

When visited in 1986 the site appeared to be on rising ground above a large marshy area which could, at one time, have been a small lake, filled by the waters of the river Fail. There is a large rubbish dump, still in use, on the east side of this marshy area. Gordon (1868, 1, 296) says that the buildings were at one time 'surrounded by the Loch' and that 'a gable and part of the side wall of the manor house of the chief or minister are still standing'. Both Cuthbertson (1939, 139) and Dillon (1958, 68) mention these ruins standing there; Dillon says until the 1950's when the stones were taken away to provide hardcore under the runways of Prestwick Airport. This fact was confirmed by a Mrs. Douglas who lived in a cottage on the road opposite where these ruins may have stood. This cottage was built of large blocks of brown and white-grey sandstone, which could have also been from the monastic ruins. Mrs. Douglas asserted that she had found human bones in the garden behind her house. In a field to the west of this cottage there are vague signs of east-west banks, and by the side of what must have been the main road before it was by-passed by the A719, was a rectangular fishpond still containing water. This was adjacent to a house called Fail Mill House.

Dunbar (East Lothian)

Sources: Groome 1895-1900, 408.
               Wordsworth 1983, 478-488

Dunbar and Thelsford are the only excavated sites in the British Isles. The excavation of 'Friarscroft' in April and May 1981, described by Wordsworth (1983, 478-488) as 'a limited exercise' proved that the only standing building on the site, known as the Dovecote, was in fact the tower of the Trinitarian church, but the claustral buildings were not located, in spite of extensive trenching of the area to the south of the tower. If these features had been as insubstantial as the wooden structures found at Thelsford, it would have been difficult to have seen them in machine trenching. However Wordsworth (1983, 479 and 487) is probably correct that the absence of claustral buildings is due to the fact that the single chaplain for this church resided in the tower, and that the rest of the community was adjacent to the Maison Dieu hospital, which they maintained, 500 m to the south of this site. Wordsworth (1983, fig. 1) has an area plan showing the location of both these properties, a site plan (fig. 2) and a plan of the east end of the church (fig. 3).

It is worth mentioning that two other of the Scottish houses have documentary sources for the existence of monastic ruins after the dissolution.

Peebles is said in Chambers (1864, 294), Gordon (1868, 1, 299) and Groome (1895-1900, 3, 160-1), to have retained the church of the Holy Cross, with cloisters on the north side, until the early 19th century. Gordon gives the measurements of the church as 102 ft by 32 ft (31 x 9.75m) and the cloister as 32ft (9.75m).

Aberdeen is well documented in Anderson (1909, see index for many charters of the 'Red Friars'); Cowan and Eason (1976, 108) say that the church was still standing in the 18th century.

Adare (Limerick) (plan, fig. 78)

Sources: Dunraven 1865, 36-67
               Gwynn and Hadcock, 1970, 217

The church of Holy Trinity stands on the south side of the main road through Adare (on the banks of the River Maigue) in the centre of the town. It's earlier dedication is said to have been to St. James but it was later known as White Abbey. An extensive review of the history of this Trinitarian priory, the only one of the order in Ireland, in Dunraven (1865, 36-67) has four plates showing the state of the ruins at various times, with an explanation of these plates. Pl. 2 (explanation p.291) is said to have been taken from 'an old tinted sketch' executed before 1800 and shows the priory almost complete, except for the roof. Pl. 3 (explanation p.291) shows 'The Village of Adare and Ruins of the Trinitarian Abbey prior to the year 1810' with the ruined tower of the church surrounded by thatched cottages and a large two storied building on the opposite side of the road, known as 'Adare Inn or Club-house'. On the gable end are two circular recesses containing the Trinitarian cross; this may well have been the guest house of the priory. In 1811 Lord Dunraven created a 'new town' and many of these cottages have disappeared, but the Catholic church which was a rebuild of the Trinitarian church (extended in 1852) is much the same now. Dunraven (1865, 65) says that at the beginning of the 19th century the ruined church had been used as 'a ball-court'. Pl. 13 (explanation p.293) shows the plan of the church and conventual buildings, with the walls of the ancient church and monastic buildings drawn in black (plan, fig. 77). The cloisters are to the north and now occupied as a convent and school, in whose garden is the complete monastic dovecote; this is circular with a conical stone roof pierced with holes. Pl. 14 (explanation p.293) shows a view, facing north, with, on the right, the roofless gable of the monastic ? kitchen and a section of the perimeter wall, with a ruined building adjoining it. These views are of great interest to Trinitarian historians, as they show the roofless buildings of the original church and claustral area. I am grateful to Lord Dunraven for allowing me to use the plan from 'Memorials of Adare' pl. 13.

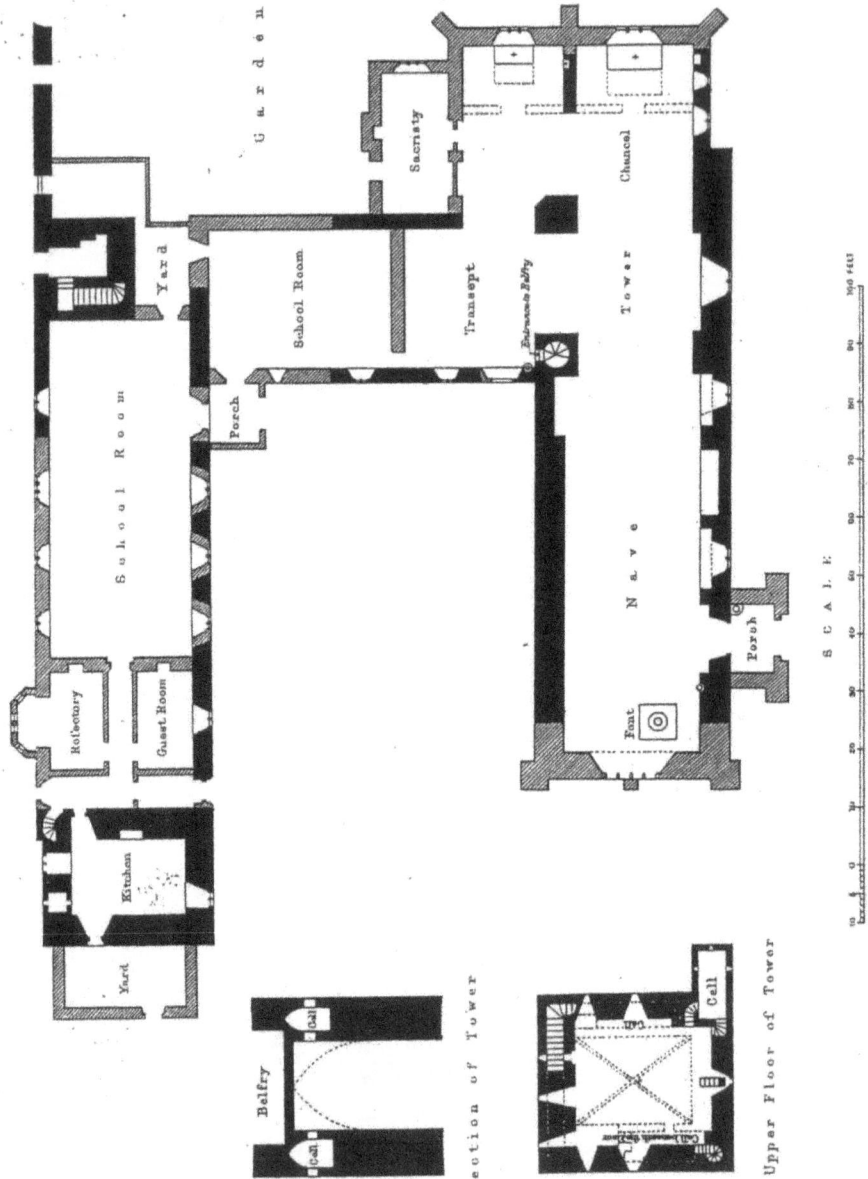

PLAN OF THE
TRINITARIAN ABBEY,
AT ADARE NOW THE
CATHOLIC CHURCH.

Fig 78

Plate X
Holy Trinity, Hounslow in 1795 from Lysons 'Environs of London, 3. Middlesex'

Chapter 10
BIBLIOGRAPHY

Aldridge 1991 N.R. Aldridge, An Archaeological Study of the Trinitarian Priory at Headcorn, Kent. (Unpublished thesis).

Anderson 1909 P.J. Anderson, *'Aberdeen Friars'* (H.M.P. Aberdeen, 1909).

Andrews 1912 H.C. Andrews, 'The Hermit of Hertford and Christ Church, London' *Herts. Mercury*, 78, No. 4022, 2, 6th January, 1912.

Andrews (undated) W.F. Andrews, 'Ecclesiastical Buildings in the past in Hertfordshire', *Herts. Mercury*(undated).

Antonin 1925 R.P. Antonin, *Les Origines de l'Ordre de la Tres Sainte Trinite* (St. Cajetan, Rome, 1925).

Aston ed. 1988 M. Aston ed., *Medieval Fish, Fisheries, and Fishponds in England* (Brit. Archaeol. Rep., British Series 182, Oxford, 1988)

Atkin *et al* 1988 M. Atkin, A. Carter, and D.H. Evans, 'Excavations in Norwich 1971-78, Part II' *East Anglia Archaeology* 26 (1988)

Atkins 1957 P. Atkins, *Headcorn, its Parish Church and People. Short Notes from a History of Headcorn* (Church Guide, 1957)

Aungier 1841 G.J. Aungier, *The History and Antiquities of Syon Monastery, the Parish of Isleworth and the Chapelry of Hounslow* (London, 1841)

Baker *et al* 1979 D. Baker, E. Baker, J. Hassall, and A. Simco, 'Excavations in Bedford 1976-1977', *Bedfordshire Archaeol.J.* 13 (1979), 1-309.

Barfield (forthcoming) L.H. Barfield, 'The Flints, in N. Palmer, *Tiddington Roman Settlement* (Forthcoming).

Barton and Holden 1978 K.J. Barton and E.W. Holden, 'Excavations at Bramber Castle, Sussex, 1966-67, *Archaeol.J.* 134 (1977), 11-79.

Bashford 1955 H.H. Bashford, "Present and Past Churches at Easton Royal', *Wiltshire Archaeol. Natur. Hist. Mag.* 56 (1955), 66-7.

Bashford 1977   H.H. Bashford, *Easton Royal, A Short History* (Marlborough College Press, 1977)

Bate 1924   G.E. Bate, *A History of the Priory and Church of the Holy Trinity, Hounslow* (Thomasons, Hounslow, 1924)

Bazire 1968   J. Bazire, *The Metrical Life of St. Robert of Knaresborough* (Early English Text Society, O.U.P., London 1968).

Beaver 1968   S.H. Beaver, *The Geology of Sands and Gravels* (Sand and Gravel Association of Great Britain, London, 1968).

Bell 1902   Mrs. Arthur Bell, *Lives and Legends of the Great Hermits and Fathers of the Church, with other Contemporary Saints* (George Bell, London, 1902)

Benedictine Book 1989   Benedictine monks of St. Augustine's Abbey, Ramsgate, *The Book of Saints*, (A & C Black 1989).

Beresford 1975   G. Beresford, *The Medieval Clayland Village: Excavations at Goltho and Barton Blount* (Medieval Archaeol. Monograph Series No. 6, 1975).

Beresford 1978   G. Beresford, 'Excavation of a Moated house at Wintringham, Huntingdonshire'. *Archaeol. J.* 134 (1977), 194-286.

Beresford and
St. Joseph 1979   M.W. Beresford and J.K. St. Joseph, *Medieval England: An Aerial Survey* (C.U.P., Cambridge, 1979).

Bernard 1697   E. Bernard, *Catalogue of Mss. Angliae ii* (Oxford, 1697).

Bickley 1923   W.B. Bickley, 'Abstract of the Bailiffs' Accounts of Monastic and Other Estates, in the County of Warwick *Dugdale Society* II (1923) 122-5.

Biddle *et al* 1961   M. Biddle, L. Barfield and A. Milward, 'Excavation of the Manor of the More, Rickmansworth, Hertfordshire', *Archaeol. J.* 116 (1959), 136-199.

Blomefield 1808   F. Blomefield, *An Essay towards a Topographical History of the County of Norfolk*, 9 (London, 1808).

Bond 1914   F. Bond, *Dedications and Patron Saints of English Churches* (O.U.P., London, 1914).

Brand 1789   J. Brand, *History of Newcastle-upon-Tyne* (Newcastle, 1789).

Braun 1970   H. Braun, *Parish Churches, their Architecture and Development in England* (Faber and Faber, London, 1970).

Braun 1971   H. Braun, *English Abbeys* (Faber and Faber, London, 1971).

Brears 1971   P.D. Brears, *The English Country Pottery: Its History and Techniques* (David & Charles, Newton Abbott, 1971).

Brittain 1925   F. Brittain, *Saint Radegund, Patroness of Jesus College Cambridge* (Bowes and Bowes, Cambridge, 1925).

Bryant and Steane 1971 & 1975   G.F. Bryant and J.M. Steane, 'Excavations at the Deserted
                                  Medieval Village at Lyveden', *J. Northampton Mus.* 9 (1971) 1-94 and 12
                                  (1975), 1-160.

Butler 1974   L.A.S. Butler, 'Medieval finds from Castell-y-Bere, Merioneth', *Archaeol.
                                  Cambrensis* 123 (1972), 78-112.

Butler and Given-Wilson 1979   L. Butler and C. Given-Wilson *Medieval Monasteries of Great
                                  Britain* (Michael Joseph, London, 1979).

Butzer 1982   K.W. Butzer, *'Archaeology as Human Ecology'*, (C.U.P., Cambridge, 1982).

Caley ed. 1810   J. Caley ed., *Valor Ecclesiasticus temp. Henr. VIII, auctoritate regia
                                  institutus* (P.R.O., 1810-34).

Cattermole and
Cotton 1983   P. Cattermole and S. Cotton, 'Medieval Parish Church Building in Norfolk',
                                  Norfolk Archaeol. 38 (1983), 235-79.

Chambers 1864   W.R. Chambers, *History of Peebleshire*, (W and R Chambers, Edinburgh,
                                  1864).

Chatwin 1926   P.B. Chatwin, 'The Priory, Warwick' *Trans. Birmingham Warwickshire
                                  Archaeol. Soc.* 51 for 1925-26 (1926), 53.

Chatwin 1936   P.B. Chatwin, 'The Medieval Patterned Tiles of Warwickshire', *Trans.
                                  Birmingham Warwickshire Archaeol. Soc.* 60 (1936), 1-41.

Cherry 1973   J. Cherry, 'The Medieval Jewellery from the Fishpool, Nottinghamshire,
                                  hoard', *Archaeologia* 104 (1973), 307-21.

Chettle 1947   H.F. Chettle, 'The Trinitarian Friars and Easton Royal' *Wiltshire Archaeol.
                                  Natur. Hist. Mag.* 51 for 1946 (1947), 365-77.

Christie and
Coad 1981   P.M. Christie and J.G. Coad, 'Excavations at Denny Abbey', *Archaeol. J.*,
                                  137 for 1980 (1981), 138-279.

Clark ed. 1890   A. Clark ed. *Survey of the Antiquities of the City of Oxford*, composed
                                  in 1661-6 by A. Wood, 2, Adenda and Indexes, (Oxford Hist. Soc., 1890).

Clark ed. 1899   A. Clark ed. *Survey of the Antiquities of the City of Oxford*, composed in
                                  1661-6 by A. Wood, 3, Adenda and Indexes (Oxford Hist. Soc., 1899).

Clarke 1984   H. Clarke, *The Archaeology of Medieval England* (British Museum, London,
                                  1984).

Clark-Maxwell 1926   W.G. Clark-Maxwell, 'Some Letters of Confraternity', *Archaeologia* 75
                                  (1926), 19-60.

Clark-Maxwell 1929   W.G. Clark-Maxwell, 'Some Further Letters of Fraternity', *Archaeologia* 79
                                  (1929), 179-216.

Clay 1928   C. Clay, 'The Seals of the Religious Houses of Yorkshire', *Archaeologia* 28
                                  (1928), 1-36.

Clay 1966 R.M. Clay, *The Medieval Hospitals of England* (Frank Cass, London, 1966).

Clissold 1977 S. Clissold, *The Barbary Slaves* (PBS Book Club, Abingdon, 1977).

Cook 1961 G.H. Cook, *English Monasteries in the Middle Ages* (Phoenix, London, 1961).

Cook 1968 G.H. Cook, *Medieval Chantries and Chantry Chapels* (John Baker, London, 1968).

Cooke 1920 W.H. Cooke, *Places of Interest in East Norfolk*, hand written MS (Stalham, 1920).

Cotman 1819 J.S. Cotman, *Engravings of the Most Remarkable Sepulchral Brasses in Norfolk*, London, 1819.

Coulton 1933 G.C. Coulton, *Scottish Abbeys and Social Life*, (C.U.P. Cambridge, 1933).

Cowan and Easson 1976 I.B. Cowan and D.E. Easson, *Medieval Religious Houses of Scotland* (Longman, London, 1976).

Cox 1923 J.C. Cox, *English Church Fittings, Furniture and Accessories* (Batsford, London, 1923).

Cummins 1924 Abbot Cummins, 'Knaresborough Cave Chapels', *Yorkshire Archaeol. J.* 28 (1924), 80-8.

Cuthbertson 1939 D.C. Cuthbertson, *Quaint Scots of Bygone Days*, (Eneas Mackay, Stirling, 1939).

Daniel 1991 P.L. Daniel 'The Order of the Holy Sepulchre in England in the Middle Ages'. (Unpublished 1991).

Davies 1958 G.R.C. Davies, *Medieval Cartularies of Great Britain* (Longmans Green, London, 1958).

Deslandres 1903 P. Deslandres, *L'Ordre des Trinitaires pour le Rachat des Captifs* (Paris, 1903).

Dickinson 1950 J.C. Dickinson, *The Origins of the Austin Canons and their Introduction into England* (S.P.C.K., London, 1950).

Dillon 1958 W.J. Dillon, 'The Trinitarians of Failford', *Ayrshire Collections* 2nd series 4 (1958), 68-132.

Drewett 1975 P. Drewett, 'Excavations at Hadleigh Castle, Essex 1971-72', *J. Brit. Archaeol. Ass.* 38 (1975), 90-154.

Drewett 1976 P. Drewett, 'Excavations of Great Hall at Bolingbroke Castle, Lincolnshire, 1973', Post-Medieval Archaeol., 10 (1976), 1-35.

Dugdale 1730 W. Dugdale, *History of Warwickshire* (Revised by W. Thomas and printed for John Osborn and Thomas Longman, London, 1730).

Dugdale, Mon.
Angl. 1830   W. Dugdale, *Monasticon Anglicanum, A History of the Abbies and Other Monasteries Hospitals and Friaries in England and Wales*, vi, iii; ed. J. Caley, H. Ellis, Rev. Bulkeley-Bandinell (Longmans, London, 1830).

Dunraven 1865   Caroline, Countess of Dunraven, *'Memorials of Adare Manor with Historical Notices by her Son, the Earl of Dunraven'*, (privately printed by Parker, Oxford, 1865).

Durham 1978   B. Durham, 'Archaeological Investigations in St. Aldate's, Oxford', *Oxoniensia* 42 (1977), 83-203.

Eames 1980   E.S. Eames, *Catalogue of Medieval Lead-Glazed Earthenware Tiles in the Department of Medieval and Later Antiquities British Museum*, 2 vols. (Trustees of the British Museum, 1980).

Encyclopaedia
Brittanica 1982   *Encyclopaedia Brittanica* 15th edition (Benton, London, 1982).

Evans 1949   J. Evans, *English Art 1307-1461* (O.U.P., Oxford, 1949).

Fairfax-Lucy 1958   A. Fairfax-Lucy, *Charlecote and the Lucys* (O.U.P., London, 1958).

Farmer 1987   D.H. Farmer, *The Oxford Dictionary of Saints*, (O.U.P., Oxford, 1987).

Fiennes 1982   C. Fiennes, *The Illustrated Journeys of Celia Fiennes, 1685-c.1712*, ed. C. Morris (MacDonald, London, 1982).

Fosbroke 1843   T.D. Fosbroke, *British Monachism or Manners and Customs of the Monks and Nuns of England* (Nattali, London, 1843).

Foster 1990   M.R. Foster, 'Durham Monks at Oxford *c.* 1286-1381: a House of Studies and its Inmates', *Oxoniensia*, 55 (1990), 99-114.

Fuller 1811   T. Fuller, *The History of the Worthies of England;* first printed in 1662, new edition by J. Nichols, Rivington (Payne et al, London, 1811).

Furley 1878   R. Furley, *Annals of Headcorn, Kent* (Igglesden, Friend and Igglesden, Ashford, 1878).

Gairdner 1904   J. Gairdner (ed.), *The Paston Letters* (London, 1904).

Gasquet 1905   Abbot Gasquet, *English Monastic Life* (Methuen, London, 1905).

Gomme 1902   G.L. Gomme, *Topographical History of Worcestershire and Yorkshire* (Gentleman's Magazine Library, Elliot Stock, London, 1902).

Gordon 1868   J.F. Gordon, *Monasticon; An Account of all the Abbeys, Priories, Collegiate Churches and Hospitals in Scotland* 1 (John Tweed, Glasgow, 1868).

Gough 1786-96   R. Gough, *Sepulchral Monuments in Great Britain*, 2 vols. (London 1786-96).

Greene 1972   J.P. Greene, 'Norton Priory', *Current Archaeol.* 31 (1972), 206-20.

Greene 1974   J.P. Greene, 'Norton Priory', *Current Archaeol.* 43 (1974), 246-50.

Greene 1980   J.P. Greene, 'Norton Priory', *Current Archaeol.* 70 (1980), 343-9.

Groome 1895-1900   F. Groom, *Ordnance Gazetteer of Scotland*, 2 and 3, (William Mackenzie, London, 1895-1900).

Gwynn and Hadcock
1970   A. Gwynn and R.N. Hadcock, *Medieval Religious Houses, Ireland*, (Longman, London, 1970).

Hargrove 1809   E. Hargrove, *History of Knaresborough* (Knaresborough, 1809).

Hartley 1974   L.S. Hartley, 'A Typology of Brick' *J. Brit. Archaeol. Ass.* 37 (1974), 63-87.

Harvey 1978   J.H. Harvey, *The Perpendicular Style*, (London, 1978).

Harvey Bloom 1906   J. Harvey Bloom, *'Seals of England"* (McKuen, London, 1906).

Hassall 1978   T.G. Hassall, 'Oxford. The City of Walls', *Archaeol. J.* 135 (1978), 258-262.

Hasted 1782   E. Hasted, *History and Topographical Survey of the County of Kent*, 2 (Simmons and Kirby, Canterbury, 1782).

Hebermann *et al.* 1907   Hebermann, Pace, Allen, Shaha and Wynne, ed., *The Catholic Encyclopaedia*, 15, (Caxton, London, 1907).

Hilton and Rahtz 1967   R.H. Hilton and P.A. Rahtz, 'Upton Gloucestershire, 1959-1964', *Trans. Bristol Gloucestershire Archaeol. Soc.* 85 (1966), 70-146.

Hirst *et al.* 1983   S.M. Hirst, D.A. Walsh and S.M. Wright, *Bordesley Abbey II* (Brit. Archaeol. Rep. British Series III, Oxford, 1983).

H.M.S.O. 1970   *Archaeological Excavations 1969* (Ministry of Public Buildings and Works, H.M.S.O., London, 1970).

Hobley 1971   B. Hobley, 'Excavations at the Cathedral and Benedictine Priory of St. Mary, Coventry's, *Trans. Birmingham Warwickshire Archaeol. Soc.* 84 (1967-70), 45-139.

Holling 1977   F. Holling, 'Reflections on Tudor Green', *Post-Medieval Archaeol.* 11 (1977), 61-79.

Hooke 1985   D. Hooke (ed.) *Medieval Villages*, (5, Oxford Univ. Ctte. for Archaeol., 1985).

Hurst 1899   H. Hurst, *Oxford Topography*, 3 (Oxf. Hist. Soc. Oxford, 1899).

Hurst 1964   J.G. Hurst, 'White Castle and the Dating of Medieval Pottery', *Medieval Archaeol.* 6-7 (1964), 135-55.

Hurst 1984   J.G. Hurst, 'The Wharram Research Project: Results to 1983', *Medieval Archaeology*, 28 (1984), 99.

Hurst and Hurst 1971   D.G. and J. Hurst, 'Excavations at the Medieval Village of Wythemail', *Medieval Archaeol.* 13 (1969), 147-203.

James 1982   H. James, 'Excavations in Wootton Wawen Churchyard 1974 and 1975',
                      Trans. Birmingham Warwickshire Archaeol. Soc. 90 (1980), 37-48.

Jameson 1905   Mrs. Jameson, *Legends of the Monastic Orders* (Longmans, Green & Co.,
                      London, 1905).

Jennings 1970   B. Jennings, ed. for Harrogate WEA Local History Group, *A History of
                      Harrogate and Knaresborough* (Advertiser Press, Huddersfield, 1970).

Jope 1956   E.M. Jope, 'The Tinning of Iron Spurs: A Continuous Practice from the
                      Tenth to the Seventeenth century', *Oxoniensia* 21 (1956), 35-42.

Jope and Threlfall 1959 E.M. Jope and R.J. Threlfall, 'The Twelfth Century Castle at Ascot Doilly,
                      Oxfordshire', *Antiq. J.* 39 (1959), 219-73.

Kent Manorial and
Moated Sites   Kent Manorial & Moated Sites Group, Moated Sites in Kent - December
                      1978, Group 1979 *Moated Sites Res. Grp. Rep.* 6 (1979).

Klingelhofer 1978   E. Klingelhofer, 'Barrack Street Excavations, Warwick, 1972', *Trans.
                      Birmingham Warwickshire Archaeol. Soc.* 88 (1978), 87-104.

Knowles 1956   D. Knowles, *The Religious Orders in England*, vol. 1 (C.U.P., Cambridge,
                      1956).

Knowles and
Hadcock 1971   D. Knowles and R.N. Hadcock, *Medieval Religious Houses, England and
                      Wales.* (Longmans, London, 1971).

La Cour 1961   V. La Cour, *Naesholm* (Copenhagen, 1961).

Lambarde 1826   W. Lambarde, *A Perambulation of Kent* (Bollifant, London, edition of
                      1826).

Lambrick and
Woods 1976   G. Lambrick and H. Woods, 'Excavations at the Dominican Priory, Oxford',
                      Oxoniensia 41 (1976), 168-231.

Lawrence 1984   C.H. Lawrence, *Medieval Monasticism* (Longman, London, 1984).

Lee-Warner 1879   J. Lee-Warner, 'The Stapletons of Ingham', *Norfolk Archaeol.* 8 (1879), 194-
                      209.

Le Strange 1973   R. Le Strange, *Monasteries of Norfolk* (Yates, Kings Lynn, 1973).

Liddlesdale
Palmer 1930   R. Liddlesdale Palmer, *English Monasteries in the Middle Ages* (Constable,
                      London, 1930).

Limbrey 1975   S. Limbrey, *Soil Science and Archaeology* (Academic Press, London, 1975).

Little 1979   B. Little, *Abbeys and Priories in England and Wales* (Batsford, London,
                      1979).

LMMC 1940 and 1954   *'Medieval Catalogue'*, London Museum Catalogue No. 7, (H.M.S.O. 1940,
                      reprinted 1954).

Loggan 1675	D. Loggan, *Oxonia Illustrata* (Oxford, 1675).
Lopez 1714	D. Lopez, *Noticias Historicas del Ordern de la Santissima Trinidad Redempcion de Captivos en Inglaterra, Escocia y Hibernia* (Madrid, 1714).
Lysons 1795	D. Lysons, *Environs of London. 3. Middlesex* (London, 1795.
Martindale 1989	A. Martindale, 'The Knights and the Bed of Stones: a Learned Confusion of the Fourteenth Century', *J.B.A.A.* 142 (1989).
Mawer and Stenton 1912	A. Mawer and F.M. Stenton, *The Place Name of Warwickshire* (English Place Names Society 13, C.U.P. Cambridge, 1912).
Maxwell Lyle 191	H.C. Maxwell Lyle (ed.), *Calendar of Patent Rolls of Edward III and Richard II* (H.M.S.O. London, 1911).
Mayes and Scott 1984	P. Mayes and K. Scott, *Pottery Kilns at Chilvers Coton, Nuneaton* (Medieval. Archaeol. Monograph Series No. 10, 1984).
Midmer 1979	R. Midmer, *English Medieval Monasteries (1066-1540)* (Book Club Associates, London, 1979).
Moorhouse 1971	S. Moorhouse, 'Finds from Basing House, Hampshire: Part Two', *Post-Medieval Archaeol.* 5, (1971), 35-76.
Moorhouse 1972	S. Moorhouse, 'Medieval Distilling Apparatus of Glass and Pottery', *Medieval Archaeol.* 16 (1972), 79-121.
Moorhouse 1983	S. Moorhouse, 'Documentary Evidence and its Potential for Understanding the Inland Movement of Medieval Pottery', *Bull. Medieval Pottery Res. Group* 7 (1983), 45-87.
Musty 1959	J.W.G. Musty, 'A Pipe-line Near Old Sarum; Prehistoric, Roman and Medieval Finds Including Two Twelfth century Lime-kilns', *Wilts. Archaeol. Natur. Hist. Mag.* 57 (1959), 179-91.
Musty 1978	A.E.S. Musty, 'Exploratory excavation within the monastic precinct, Waltham Abbey, 1972, *Essex Archaeology and History* 10 (1978), 127-73.
Mynard 1970	D.C. Mynard, 'Medieval Pottery of Potterspury Type', *Bull. Northamptonshire Fed. Archaeol. Soc.* 4 (1970), 49-55.
Neale 1824-5	J.P. Neale, *Views of the most Interesting Collegiate and Parochial Churches in Great Britain*, 2 vols. London 1824-5.
Newcourt 1708	R. Newcourt, *Repetorium Eccles. Parochiale London, Parochial History of the Diocese of London, vol. 1*, (London, 1708).
Notes Queries Hertfordshire 1912	"The Hermit of Hertford and Christ Church, London'. *Hertfordshire Archaeol. Notes and Queries*, January 1912.
Oliver 1831	T. Oliver, *A New Picture of Newcastle-upon-Tyne*, (Newcastle, 1831).
Ordnance Survey 1978	Ordnance Survey, *Monastic Britain*, (Southampton, 1978).

140

Oswald 1962-3   A. Oswald, 'Excavation of a Thirteenth Century Wooden Building at Weoley Castle, Birmingham, 1960-61', *Medieval Archaeol.* 6-7 (1962-63), 109-134.

Oxoniensia 1943-4   'East Gate Oxford and its Neighbouring Properties in 1624/5' in Notes and News *Oxoniensia*, 8-9 (1943-4), 203-5.

Pantin ed. 1960   W.A. Pantin ed., H.E. Salter, 'Survey of Oxford' *Oxford Hist. Soc.* New Series, 14, Vol. 1 (1960), 197.

Park 1988   D. Park, 'A lost 14th century Altar Piece from Ingham', *The Burlington Magazine* 130 (1988).

Payne 1979   R. Payne, *Five Moated Sites in the Parish of Headcorn*, (Unpublished B.A. dissertation, University of Durham 1979).

Pestell 1991   T.J. Pestell, *'The Archaeology of Ingham Priory: a Case Study with reference to the Trinitarian Order in England'*, (unpublished B.A. dissertation, University of Cambridge, 1991).

Pevsner 1962   N. Pevsner, *Buildings of England North East Norfolk and Norwich*, (Penguin, London, 1962).

Pevsner 1980   N. Pevsner (J. Newman) *Buildings of England, West Kent and the Weald*, (Penguin, London, 1980).

Pitts 1978   M. Pitts, 'Towards an understanding of Flint industries in post-glacial England', *Bull. Inst. Archaeol. Univ. London*, 15, 1978.

Platt 1984   C. Platt, *The Abbeys and Priories of Medieval England*, (Secker and Warburg, London, 1984).

P.R.O. 1964   *'Lands of the Dissolved Religious Houses', P.R.O. Lists and indexes, Suppl.* Series III 1-3, (New York, 1964).

P.R.O. Seals 1968   'A Guide to Seals in The Public Record Office', *P.R.O. Handbook* No. 1, (H.M.S.O., London, 1968).

Rackham 1972   B. Rackham, *Medieval English Pottery*, (Faber and Faber, London 1972).

Rahtz 1959   P.A. Rahtz, 'Humberstone Earthwork, Leicester' *Trans. Leicestershire Archaeol. Hist. Soc.* 35 (1959), 1-32.

Rahtz 1966   P.A. Rahtz, 'Kenilworth Castle, 1962' *Trans. Birmingham Warwickshire Archaeol. Soc. 81* (1966), 55-73.

Rahtz and Hirst 1976   P. Rahtz and S. Hirst, *Bordesley Abbey, Redditch, Hereford-Worcestershire. First Report on Excavations 1969-1973*, Brit. Archaeol. Rep., British Series 23, Oxford, 1976.

Roberts 1980   H.E. Roberts, *Medieval Monasteries and Minsters of English and Wales*, (S.P.C.K., London, 1949).

Robinson 1980   D.M. Robinson, *The Geography of Augustinian Settlement*, i, Brit. Archaeol. Rep. British Series 80, Oxford, 1980.

Runcorn Development
Corporation 1972   J.P. Greene, 'Norton Priory Excavation 1972. Interim Report on the 1972
                       season', *Runcorn Development Corporation*, 1972.

Runcorn Development
Corporation 1973   J.P. Greene, 'Norton Priory Excavation 1973'. Interim Report on the 1973
                       season', *Runcorn Development Corporation*, 1973.

Russell-Smith 1956   F. Russell-Smith, 'The medieval "Brygyrdyl",' *Antiq. J.* 36 (1956), 218-21.

Salt 1911   W. Salt, 'Collections for a History of Staffordshire', *William Salt Archaeol.
                       Soc.* (Staffordshire Record Soc.) (1911), 269.

Stothard 1817   C. Stothard, *The Monumental Effigies of Great Britain*, (London, 1817).

Saunders 1980   A.D. Saunders, 'Lydford Castle, Devon', *Medieval Archaeol.* 24 (1980), 123-
                       86.

Streeten 1983   A. Streeten, *Bayham Abbey*, Sussex Arch. Soc. Monograph, No. 2, 1983.

Tanner 1787   T. Tanner, *Notitia Monastica*, ed. J. Nasmith, (University Press, Cambridge
                       1787).

Thordeman 1939   B. Thordeman, *Armour from the Battle of Wisby 1361*, (Stockholm, 1939).

Trans. Birmingham
Warwickshire
Archaeol. Soc. 1930   Notes, 1927, *Trans. Birmingham Warwickshire Archaeol. Soc.* 52, (1927).

V.C.H. Berks. 1907   *Victoria History of the County of Berkshire, 2, Religious Houses of
                       Berkshire*, (Constable, London, 1907).

V.C.H. Herts. 1912   *Victoria History of the County of Hertfordshire, 3.* (Constable, London,
                       1914).

V.C.H. Herts. 1914   *Victoria History of the County of Hertfordshire, 4.* (Constable, London,
                       1914).

V.C.H. Kent 1926   *Victoria History of the County of Kent*, ed. W. Page. 2. (St. Catherine Press,
                       London, 1926).

V.C.H. Middlesex 1962 *Victoria History of the County of Middlesex, 3* ed. S. Reynolds, (O.U.P.
                       London 1962).

V.C.H. Norfolk 1906   *Victoria History of the County of Norfolk, 2. Religious Houses of Norfolk.*
                       (Constable, London, 1906).

V.C.H. Oxon. 1907   *Victoria History of the County of Oxford*, ed. W. Page, 2. (Constable,
                       London, 1907).

V.C.H. Oxon. 1979   *Victoria History of Oxfordshire 1*, ed. A. Crossley, 4. (O.U.P. London,
                       1979).

V.C.H. Warks. 1908   *Victoria History of the County of Warwick. 2 'Religious Houses of
                       Warwickshire'.* (Constable, London, 1908).

142

V.C.H. Wilts. 1956   *Victoria History of the County of Wiltshire:* A History of Wiltshire 3. (O.U.P., London, 1956).

V.C.H. Yorks. 1913   *Victoria History of the County of York*, ed. W. Page. 3. (Constable, London, 1913).

Von Kralik 1919   R. Von Kralik. *Gesichte des Trinitatien Ordens.* (Vienna, 1919).

Walsh 1967   Walsh, *New Catholic Encyclopaedia* (McGraw Hill, New York, 1967).

Webster and Cherry 1973   L.E. Webster and J. Cherry, 'Medieval Britain in 1971', *Medieval Archaeol.* 16, 1972 (1973), 175-6.

Webster and Cherry 1980   L.E. Webster and J. Cherry, 'Medieval Britain in 1979', *Medieval Archaeol* 24, (1980), 242.

Webster and Hobley 1965   G. Webster and B. Hobley, 'Aerial Reconnaissance over the Warwickshire Avon', *Archaeol. J.* 121, 1964 (1965), 1-22.

Wheater 1907   W. Wheater, *Knaresburgh and its Rulers,* (Jackson, Leeds, 1907).

Whitcomb 1956   Norma R. Whitcomb, *"The Medieval Floor-Tiles of Leicestershire'.* Leicestershire Archaeol. Hist. Soc., 1956.

Wight 1972   J.A. Wight, *"Brick Building in England from the Middle Ages to 1550",* (John Baker, London, 1972).

Williams 1979   J.H. Williams, *'St. Peter's Street, Northampton, Excavations 1973-1976',* Northampton *Development Corporation, 1979.*

Wilson 1980   C. Wilson, *The Origins of the Perpendicular Style and its' Development to circa 1360,* unpublished PhD thesis, Coutauld Institute of Art, (1980) 248-50.

Wilson and Hurst 1967   D. Wilson and D.G. Hurst, 'Medieval Britain in 1965' *Medieval Archaeol* 10, 1966, (1967), 182.

Wilson and Hurst 1971   D. Wilson and D.G. Hurst, 'Medieval Britain in 1969', *Medieval Archaeol* 14, 1970, (1971), 169.

Windeatt 1880   E. Windeatt, An Historical Sketch of Totnes, *Rep. Trans. Devonshire Ass.* 12 (1880), 166-7.

Wise 1991   P.J. Wise, 'Wasperton', *Current Archaeol.*, 126 (1991), 256-9.

Wordsworth 1983   J. Wordsworth, 'Friarscroft and the Trinitarians in Dunbar', *Proc. Soc. Antiq. Scot.*, 113 (1983), 478-488.

Youngs, Clark and Barry 1987   S.M. Young, J. Clark and T. Barry, 'Medieval Britain and Ireland in 1986', *Medieval Archaeol.* 31, (1987) 155-6.

Youngs, Clark,
Gaimster and
Barry 1988   S.M Youngs, J Clark, D.R.M. Gaimster and T. Barry, 'Medieval Britain and
                     Ireland in 1987', *Medieval Archaeol.* 32, (1988), 270-1.

www.ingramcontent.com/pod-product-compliance
Lightning Source LLC
Chambersburg PA
CBHW060959030426
42334CB00033B/3293